Visitor's Guide to the Bahamas
The Out Islands

By

Blair Howard

Copyright © 2012 Blair Howard

All rights reserved. No part of this publication may be reproduced, stored in a retrieval system, or transmitted in any form, or by any means, electronic, mechanical, photocopying, recording, or otherwise, without the written permission of the publisher.

This guide focuses on recreational activities. As all such activities contain elements of risk, the publisher, author, affiliated individuals and companies disclaim responsibility for any injury, harm, or illness that may occur to anyone through, or by use of, the information in this book. Every effort was made to insure the accuracy of information in this book, but the publisher and author do not assume, and hereby disclaim, liability for any loss or damage caused by errors, omissions, misleading information or potential travel problems caused by this guide, even if such errors or omissions result from negligence.

Important Note: The rates, fees and prices, and especially the entrance fees to the many attractions, quoted throughout this book were current at the time of writing. However, they are all subject to change without notice and they do, almost weekly, thus the prices quoted herein are given only as a rough guide as to what you might expect to pay. The author therefore disclaims any liability for such changes and urges you to check, either by phone or online for current rates before you travel.

Planning a visit to the Out Islands of the Bahamas?

If so, you'll find this book to be an invaluable guide. Everything you need to know to plan your visit is included.

This guide includes up-to-date information about the best hotels, attractions, things to do, touring the islands, restaurants, the beaches, snorkeling, guided tours, hiking, dive sites, dive operators, fishing guides and much more.

The book also includes up-to-date practical information: everything you need to know to make your visit to the Out Islands a success.

The Visitor's Guide to the Out Islands of the Bahamas is the most complete travel guide to the islands available.

What's included:

The Abacos

The Exumas

Eluethera

Long Island

Cat Island

The Inaguas

San Salvador

Bimini

The Berry Islands

Mayaguana Island.

Table of Contents

Introduction 4
The Abacos 11
   History 11
   Getting There 12
      By Air 12
      By Mail Boat 14
      By Private Boat 15
      Package Vacations 17
Before You Go 18
   Travel Documents 18
   Customs 18
   Departure Taxes 18
   Disabled Travelers 18
The People 20
   Language 20
   People to People 21
Eating & Drinking 22
   Feast from the Sea 22
   Fishy Delights 22
   Traditional Foods 23
   Drinks 24
   Tipping 24
Accommodations 25
   Hotel Classification Guide 25
   Out Islands 25
   Package Deals 26
   Meal Plans 26
Practical Information 27
   Banking 27
   Bicycles & Mopeds 27
   Buses 27
   Casinos 28
   Climate 28

  Currency 28
  Dress 29
  Electricity 29
  Ferries 29
  Internet 30
  Mail Boats 30
  Photography 31
  Medical 32
  Rental Cars 33
  Shopping Hours 33
  Taxis & Tours 33
  Telephones 34
  Cell Phone s 34
  Time 35
 How to Use This Book 36
  Tourist Information 36
  Bahamas Tourist Offices 37
 A Land of Adventure 38
  Bird Watching 38
  Boating 38
  Sea Kayaking & Sailing in the Exumas 39
  Powerboat Adventures 39
  Golf 40
  The Best Courses 40
  Hiking & Bicycling 40
  Honeymooning 41
  Shelling 42
  Sport Fishing 42
  The Lure of Fishing 42
  Blue-Water Fishing 43
  Bonefishing 45
  Tournaments 47
  Fishing Licenses & Permits 48
  Marine National Parks 49
  Sightseeing 50
  Scuba Diving 50

Dive Sites	50
Snorkeling	51
Dangers	51
Wreck Diving	53
SAFETY	53
Sun Seeking	53
Shopping	53
Holidays	54
Bahamas Holiday Calendar	54
The Abacos	56
Getting Around	56
By Ferry	56
By Bicycle, Moped or Car	56
Marsh Harbour	57
Walking	58
South from Town	58
North from Town	59
Driving	59
Man-O-War Cay	59
Exploring	60
Elbow Cay & Hope Town	60
Exploring	60
The Artist	61
Green Turtle Cay & New Plymouth	61
Exploring	62
Treasure Cay	62
Great Guana Cay	63
Walker's Cay	64
Bird Watching & Nature Tours	64
The Different of Abaco	64
On The Water	65
Sport Fishing	65
Boat Rentals	66
Fishing Tournaments	67
Fishing/Accommodation Packages	67
Fishing Guides	70

Diving & Snorkeling	71
Abaco's Best Dive Sites	72
Marsh Harbour:	72
Pelican Cays National Land & Sea Park	72
Green Turtle Cay	73
Walker's Cay	73
Shipwrecks	74
The USS Adirondack	74
The USS San Jacinto	75
The Viceroy	75
The H.M.S. Mermaid	75
The Bonita	76
The Barge	76
The Demira	76
Best Snorkeling Sites	76
Angelfish Reef	77
Blue Strip Reef	77
Crawfish Shallows	77
Elkhorn Park	77
Fowl Cay Reef	77
Hope Town Reef	77
Jeanette's Reef	77
Meghan's Mesa	77
Pirates Cathedral	77
Pelican Park	77
Smugglers Rest	77
Spanish Cannon	78
Sandy Cay Reef	78
Dive Operators	78
Dive Abaco	78
Brendal's Dive Center International	78
Dive Guana	78
Froggies Dive Shop	79
Walker's Cay Undersea Adventures	79
The Dive Shop	79
The Hope Town Dive Shop	79

    Dive/Accommodation Packages 80
        The Conch Inn 80
        Schooner's Landing Resort...80
        The Green Turtle Club...81
        Walker's Cay Hotel and Marina 81
    Dining 82
    Elbow Cay 82
        Great Abaco & Marsh Harbour 83
        Great Guana Cay...85
        Green Turtle Cay 86
    Accommodations 88
        Hotel Meal Plans..88
        Elbow Cay 88
        Great Guana Cay...90
        Green Turtle Cay 92
        Man-O-War Cay 94
        Marsh Harbour..94
        Spanish Cay 95
        Treasure Cay 96
        Walker's Cay 96
        Wood Cay 97
Andros..98
    Geography & Wildlife 98
    History 99
    Getting There 99
        By Air 99
        By Mail Boat..101
        By Private Boat...102
    Getting Around 102
        By Bicycle 102
        By Car..103
        Fishing Camps 104
    Sightseeing..104
        Andros Lighthouse...104
    On The Water 105
        Sport Fishing..105

Boat Rentals 105
　　　Diving 105
　　　Best Dive Sites 106
　　　Shipwrecks 107
　　　Best Snorkeling Sites 107
　Dive Operators 108
　　　Small Hope Bay Lodge 108
　Dive/Accommodation Packages 108
　　　Small Hope Bay Lodge 109
　Where to Stay & Eat 109
　　　Dining 109
　　　Accommodations 109
　　　Hotel Meal Plans 109
Bimini 112
　History 112
　Getting There 113
　　　By Air 113
　　　By Mail Boat 114
　　　By Sailboat 114
　　　The Flings: 114
　On The Water 115
　　　Fishing 115
　　　Fishing/Accommodation Packages 115
　　　Fishing Tournaments 116
　Diving 117
　　　Best Dive Sites 117
　　　Dive Operators 118
　　　Spotted Dolphins 118
　　　Dive/Accommodation Packages 118
　　　Best Snorkeling Spots 119
　Where to Stay & Eat 120
　　　Dining: 120
　Accommodations 120
　　　Hotel Meal Plans 120
Eleuthera 122
　History 122

Getting There 122
   By Air 122
   By Fast Ferry 124
   By Mail Boat..125
   By Private Plane 125
   By Private Boat...126
Package Vacations 126
   American FlyAAWay Vacations 127
   Apple Vacations..127
Getting Around 127
   Island Driving Tour 128
   Bicycling or walking...130
   Day Trips to Harbour Island 130
On The Water 132
   Fishing 132
   Boat Rentals...133
   Diving 133
   Best Dive Sites...133
   Shipwrecks...134
   Best Snorkeling Sites..135
   Cousteau Snorkeling Adventures 136
   Dive Operators...136
   Romora Bay Club Dive Shop 136
   Valentine's Dive Center 136
Where to Stay & Eat 137
Dining: 137
   Gregory Town..137
   Hatchet Bay 137
   Palmetto Point..137
   Harbour Island 137
Hotel Meal Plans...138
Accommodations 138
The Exumas 141
Exuma Cays Land & Sea Park....................................141
  History 141
   Rolle's Heirs 142

- Getting There 142
  - By Air 142
  - By Mail Boat 143
  - By Private Boat 144
- Getting Around 144
  - By Taxi 145
  - George Town On Foot 145
  - Touring by Bus 146
  - Touring by Motor Scooter 146
  - Touring by Bike 146
  - Touring by Car 146
- Nightlife 148
- On The Water 148
  - Sea Kayaking & Sailing 148
  - Fishing 151
  - Fishing Tournament 152
  - Fishing Packages 152
  - Boat Rentals 153
  - Powerboat Adventures 153
  - Diving & Snorkeling 154
  - Best Dive Sites 154
  - Dive Operators 155
  - Dive/Accommodation Packages 155
- Where to Stay and Eat 155
  - Dining 155
- Accommodations 156
- THE Other out Islands 159
- The Acklins & Crooked Island 160
  - History 160
    - Columbus Was Here 160
  - Getting There 161
    - By Air 161
    - By Mail Boat 161
    - By Private Boat 161
  - Sightseeing 161
    - Bird Rock Lighthouse 161

- Crooked Island Caves 162
- French Wells 162
- Marine Farm 162
- Dining 162
- Accommodations 162
- The Berry Islands 163
  - Getting There 164
    - By Air 164
    - By Mail Boat 164
    - By Private Boat 164
  - On The Water 164
    - Boat Rentals 164
    - Diving & Snorkeling 165
  - Dining: 165
  - Accommodations 165
- Cat Island 167
  - Getting There 167
    - By Air 167
    - By Mail Boat 168
    - By Private Boat 168
  - Sightseeing 168
    - The Hermitage 168
    - The Deveaux Plantation 169
  - On The Water 169
    - Boat Rentals 169
    - Diving & Snorkeling 169
    - Best Snorkeling Sites 170
  - Dining 171
  - Accommodations 171
- The Inaguas 174
  - Getting There 174
    - By Air 174
    - By Mail Boat 174
  - Sightseeing 174
    - Inagua National Park 174
    - Henri Christophe's Treasure 175

Morton Bahamas Salt Company	175
Matthew Town Lighthouse	176
On The Water	176
Dining	176
Accommodations	177
Long Island	**178**
History	178
The Adderleys	179
Getting There	179
By Air	179
By Mail Boat	179
Vacation Packages	180
Sightseeing	180
The Adderley Plantation	180
Columbus Point	181
Conception Island	181
Deadman's Cay Caves	181
Churches	181
On The Water	182
Diving & Snorkeling	182
Best Dive Sites	182
Best Snorkeling Sites	184
Dive Shop	184
Sport Fishing	185
Boat Rentals	185
Dining	185
Accommodations	186
San Salvador	**188**
History	188
John Watling	188
Getting There	189
By Air	189
By Mail Boat	189
By Private Boat	189
Package Vacations	190
Sightseeing	190

Cockburn Town	191
Sandy Point	192
Watling's Castle	192
Wrecking	192
Lookout Tower	192
Dripping Rock Cave	193
Graham's Harbour	193
Father Schreiner's Grave	193
North Victoria Hill	193
New World Museum	193
The Columbus Monuments	194
Dixon Hill Lighthouse	194
Going on Foot	195
Walking & Hiking	195
On The Water	195
Diving & Snorkeling	195
Best Dive Sites	196
Best Snorkeling Sites	197
Dive Operators	198
Dining	198
Accommodations	199
Rum Cay	202
Mayaguana island	203
Tourist Information	204
Communications	205
Accommodations	205
Baycaner Beach Resort, Pirate's Well	205
Dress	206
Medical	206
Money Matters	207
Photography	207
Things You Need to Know	207
How to Get There:	208
Mail Boat Schedules	208
At a Glance	209
Airlines Serving the Islands	209

Getting There 211
Mail Boat Schedules 215
Fishing Guides on all the Islands 219
Dive Operators 221
Accommodations 222
    The Abacos 223
    Andros..223
    The Exumas 225
    Grand Bahama 225
    Nassau-New Providence 226

Introduction

The Out Islands of the Bahamas are as close as you can get to paradise; the beaches, many of them ranked among the most beautiful in the world, are vast, silent, often deserted, stretches of pale pink sand bounded with waving palm trees. The Out Islands are dotted with tiny villages, populated by the nicest people on the planet. Oh what joy! I've been visiting, and writing about, the Out Islands of the Bahamas for more than 20 years. During that period, things have changed slowly and mostly for the better. But, even if they hadn't changed, these are still the magical islands I fell in love with all those years ago.

It's still a real thrill to fly in from the west and gaze down at one tiny islet after another, each one surrounded by the emerald green, crystal water of the Grand Bahama bank. These islands are the most beautiful places on Earth. Whether it's the combination of the ever-present English culture, its sub-tropical setting, or something else, there's something very special about these islands in the western Atlantic that, once experienced, is never forgotten.

There are some 700 islands in The Bahamas and at least 2,000 more much smaller islets, called cays (pronounced Keys), that lie scattered over 750 miles of the western Atlantic Ocean. These islands have provided generations of seafarers and travelers with more adventure than many of them might ever have imagined. New Providence Island (Nassau) and Grand Bahama Island (Freeport) are the principle islands of the archipelago.

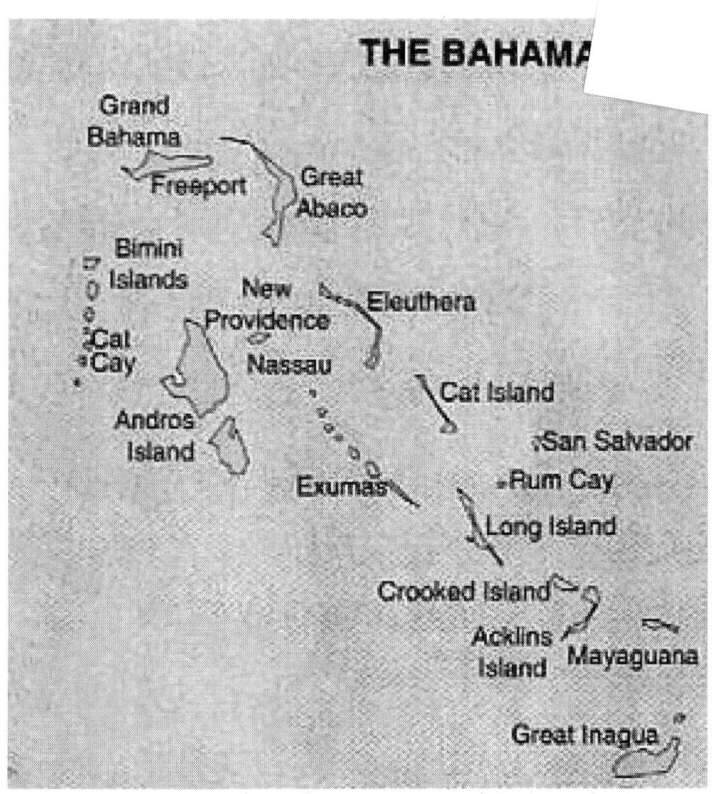

Beyond Nassau and Freeport lie the 13 inhabited islands or island groups that make up the Out Islands of The Bahamas. These are the Abacos, Andros, Eleuthera, Cat Island, Long Island, Bimini, the Berry Islands, Crooked Island, San Salvador, the Inaguas, the Exumas, Ragged Island, Rum Cay and Mayaguana. They are magical places, each with a character all its own. It's here in these tiny backwater paradises that adventures really begin. This is the land of the treasure hunter, scuba diver, beachcomber, explorer and hiker.

It's where the old world ends and the new one begins, a land of emerald seas, snow-white sands and mysterious blue holes, where you can wander deserted beaches for hours on end and never set eyes on another living soul. Although there are no shopping malls, night clubs, casinos or any of the other major attractions that lure visitors to the two main islands of the Bahamas, life goes on here much as it has for more than 300 years, quietly, unchanged.

There's another world beyond the two major tourist destinations, Nassau and Freeport: The Out Islands have long been a popular destination for sailors, sport fishermen and divers. Today, due to some aggressive marketing and increased accessibility, they are fast becoming popular with other active travelers.

Far away from the bustling streets and tourist attractions of Nassau and Freeport, the rest of the Bahamian population, some 40,000 people, pursue their everyday lives. They live in sparsely settled little towns and villages from one end of the island chain to the other. Most Out Island residents have never left their island.

The little towns and villages are an odd mixture of the old and the new. Here and there across the Out Islands you'll find impressive colonial manor houses right alongside half-finished concrete structures that will one day, as money permits, become the homes of fishermen and farmers.

In the many villages of the outer islands to the southeast, the traditional pattern of farming and fishing prevails. Fruits and vegetables are grown throughout the Out Islands, along with pigs, sheep, goats and turkeys, while crayfish (Bahamian lobster), lumber, and pulpwood are exported, chiefly to the United States.

Thick vegetation, mostly shrubs and bushes, covers most of

the Out Islands. Each is a tiny land of dunes and rocks, sea grass, spider lilies, seagrape, mangrove, casuarina and palm. Each is a land of endless shores, tiny bays and rocky inlets, where the colorful families of the ocean live, play and die in the crystal-clear waters of the reefs.

Marsh Harbour, on Abaco Island, is the third-largest city in the Bahamas. This dusty little town is somewhat reminiscent of an American frontier cattle town of the 1880s. In contrast, the neat little painted villages of **Hope Town**, on Elbow Cay, and **New Plymouth**, on Green Turtle Cay, might well have been lifted up and flown in straight from New England.

If it's seclusion you're after, you'll find it in the Out Islands. The flat terrain and the long dusty roads, often devoid of travelers and always in various stages of disrepair, lend themselves well to walking or bicycling. Anglers no longer will need to tell tales of the one that got away. The bonefish here fight each other to take the hook and big game fish aren't as wary as they are off the coast of Florida. Shipwrecks, coral reefs, and mysterious blue holes dot the vast stretches of empty flats and shallow reefs. There are beaches where the sand is the color of pink champagne and there's not an empty soda can to be seen anywhere; where you can wade in the shallow waters, lie in the sun, or cast a line into the gently rolling surf. You might hook a chunky snapper and bake it over a small fire as the sun goes down. Get lucky and you could be eating fresh lobster instead of snapper.

These are the islands of romance where couples can leave the bustling mainland and all its distractions behind. Sunshine, warm breezes, tropical drinks, soft music and solitude make for an unforgettable experience. If, after a week together here in the Out Islands, you don't get to know one another intimately, you never will.

Dotted around the Out Islands are a dozen or so resorts (some more deserving of the title than others) and perhaps five times as many small hotels and B&Bs. Accommodations run the gamut from Spartan to delightful and almost luxurious. Don't expect all the modern conveniences here: telephone s and televisions are rarities. Air-conditioning is available almost everywhere, but be sure you confirm before you book. The absence of climate control in your room, if you're not prepared for it, can be a vacation breaker.

Upscale restaurants and fine dining, as we know them, are the exception rather than the rule, but these islands do boast of some of the best little holes in the wall I've ever come across. The atmosphere in these sometimes raunchy little cafés and restaurants, and the often outrageous local cuisine, makes eating out an experience to remember. But even those who like fine dining and a good bottle of wine will find opportunities to indulge. The Romora Bay Club on Harbour Island is one, the Green Turtle Club on Green Turtle Cay in the Abacos is another.

Adventures on land and sea abound in the Out Islands. Most

of them, though, require a modicum of self-organization. Throughout the following pages you'll find references to beaches, dive sites, snorkeling, bicycling and walking opportunities. Very few of these activities, with the exception of scuba diving, can be formally structured. A good map and the ability to make friends with the locals – local knowledge can produce golden opportunities – is all you need. Hotel employees are also a good source for local secrets. Other than that, you'll need to head out on your own and see what you can find.

Most people have heard of Nassau, some have heard of Freeport and Grand Bahama, but very few have heard of the Out Islands. If you really want to get away from life in the fast lane, enjoy a few quiet days in the sun on some of the most beautiful and unspoiled beaches in the world, the opportunities offered by the Out Islands are almost limitless.

Note: *With rare exceptions, hotel standards in the Bahamas are not what you get on the US mainland, or in Europe. Due to the fact that almost everything has to be imported, and is therefore expensive, there is a definite trend to put off until tomorrow what should be done today. Hotels that might have been considered fairly upscale five years ago can quickly become slightly seedy as time and weather take their toll. Don't expect too much, especially in the Out Island, and for sure don't let a little inconvenience spoil your vacation.*

The first foreigners to visit the Abacos were **Spanish** explorers. They called the islands Habacoa, from the Spanish phrase, "haba de cacau," a rough description of the islands' limestone substructure.

Juan Ponce de Leon is supposed to have stopped by the islands in 1513, during his search for the fabled Fountain of Youth, but he found nothing of value except the local inhabitants, a small number of Lucayan Indians. These he quickly enslaved and, by 1550, the poor Lucayans had died out completely.

Then the pirates arrived. They, too, found little of value. They realized, however, that the remote location and the hundreds of tiny cays, bays and inlets made fine hideouts, and the rocky coastline was a great asset in increasing their second source of income, wrecking.

Note: It's said that more than 500 galleons, some still laden with treasure, lie at the bottom of the ocean around the Abacos; many of them are the victims of wreckers.

Following the pirates, and after the end of the American War of Independence, a new breed of adventurer arrived on the Abacos. **Loyalists** from Virginia, the Carolinas and New England put down roots at **Charleton**, near Treasure Cay in the center of the Abacos. But their crops failed and, finally, the town was destroyed in a hurricane. By the late 1700s, Charleton had been abandoned and, in 1784, a new settlement, **Elizabeth Harbour**, some 18 miles to the south, had been established with help from friends on nearby Eleuthera. There, the colonists took to fishing and, once again, to farming. The little settlement of Elizabeth Harbour eventually became **Marsh Harbour**.

New settlers came and stayed on the Abacos, bringing with them an assortment of skills. The islands became an important center for small shipbuilding. Soon, due to the high quality of the islanders' craftsmanship, sloops, fishing boats, and dinghies built on the Abacos became prized throughout the Bahamas.

In the early 1970s came the movement toward Bahamian **independence**. The white population of the Abacos remained fiercely loyal to Britain; they even tried to secede from the Bahamas. In the end, however, independence came to the islands.

Today, although the little settlements on Man-O-War Cay – Hope Town and Green Turtle Cay – are still predominantly white, the residents of the Abacos have somewhat reluctantly come to terms with their new situation. The Abacos are prosperous – a popular tourist destination – and they are playing an increasingly important part in the Bahamian tourist industry.

Getting There

By Air

The Abacos are well served, both locally and from the

mainland. **American**, **Continental**, and **USAir** offer service from most US gateway cities.

Visitors from Europe can travel from London and other major continental cities on the same three airlines, or on other code-sharing partner airlines, making connections in the US through Miami, Atlanta, Orlando, and elsewhere. Also, your travel agent can hook you up with package operators – British Airways Holidays, Thomas Cook, or American Express Holiday, to mention just a few.

Flying in to the Abacos, you arrive at one of two international airports, both tiny. **Treasure Cay Airport** is in the middle of that island and serves Green Turtle Cay, Manjack Cay, Cooper's Town, and the rest of Little Abaco, while **Marsh Harbour Airport**, farther south, serves Hope Town, Man-O-War Cay, and Great Guana Cay.

To March Harbour From:	Airline
Nassau	**Bahamasair** operates regular daily schedules, 800-222-4262. Round-trip fare, $96.
Freeport	**Major Air**, 242-352-5778.
Fort Lauderdale	**Gulfstream** (Continental Airlines Connection), 800-231-0856; **Island Express**, 954-359-0380; **Air Sunshine**, 800-327-8900; **Bel Air Transport**, 954-524-9814. Round-trip fare, $99.
Miami	**American Eagle**, 800-433-7300; **Gulfstream** (Continental Airlines Connection), 800-231-0856. Round-trip fare, $158.
Orlando	**USAirways Express**, 800-622-1015. Round-trip fare, $158.
West Palm Beach	**Bahamasair** operates regular daily schedules, 800-222-4262, **USAirways**

	Express, 800-622-1015. Round-trip fare, $160.

To Treasure Cay with access to Green Turtle Cay and Spanish Cay. From:	Airline
Nassau	**Bahamasair** operates regular daily schedules, 800-222-4262. Round-trip fare, $96.
Freeport	**Major Air**, 242-352-5778. Round-trip fare, $99.
Fort Lauderdale	**Gulfstream** (Continental Airlines Connection), 800-231-0856; **Island Express**, 954-359-0380; **Air Sunshine**, 800-327-8900; **Twin Air**, 954-359-8266. Round-trip fare, $160.
Miami	**Gulfstream** (Continental Airlines Connection), 800-231-0856. Round-trip fare, $158.
Orlando	**USAirways Express**, 800-622-1015. Round-trip fare, $160.
West Palm Beach	**Bahamasair** operates regular daily schedules, 800-222-4262; **USAirways Express**, 800-622-1015. Round-trip fare, $160.

By Mail Boat

MV Legacy leaves Potter's Cay, Nassau, for Marsh Harbour, Treasure Cay, Green Turtle Cay and Hope Town on Tuesday at 8 pm, returning on Thursday at 7 pm. Sailing time is 12 hours. The fare, one-way, is $45.

Bahamas Ferries now operates a direct service from Nassau aboard the *Sea Wind*. The trip to Sandy Point takes an hour and 50 minutes. A round-trip costs $99 per adult or $55 for children (free under two). 242-323-2166 for information and bookings.

Mail boat schedules depend on the weather, and therefore can be a little erratic. They do stick to the schedule most of the time but it's best to call ahead and make sure. 242-393-1064.

By Private Boat

During recent years, the Abacos have become a popular sailing destination. For more than 130 miles, stretching north and south, the two major islands, along with dozens of tiny islets and cays, present a wealth of opportunities. While you can visit a limitless number of secluded, often deserted, inlets, bays and anchorages, you're always secure in the knowledge that civilization is never very far away. Official ports of entry are Walker's Cay, Green Turtle Cay, Marsh Harbour, Sandy Point, and Spanish Cay.

There's a marina at the south end of **Spanish Cay**. Facilities include 75 slips with a maximum depth of nine feet, showers, fuel, a Laundromat, shops and a restaurant. 888-722-6474, fax 561-655-0172, VHF 16.

Green Turtle Cay has two facilities, the **Green Turtle Club** and the **Green Turtle Shipyard**. They have a combined total of 44 slips and a maximum depth of eight feet. Other facilities include showers, fuel, shops, restaurant, Laundromat and satellite TV. 242-365-4271, fax 242-365-4272, VHF 16.

The **Bluff House Beach Hotel** on Green Turtle Cay at White Sound offers 20 slips with a maximum depth of 10 feet. There's also a restaurant, Laundromat, showers, fuel service, and a shop. 242-365-4247, fax 242-365-4248, VHF 16.

At **Treasure Cay**, the **Treasure Cay Hotel Resort & Marina** is a full-service operation with 150 slips with a maximum depth of 12 feet. It also has on-shore accommodations, a repair shop, fuel service, a Laundromat, showers, a restaurant, and several shops. There's a 50-ton travel lift nearby. 800-327-1584, fax 242-365-8847, VHF 16.

The marina at the **Guana Beach Resort** on Abaco offers 22 slips with a maximum depth of 10 feet, along with on-shore accommodations, a popular bar and restaurant, an excellent beach with pink sand and several shops close by. If, however, you're looking for fuel or showers, you'll need to go elsewhere. 242-365-5133, fax 242-365-5134, VHF 16.

The **Abaco Beach Resort and Boat Harbour Marina** is very popular. Facilities include 180 full-service slips with a maximum depth of 10 feet, repair service, fuel, a modern bathhouse with hot showers and dressing rooms, shops, a great restaurant, and a sailor's bar. 800-468-4799, fax 242-367-2819, VHF 16.

There are more marinas scattered across the Abacos: **Admiral's Yacht Haven, Harbour View Marina, Hope Town**

Harbour Marina on Elbow Cay, **Marsh Harbour Marina, Mango's Marina,** and the **Conch Inn Marina,** which has a great outdoor/indoor bar and restaurant, as well as more than 30 full-service slips, postal service, and mini-market; there's even a dive shop on the property. Call the Conch Inn Hotel and Marina at 800-688-4752 or 242-367-4000.

Package Vacations

Unless you're a completely independent traveler, a package vacation is the best way to visit the Abacos, especially if you've not been before. Several companies offer air/hotel-inclusive packages with a variety of hotels to choose from; contact a reliable travel agent for a presentation of all the options. I recommend a package by **American Airlines FlyAAWay Vacations** (800-321-2121, www.aavacations.com) because they supply their own air portion of the vacation. This is an advantage if something goes wrong, especially when flights are delayed or cancelled. An airline will always see that their own customers are looked after before those of package operators.

American Airlines does not offer packages into Treasure Cay International Airport because they do not serve that airport. **Destination Bahamas** is a wholesaler that packages a more diverse number of properties with air on Abaco. Their number for reservations is 1-800-224-2627. More information on this wholesaler or alternatives can be found at www.bahamas.com.

Both of the airports and the docks are well served by independently owned taxis, and you'll find them waiting to meet all of the inter-island ferries. Fares are reasonable, starting at around $12 for two people to ride from Treasure Cay or Marsh Harbour to any of the local hotels or ferry docks.

If you're traveling to Green Turtle Cay or Hope Town, take a taxi from the airport to the dock. The inter-island ferries are scheduled to coincide with incoming air services.

Before You Go
Travel Documents

To enter the Bahamas you'll need two things: a return or onward-bound ticket and a valid passport. A visa is not required. US immigration officials will want to see proof of US citizenship on your return. See the State Department website for details at http://travel.state.gov/bahamas.html.

Canadian and British citizens visiting for three weeks or less may enter by showing the same documents as required for US citizens. Citizens of British Commonwealth countries do not need visas.

Customs

Dutiable items, such as furniture, china and linens, must be declared. Each adult may bring in duty-free 200 cigarettes, or 50 cigars or one pound of tobacco and one quart of alcohol.

US residents, including children, may take home duty-free purchases valued up to $800, and up to 67 ounces of alcohol per person over the age of 21. Canadian citizens may take home up to $200 in purchases, including up to 200 cigarettes, 50 cigars, two lbs of tobacco and 40 oz of alcohol. Residents of Great Britain may take home up to £32 in duty-free purchases and each adult visitor is allowed 200 cigarettes or 50 cigars or one pound of tobacco and a liter of alcohol without paying duty.

Departure Taxes

At the time of writing, the government departure tax of $15 is included in the cost of most airline tickets. Children under six are exempt. There is an additional $10 security fee for international passengers departing from Freeport, Grand Bahama.

Disabled Travelers

If you're disabled, or traveling with someone who is disabled, make all your arrangements well in advance. Be sure that you let everyone involved know the nature of the disability so that accommodations and facilities can be arranged to meet your needs. On the whole, you'll find most hotels, tour operators, and other facilities are well equipped to handle the needs of disabled visitors.

The People

The Bahamas, still very much steeped in their traditional British heritage, are inhabited by a hodgepodge of black and white races of African-American, Continental European, and African origin, among others. Less than 40 years ago, blacks on the islands were not allowed in any of the nation's restaurants, theaters, and hotels, although they represented more than 80Phoneof the population. That is all changed now and, although several islands remain predominantly white, Bahamians of all colors integrate freely with one another.

With independence from Britain in 1973, and with tourism becoming the mainstay of the Bahamian economy, black people, once the poorest members of the population, have increasingly improved their lot.

The bulk of the wealth is still in white hands, but more and more black-owned business are making a contribution. Where once they were not allowed, black Bahamians have found their way into administration and management. And while many young Bahamians still leave the islands in search of something better, it seems most of them return sooner or later.

Bahamians, black or white, are very friendly and outgoing. The always cheerful "good morning," the happy smile, and the eagerness to help, whether it's with directions or service, often borders on the cloying. But rest assured, it's done with an almost naïve genuineness and a desire to please.

Language

The language spoken on the islands is English – at least it's called English. The old language has been shaped and reshaped over more than 300 years by a potpourri of cultures, of which the British and Caribbean have had no small influence. Some say the Bahamian accent is decidedly West Indian, others say it has a sound all its own. If it's spoken quickly, it's almost impossible for an outsider to understand. The secret is to listen carefully, and don't be afraid to ask the speaker to repeat – that will often bring a delighted grin to his or her face.

People to People

If you want to get to know the real Bahamians, go out and meet the people. This is easily achieved through the government-sponsored "People to People" program offered by the Ministry of Tourism. It gives visitors the opportunity to meet and socialize with Bahamians, meeting them in their homes and participating in their social and cultural events. Get involved and you'll be invited to a variety of activities and social events. These might include performances by a local theater group, sporting events, or afternoon tea with a Bahamian family. For more information, contact the People-to-People Unit at the Tourist Information Center at Rawson Square in Nassau, at one of the information booths at the Nassau International Airport, or on Bay Street next to the Straw Market, at Prince George Dock, where the Ministry of Tourism's main office is located. In Freeport, there's a tourist office at the International Bazaar. In the Out Islands there are offices on Abaco, Eleuthera and the Exumas. To find out more on the Internet, go to www.bahamas.com, click on People at the left of the screen, then click on People-to-People Programme.

Eating & Drinking

Bahamian food is an adventure in itself. The larder of the Bahamas is the sea that surrounds it; seafood is the staple.

Feast from the Sea

The conch – pronounced "konk" – is chief among the many varieties of goodies gathered from the ocean. Claimed by the locals to be an aphrodisiac, conch can be prepared in numerous ways: for conch salad the flesh is chopped, spiced, and eaten raw with vegetables and lime juice; cracked conch is beaten and fried; and, finally, there are conch fritters. Be sure to try conch salad before you leave; it's delicious.

Fish, especially grouper, is the principal fare of the Bahamian people. It's served many ways, for breakfast, lunch and dinner. The Bahamian lobster (Americans call it crayfish) is plentiful, often large, and not as expensive as it is in the States. Try minced lobster, a mixture of shredded lobster meat cooked with tomatoes, green peppers and onions, and served in the shell.

Fishy Delights

Fish is prepared in a number of ways, the names of which are often confusing. Boil fish is served for breakfast. It's cooked with salt pork, green peppers and onions, and served with a generous portion of grits. Stew fish is prepared with celery, tomatoes, onions, and spices, all combined in a thick brown gravy; it is also served for breakfast. Steamed fish is cooked in a tomato base and is as tasty as it is novel. And nowhere else will you find anything like this:

Traditional Foods

Bahamians also eat a lot of crab, chicken, pork, and mutton. Almost everything is served with huge portions of peas and rice – a concoction of pigeon peas, peppers, celery, tomatoes, and rice, seasoned and cooked until golden brown.

For dessert, try guava duff, a Bahamian delicacy made by spreading guava fruit pulp on a sheet of dough. It's then rolled and boiled, cut into slices and served with a thick white sauce.

Other than fish, most of the food eaten on the islands is imported, which makes it somewhat expensive. While restaurants on the Out Islands tend to serve mostly Bahamian foods, more and more American fare is making its way onto Bahamian tables. You can find a good steak or prime rib and the inevitable French fries at most of the popular restaurants in Nassau and Freeport. And almost all of the American fast-food chains are represented: McDonalds, Burger King, KFC. There's even a Pizza Hut on Abaco. But to avoid the local food is to miss a great eating experience.

Drinks

Popular drinks are the Bahama Mama, the Goombay Smash, and the Yellow Bird. Bahamians also drink lots and lots of beer, mostly the local brew: a fine golden beer called Kalik. Be sure to try it. Imported beers from America and Europe are also available but, like everything else that has to be imported, they're expensive. For something really different, try one of the locally brewed sodas with exotic names.

All drinks on the islands are expensive. Be prepared to pay up to $7 for a bottle of beer in a restaurant, $7 for cocktails. Even non-alcoholic cocktails kids can consume in large quantities are pricey. A Coke or locally made soda can cost up to $4.

During the day, hot tea is the drink of preference. If you want iced tea, be sure to specify that when ordering. On most of the islands, the water is pure and safe to drink straight from the tap.

Nassau's water is imported from Andros by ship and, by the time it reaches the consumer, the taste is not what you might like. It's best to drink only bottled water in Nassau because of that.

Tipping

It's standard to add a 15% charge to restaurant checks and the same with room service in the large hotels. If you don't see a gratuity on the bill, ask. Hotels add an 8%-10% service charge to their rates, so there's no need to leave a room tip. Tour guides expect to receive $2 to $5 per person, and cab drivers usually receive 10%-15% of the fare.

Accommodations

Hotels range in quality from Tourist Class through Superior Deluxe. Remember, however, that you are not dealing with the same standards you have grown used to in the United States, Canada or England. Even the top-rated hotels are almost always busy, and geared to accommodate the vacationing public, rather than business people. In general, this means that, unless you book the best room your particular hotel has to offer, your accommodations will probably be no better than average. Clean and comfortable, yes; luxurious, hardly.

Hotel Classification Guide

SUPERIOR DELUXE: Exclusive, elegant, luxury hotels offering the highest standards of accommodations, service and facilities.

DELUXE: Outstanding hotels with many of the features and amenities offered by those classed as Superior Deluxe, but less expensive.

SUPERIOR FIRST CLASS: Above-average hotels, often older, but well-maintained. Accommodations are comfortable and tastefully furnished.

FIRST CLASS: Facilities are not as extensive as those at hotels in the more expensive categories, but these hotels are dependable and comfortable.

SUPERIOR TOURIST CLASS: Budget properties, mostly well-kept and maintained. Facilities are few, but the rooms are generally clean and comfortable, if sometimes spartan.

TOURIST CLASS: Low budget, with few or no facilities. Not for the discriminating traveler.

Out Islands

On the Out Islands – the Abacos, Eleuthera, the Exumas, Andros, Long Island, Cat Island, etc. – accommodations can be basic; many are not air-conditioned. There are very few hotels rated better than First Class. Also, most Out Island hotels do not have TVs or telephones in the rooms, although they all have them in the main buildings. If you want to get away from the stresses of everyday living, it can be nice to leave the television and telephone back on the mainland.

Package Deals

If your vacation is a package provided by a major operator, you can generally expect your hotel to be clean and comfortable. Package operators inspect their client hotels regularly and require certain minimum standards. This doesn't mean you get better service or accommodations, just that you can be assured of certain standards.

Hotels are listed in order by rate, the least expensive first. Actual rates, when not quoted within the text, are shown at the back of the book in the At a Glance section.

Meal Plans

CP (Continental Plan) includes a continental breakfast.

EP (European Plan) denotes no meals, although restaurant facilities are available either on the property or nearby.

MAP (Modified American Plan) denotes breakfast and dinner.

FAP (Full American Plan) includes all meals.

All-Inc. (All-Inclusive Plan) includes all meals, beverages (alcoholic and soft), watersports, tennis and golf, if available.

All hotel rates quoted are subject to a 4Phoneroom tax and a 4Phoneresort levy; gratuities are extra.

Practical Information
Banking

Banking is big business in the Bahamas. Long recognized as a tax haven, both Nassau and Freeport are home to more than their fair share of counting houses. And for visitors to the islands that's good. There's always a bank around the next corner.

In Nassau and Freeport/Lucaya, banks are open from 9:30 am until 3 pm, Monday through Thursday, and from 9:30 am until 5 pm on Friday. If you rely on credit cards for your cash, there are international ATMs located at strategic spots on both of the major islands, including the casinos. As one might expect, banking hours vary in the Out Islands. In fact, banks on some islands open only on certain days of the week, and then only for a few hours.

Bicycles & Mopeds

Bicycles are popular on the islands. Visitors love them. They are inexpensive to rent, convenient, easy to park, and nowhere is really too far away. The only concern is that you'll be riding on the "wrong" side of the road. You can rent mopeds and bicycles at most hotels and resorts, or at nearby cycle shops. At the time or writing, the going rates for mopeds range from about $20 to $30 a day – a half-day might cost anywhere from $10 to $20 – and you'll be asked to leave a small deposit, usually about $30. Bicycles run about $18 a day.

Buses

Bus travel can be an adventure. And if you want to meet the people, there's no better way to do it than finding your way around Nassau by bus. For 75¢, it's a great way to travel. Bahamians are very friendly and will come to your aid quickly with directions. (The only problem is understanding the waving hands and the fast talk.) On Grand Bahama, the buses connect Freeport with Lucaya, the hotels, the beaches, Port Lucaya and, of course, the International Bazaar.

Casinos

Visitors over the age of 18 may gamble at all four casinos in Nassau and Freeport. Children are allowed to enter the casinos only to attend shows in the casino theaters. In Nassau, there is a casino on Paradise Island at the Atlantis Resort and one at Wyndham Nassau Resort & Crystal Palace Casino on Cable Beach. In Freeport, one casino is at Our Lucaya. The other is at the Isle of Capri Casino on Royal Palm Way. There is more information on gaming and casinos in the regional chapters.

Climate

The trade winds blow almost continuously here, creating a warm, agreeable climate that varies little throughout the year. September through May, when the temperature averages 70-75°F, is the most refreshing time to visit. The rest of the year is somewhat warmer, with temperatures between 80° and 85°.

May is the rainy season.

Currency

Legal tender is the Bahamian dollar, which is always equivalent in value to the US dollar. Both US and Bahamian dollars are accepted interchangeably throughout the islands, and visitors are likely to receive change in mixed American and Bahamian currency.

Traveler's checks are accepted throughout the islands and may be cashed at banks and hotels. They will, however, add a service charge. Credit cards are widely accepted in Nassau and Freeport/Lucaya, and to a lesser extent on the Out Islands, where cash is still king. Be prepared to pay a service charge if you use American Express.

b British visitors should buy Bahamian dollars before traveling. The exchange rate often will be more favorable at home than in the Bahamas.

Dress

The dress code is casual and comfortable. Days are spent in shorts, swimsuits, slacks or jeans. Although the islands have been independent for more than 25 years, the influence of more than 250 years of British rule is still evident. You shouldn't wear swimsuits except at the pool or on the beach. Do not wear them in shops, restaurants, and on the streets of Nassau and Freeport/Lucaya.

In the evening, most people prefer to dress casual but smart – sport shirts and slacks. For more formal dining at some of the first-class restaurants and larger hotels, gentlemen should wear a tie and jacket; long skirts or cocktail dresses are preferred for ladies. On the Out Islands, except at some of the large resorts, dress is much more casual.

Electricity

All US and Canadian appliances can be used without adapters. Visitors from the United Kingdom will need adapters to 120 volts.

Ferries

Ah, this is the way to travel. Ferries in Nassau run between Prince George Dock and Paradise Island. On the Out Islands the ferry is often the only way of getting around. On Abaco, ferries run every hour or so between Treasure Cay, New Plymouth on Green Turtle Cay, and the Green Turtle Club (also on Green Turtle Cay), with various stops along the way. This round-trip takes about an hour to complete. From Marsh Harbour the ferry runs to Man-O-War Cay and back, and from Marsh Harbour to Hope Town on Elbow Cay and back. Once again, a round-trip takes about an hour. It's a lazy way to travel, but most enjoyable. There's nothing quite like a boat ride on a warm sunny day, especially when the scenery is spectacular and the sea the color of the palest jade. www.bahamasferries.com.

Internet

No much is available in the Out Islands. Most of the major hotels offer high-speed access via Ethernet cable. The cost runs from $12 to $20 per day, depending upon the hotel.

Mail Boats

Even though the Out Islands are now almost all accessible by air, mail boats still ply the waters back and forth between the islands. The boats leave Nassau from Potter's Cay – located off East Bay Street under the east Paradise Island Bridge – about once a week, stopping at one or two of the Out Islands along the way. The journey takes about 12 hours, usually overnight. Schedules are somewhat random, subject to change and postponement. The mail boat is, however, an economical way to travel the islands, a lot of fun, and perhaps the most understated and unusual adventure available. The decks are crowded with Bahamians, freight, livestock and a variety of weird cargoes.

This is also a great way to make short trips to the Out Islands. For instance, the Bahamas Daybreak III leaves Nassau on Mondays at 7 pm, arrives at Governor's Harbour on Eleuthera at midnight, and returns to Nassau at 8 pm on Tuesday. You could spend the night at the Duck Inn or the Rainbow Inn, spend the next day sightseeing, swimming, snorkeling or whatever, then catch the boat and be back in your hotel by 1:30 am, just in time to get some sleep. Unfortunately, passage cannot be arranged in advance, but only after arrival in the Bahamas. For more information, call the dock master at Potter's Cay, Phone 242-393-1064. You'll find detailed schedule and fare information within each regional chapter, and in the At a Glance section at the end of the book.

Visit www.bahamasgp.com.

Photography

The ocean wears a coat of many colors, ranging from the palest emerald green to the deepest indigo. The colors of the flowers – hibiscus, bougainvillea, goat's foot, and spider lily – seem a little brighter than anywhere else. The sand varies just a little from the palest pink to the tint of fine champagne. And then there's the clothing. Bahamians love bright colors. Light colored dresses, shirts, and hats set against rich brown skin offer rare opportunities for great photography. Gaily painted cottages, bustling streets alive with color, roadside fish markets, vast mangrove swamps, tiny harbors crowded with sailboats, lighthouses, and thousands of scenic bays, inlets, and beaches offer even more vistas for shutterbugs. If that's not enough, you can always dive into the underwater world where the colors are even brighter.

Here are some simple techniques to help you shoot better photos:

If you are shooting digital, take your laptop computer and a couple of extra memory chips. You'll also need a way to download your images – a card reader perhaps. If not a card reader, don't forget to take your camera's USB cable. If you can't take your computer, purchase a couple of 4GB chips and set your camera to shoot JPEG images at the "normal" or "medium" setting. This will allow you to shoot 1,000 images before you run out of memory. If you're using film, take more of it with you than you think you'll need, especially if you're shooting slides. Film is expensive locally and the type you prefer might not be available, especially in the Out Islands. Digital or film, you'll need extra batteries and a charger.

Digital photographers should set the ISO as low as possible – 100ISO is ideal. If you're shooting 35mm, use a low-speed film; 50 or 100ISO will produce the best results and less grain. The rule of thumb is: the lower the speed of the film, the sharper the image will be. In the interest of creating great pictures, use a low-speed film whenever you can, especially on bright sunny days. Use a high-speed film, or turn up the ISO on your digital camera, only with low light or when using a telephoto lens.

Shoot at the highest shutter speed you can. This will reduce camera shake. The longer the lens, the faster the shutter speed. You should never hand-hold a camera at a shutter speed slower than the focal length of the lens. For example you would only hand-hold a camera fitted with a 180mm lens when the shutter speed is set to 1/250 of a second or more; never slower. Likewise a 50mm lens could be hand-held with the shutter set to 1/60th of a second, but no slower.

Medical

The Bahamas are blessed with an excellent health service. The Out Islands are served by health centers, clinics and general practitioner doctors. In an emergency, patients are flown to Nassau and treated at Princess Margaret Hospital.

You should be aware that most US medical insurance plans will not cover you while traveling abroad.

Most package operators offer travel protection insurance. This may cover some limited medical emergencies. Several insurance companies also offer cancellation insurance. They can be well worth the extra cost. Perhaps the best of these is CSA Travel Protection Insurance offered through travel agents and underwritten by Commercial Union Insurance Company. For more information, call your local travel agent or Phone 800-873-9855.

Visit www.csatravelprotection.com.

Insects are not much of problem, but take along some insect repellent just in case. And don't leave home without a good sunblock.

Rental Cars

If you have a valid US, Canadian or British driver's license, you can rent a car – even on the Out Islands, although what you get there might bring on a mild heart attack. Most rental cars in the Out Islands are privately owned. Be sure to check the car's condition before you drive away.

Rates vary from around $60 to $90 per day, but are much cheaper if rented by the week.

Remember, Bahamians drive on the left side of the road. It can at first be a little disconcerting, but you'll soon get used to it.

Shopping Hours

Although shops throughout the Bahamas are now permitted to open on Sundays and some national holidays, you'll find many remain closed

Taxis & Tours

On the Out Islands, some taxis are showing their age. Almost always reliable, these taxis often offer a ride that can be an adventure all its own.

The Ministry of Tourism and the Bahamas Training College have established a number of specialty tour guide qualifications: ecotour guides, bird-watching guides, etc. On the Out Islands there are no tour buses and, as yet, few tour guides. This is where the taxi comes into its own. For as little as $16 an hour, your friendly driver will show you his island and tell you all about it. These drivers are experts on the history of their particular island, and are often able to tell the story in a form that's as entertaining as it is interesting.

Rates are often negotiable, especially if you are prepared to hire by the day. Meters are present in most cabs on the main islands, but they may not be activated. It's always best to negotiate a particular fare before embarking.

Tips are expected and a couple of dollars for a short trip will be enough. Taxis usually meet arriving flights and ferry boats, but it's advisable to make sure in advance. Speak with your hotel and have them arrange something for you if needed.

Telephones

When calling from the US, dial 242 and the local number. To call the US or Canada from the Bahamas, dial 1 + the area code and the local number.

Cell Phone s

Cell Phone use has gotten a lot easier over the last couple of years. But service on the Out Islands is limited. Do not expect to find a signal everywhere, or all the time. It's very much a potluck kind of thing.

Most manufacturers now build GSM (Global System for Mobiles) technology into their equipment as a matter of course, especially in Europe. In the US, all one needs is the properly-equipped cell phone , a call to your provider and a request for the international dialing option, and you're ready to go. The international dialing option will cost you nothing: the roaming service, however, can be quite expensive – anywhere from $1 to $5 per minute. If your Phone is not "international capable," you can always rent one from your local provider before you leave. It's not cheap – usually $40 to $50 per week – and then you'll also have to cough up for airtime, at least $1 per minute. Most of the national providers – Verizon, Cingular, etc. – offer cell Phone rental by the week. Other options in the USA include Roadpost (Phone 888-290-1606) and InTouch USA (Phone 800-872-7626). In the US, if you'd like to find out if your cell Phone will work in the Bahamas, call Phone 703-222-7161 or go online to

http://intouchglobal.com/travel.html.

Time

Time in the Bahamas coincides with that of the Eastern United States. If it's noon in Atlanta, it's noon throughout the Bahamas.

How to Use This Book

In the section on each individual island, you'll find everything you need to know to plan an enjoyable vacation. Travel planning tips, plus sections on sightseeing, shopping and the best beaches are offered. Then I focus on activities – from diving and hiking to bird-watching. The Out Islands are listed in alphabetical order.

At the end of the book you'll find a section called At a Glance – a quick reference to all you need to know; no descriptions, just names and addresses listed by category.

Tourist Information

Information is readily available throughout the Bahamas. There are, for instance, two district offices of the Bahamas Ministry of Tourism in the Out Islands, one on Eleuthera on Harbour Island and one in Governor's Harbour.. Ministry personnel are cheerful, ready and willing to help. Maps and brochures are free and yours for the asking.

Bahamas Ministry of Tourism, PO Box N-3701, Market Plaza, Bay Street, Nassau, Bahamas. Phone 242-322-7501; fax 242-328-0945.

The Grand Bahama Island Tourism Board, PO Box F-40251, Freeport, Grand Bahama Island. Phone 242-352-8365; fax 242-352-7849.

For information about the Out Islands, contact:

The Out Islands Promotion Board, 1100 Lee Wagener Boulevard, Suite 206, Ft. Lauderdale, Florida, 33315-3564. Phone 800-688-4752 (USA and Canada). In Ft. Lauderdale Phone 305-359-8099; fax 305-359-8098.

For brochures on the Bahamas, Phone 800-8BAHAMAS. You can also visit www.bahamasgo.com, where you'll find all sorts of useful information, some of which is not available anywhere else.

Bahamas Tourist Offices

150 East 52nd Street, New York, NY 10022. Phone 212-758-2777; fax 212-753-6531.

One Turnberry Place, 19495 Biscayne Blvd., Suite 809, Aventura, FL 33180. ☐305-932-0051; fax 305-682-8758.

3450 Wilshire Blvd., Suite 1204, Los Angeles, CA 90010. Phone 213-385-0033; fax 213-383-3966.

8600 W. Bryn Mawr Avenue, Suite 820, Chicago, IL 60631. Phone 312-693-1500; fax 312-693-1114.

121 Bloor Street East, Suite 1101, Toronto, ON M4W 3M5, Canada. Phone 416-968-2999; fax 416-968-6711.

3 The Billings, Walnut Tree Close, Guilford, Surrey, England, QV1 4VL. Phone 01483-448990.

A Land of Adventure

In a nation completely surrounded by the clearest waters in the world, there are plenty of watersports. And while the great outdoors is where most people want to be, there's a lot to do here beyond the beach and the ocean. The shops and the nightlife of New Providence Island and Grand Bahama Island provide diversions that allow you to have a great vacation.

General information about what's available throughout the islands is listed in this section. More specific information about the attractions and activities on individual islands is given in each chapter, and the At a Glance section at the end of the book.

Bird Watching

Guides & Self-Guided Tours

With more than 25 inhabited islands and thousands of smaller rocks and cays, there is plenty of opportunity to explore different habitats and spot some rare birds. The three endemic species are the Bahama woodstar hummingbird, the Bahama swallow and Bahama yellowthroat warbler. Other prized birds include the white-tailed tropicbird, Bahama pintail, Bahama parrot, great lizard-cuckoo, loggerhead kingbird, Bahama mockingbird and the stripe-headed tanager, to name but a few. These birds cannot be found on all of the Bahamian Islands, so a birding guide can ensure you make the best use of your time.

Boating

Rentals

There are endless possibilities for getting out and about on the water – from the self-drive rental boat available by the hour, to the full-blown chartered day-sailor yacht that comes complete with captain and crew, not to mention champagne and lobster lunches. Most of the hotels have

Hobe Cats, Sunfish or Sailfish for rent. Some even have Boston Whalers and other outboard-driven craft available. All come at a great variety of hourly or daily rates. Sometimes they are free. It's worth checking before you make your hotel reservations.

The islands have vast expanses of calm, clear open water, safe bays and inlets, and numerous convenient anchorages and marinas that offer everything from a quick lunch and a glass of cold beer to chilled champagne and a gourmet lobster dinner. All sizes of sailboats are available, with or without crew.

Arrangements can be made through any number of outlets, including your travel agent, hotel or one of the many special outfits you will find listed throughout the pages of this book.

Sea Kayaking & Sailing in the Exumas

If it's real adventure that you're looking for, consider a sea kayaking expedition in the Exumas. You can look forward to long hot days paddling the open waters between the islands of the chain, balmy nights under canvas, good food, and good company. You have to be fairly fit to handle the often-strenuous exercise of paddling for hours at a time. But the sheer vastness of the seascapes, the pristine beaches, and the crystal waters make this a one-of-a-kind experience.

Powerboat Adventures

Not for the faint-hearted, this is your chance to experience the thrills of off-shore powerboat racing in a certain degree of comfort, at least as much as one might be able to expect at speeds in excess of 50 miles per hour. Several companies offer this type of adventure, most of them operating out of Nassau. One offers day-trips to the Exumas – a truly excellent experience – and another has rides around Paradise Island. They'll take you anywhere in the Bahamas, provided you can afford the cost of a private

charter. You'll find more detailed information in the chapters on Nassau and Paradise Island and the Exumas.
Golf
Across the islands are a number of fine courses, some laid out by famous names in golf architecture: Robert Trent Jones Jr. and Sr., Pete Dye, Dick Wilson and Joe Lee, to name but a few.

The Best Courses
The best courses on the Out Islands are those at the The Club on Eleuthera, The Treasure Cay Golf Club, Sandals Emerald Reef Golf Club on Great Exuma, and the small but challenging nine-hole course on Great Harbour Cay in the Berry Islands. All 18-hole courses on New Providence, Grand Bahama and the Out Islands have a complete range of facilities, including a resident pro, rental carts and clubs. Most facilities also offer clinics and private lessons.

Hiking & Bicycling
Opportunities to enjoy an afternoon, or even a week, hiking the quiet country lanes and beaches are just about endless. There's not a single island in the entire archipelago that doesn't offer some sort of hiking route.

Most hiking routes are lonely, often dusty, and without facilities. Be sure to carry everything you need, especially an adequate quantity of water and sun block.

Bicycling offers the opportunity to see the land at a more leisurely pace than by car or taxi. While bicycles are available for rent on the two main islands, they are not quite so easily come by in the Out Islands. Some of the hotels in the Out Islands offer them free of charge to their guests, and some do rent them to guests staying at other hotels. Check with your travel agent.

There are virtually no designated walking, hiking or bicycling trails on any of the islands. These activities are very much go-as-you-please affairs, especially on the Out Islands. The main roads are the first and most obvious choice, but there are also the beaches, of course, and hundreds of unmarked side roads that often end up at a secluded beach where you can enjoy a picnic lunch and a swim. At least in the Out Islands, there's no reason why you shouldn't wander at will. The locals are friendly and willing to give ideas, directions and the benefit of their knowledge about the best places to go and sites to see. Don't be afraid to ask.

Guided bike rides are offered by some of the larger hotels on New Providence Island, Pedal & Paddle Ecoventures in Nassau, Phone 242-362-2772, and Kayak Nature Tours on Grand Bahama Island, Phone 242-373-2485. Both offer guided rides and day-trips. Both use modern, off-road bikes.

If you are going to one of the more remote islands, consider taking your own bike. Check with the airline as to procedure and costs.

Honeymooning

The Bahamas epitomize romance. From the soft sounds of the steel drum and calypso wafting gently over the beaches on a warm evening under a spectacular sunset, to deserted beaches where the palms wave gently over an emerald sea, the islands have much to offer.

There are extensive opportunities for honeymooning, or even getting married, in the Bahamas, especially on one of the Out Islands – the Abacos, Eleuthera, or the Exumas. And for a really remote, even primitive, location, try Andros.

Here are some websites specializing in Bahamas weddings and honeymoons:

www.islanddreaming.com
www.weddinginthebahamas
www.coordinators.thebahamian.com
www.out-island-wedding.com
www.honeymoontravel.com

www.honemooncruiseshopper.com

www.wedding-world.com

Check first with your travel agent when making your booking and be sure to do so well in advance. The Bahamas are a very popular honeymoon destination and many suites are booked up a year or more in advance.

Shelling

Shelling is a hobby that can bring back memories of your vacation for years to come. Put on your swimsuit, wait for low tide and then wade out to the dark spots in the water where the seaweed grows. There, conch feed in the thousands. There's always someone around willing to clean the shells for you. Sand dollars are common, and literally hundreds of exquisite shells lie on the high water line of Out Island beaches.

Sport Fishing

For many Bahamians, fishing is not just a sport, it's the way they make their living. But sport fishing here is spectacular, and you don't have to be a world-class angler to take advantage of what the islands have to offer. In fact, it's okay if you've never fished before in your life. There are plenty of skilled guides willing to take you in hand and show you exactly how it's done. A couple of hours of instruction, a fast boat or a calm, shallow-water flat, and you're in business.

The Lure of Fishing

Nothing compares with the feeling you'll get aboard a slowly trolling boat on a calm sea under a hot summer sun, a heavy rod between your knees, and a can of something cold in your hand. And then it happens. There's a jerk on your line; something's taken the bait, and in seconds you're involved in the fight of your life. But wait, the line goes slack, it's gone. No, it's still there, and suddenly the water a hundred yards from the boat explodes and the great fish is in the air. Your first sailfish hurls itself out of the water in a breathtaking arc. The sight leaves you speechless, awed and, for a moment, not knowing what to do next. And then it hits again and the fight is on. Slowly you reel in, the clutch slipping under the strain, three winds on the crank for every inch of line you gain. As suddenly as it began, it's over. Your opponent, exhausted at the side of the boat, is gaffed and hauled aboard. It's more than five feet long and weighs perhaps as much as 90 pounds – you won't know until you get it back to the scale on the dock, but it's a good one; you know it is. You go home at day's end satisfied and tired, but still excited, ready to do it all again tomorrow, the next day, next year.

There are many ways to fish in the Bahamas. Off-shore fishing is the premier choice, but there really is something for everyone and you don't need to charter an expensive deep-sea boat. You can do it from a small rental boat all by yourself, or even wade to your waist in the crystal waters of one of a hundred or more bonefish flats for a day of sport.

Blue-Water Fishing

Other than the sailfish, the king of them all is perhaps the blue marlin. Catches of the big blue typically range from 100 to 300 pounds or more. Four and five hundred pounders are not uncommon and stories of the one that got away tell of fish in excess of 1,000 pounds. Fantasy? Perhaps; perhaps not.

Tuna is another fine blue-water catch. Every spring the bluefin make their annual run through the Bahamas, and anglers leave the docks in droves to participate in any one of a dozen or more tournaments from Bimini to Walker's Cay. Catches weigh from 100 to 800, even 900 pounds. There's also blackfin and yellowfin tuna – smaller, but no less fun to catch.

Other excellent deep-water species include the kingfish or king mackerel. They can be caught through the year, although peak time is during the spring and summer.

Dolphin (the fish; not Flipper) are usually found fairly close in along the shoreline, weigh anywhere from five to 20 pounds, and are excellent to eat. Wahoo weigh 15 to 30 pounds; even 60 pounds is not unusual. They, too, make for good eating and are highly prized by sport fishermen. Wahoo are most often found lurking in the deep water off the edge of a reef. The amberjack is another prized sporting fish found most often during the summer months in the cooler, deep waters just off the edge of the reef and closer in-shore the rest of the year. Amberjack can run 20 to 40 pounds.

Sharks are common throughout the Bahamas, especially the Out Islands, and can be found in both shallow waters and deep. Bull sharks, blues, hammerheads, and tiger sharks abound. The truth is, however, that when one is caught, the fight usually lasts only as long as it takes for the shark's razor-like teeth to bite through the wire traces that hold him. Even so, you'll remember the battle for a long time to come.

The wily barracuda is found in large numbers, in shallow or deep waters. They can often be seen swimming close to the surface in the clear waters over reefs and sandy banks. Barracuda range in size from a few pounds to about 15 or 20 pounds and, small though they might be, you're sure of a good fight if you can get one on your hook.

Unfortunately, barracuda are often the victims of ciguatera poisoning and are, therefore, risky to eat.

For good eating, you can't beat grouper. Grouper – black, Nassau and yellowfin – can be found swimming lazily around, close to the bottom on the reefs throughout the Bahamas. Catches ranging from 15 to 25 pounds are the norm, and fish of 30 to 45 pounds are not uncommon. Often, your hotel will be willing to clean and cook grouper for you. There's nothing quite like a grouper steak, caught in the afternoon and eaten the same evening. The snapper too, may be caught on reefs throughout the islands. Most common are the red and gray variety and, though a fish may weigh only a pound or two, fresh-caught snapper is delicious.

Bonefishing

Bonefishing is a specialty in the Out Islands.

Inside the reef, before you reach the deep waters of the ocean where glamorous, deep-water sportfish hog the limelight, there's a second, very exciting sporting opportunity – bonefishing. The elusive bonefish, often called the ghost fish, is rapidly becoming one of the most popular sportfish on the islands. Until quite recently, bonefishing was almost unheard of among mainland anglers. Today, people from around the world flock here in search of this hard-fighting denizen of the flats.

Bonefish, so named for the huge numbers of bones in their bodies, live in deep water and come up onto the flats to feed. That's where you'll have to go to find them. Unlike most deep-water sportfish, they offer not only a good fight, but the thrill of a hunt as well.

Bonefish, like deer, must be stalked, and they are just as skittish. Make a wrong move at the wrong time and your quarry will be gone in a flash, leaving you standing alone in the water, totally frustrated, and wondering what went wrong.

Bonefish are not very big. They weigh in around six to 15 pounds, with some growing as large as 20 pounds.

You'll need a guide who knows the area and where the best flats are found. Many hotels offer bonefishing packages that include the services of a reliable and experienced guide. If not, don't be afraid to ask. The hotel desk is the best place to start, but many taxi drivers know just who to put you in touch with. Most boat rental companies and dive companies will also know of someone.

Bonefishing is good almost everywhere in the islands, from Abaco to the Acklins, and from Bimini to Eleuthera. Unlike most other sportfishing, it is good throughout the year. There are a number of ways to go about it. It's claimed that in some areas bonefish can be caught from the dock, or by casting into the surf, or from a skiff. But the best way is to hunt them down on foot on the lonely flats of the Out Islands. This is where your guide will earn his fee. He will know where to go, what bait to use – fly or jig – and he'll guide you through the basics of how to fish for the ghost.

Bonefish come up onto the flats in schools and can be seen first in the near distance as a dark stain in the crystal-clear water above the white sandy bottom, then as a vast, surging ripple on the surface of the water as maybe a hundred fish move like a flock of birds, this way and that, across the flats, tails cleaving the water. Then you see them, shadowy gray streaks flashing over the white sand, ghostly, moving fast.

To hunt bonefish, move slowly, disturbing the water as little as possible. Keep your eyes on the school, not on the sandy bottom beneath your feet. Take one step at a time, until you're close enough to try a cast. Aim tour fly or jig close to the center of the school. If you're lucky, there's a slight tug, then a stronger one, and the surface of the water explodes in a frenzy of white water and struggling fish; and he's off like a runaway horse leaving you hanging on to your rod, reel screaming, spinning, as 150 yards of line disappears seaward in what seems less than a second. Then he turns, heads in another direction as you wind in frantically to take up the slack, beginning to reel him in, fighting every inch of the way.

Bonefishing guides cost about $250 for a full day, or $150 for a half-day. Bring food and beverage. If you don't have your own gear, your guide can supply everything you need.

If you've never bonefished before, the best way is to purchase one of the packages offered by many of the islands' hotels. These require only that you bring yourself and a willingness to do as you're told. You can expect to spend anywhere from $350 for a three-night stay, to more than $2,000 for seven nights in a luxury accommodation (see individual chapters for specific details).

Tournaments

There's a year-round series of competitive fishing events designed to make things as interesting as possible for all participants, novice and veteran alike. The best-known and most popular is the Bahamas Billfish Championship Tournament, held during the spring and early summer each year at five different locations. Anglers are welcome to take part in all or as many legs as they wish. The first two legs are held in April at Bimini and Walker's Cay. In May, the tournament moves to Treasure Cay and Boat Harbour, and then ends at Chub Cay in June. For details and registration, Phone 305-923-8022.

The Bimini Big Game Club sponsors a number of tournaments. These include the mid-winter Wahoo Tournament in February, the Annual Bacardi Rum Billfish Tournament in March, the Bimini Festival in May, the Family Tournament in August, the Small B.O.A.T. Tournament for boats under 27 feet in September, and another Wahoo Tournament in November. The Bimini International Light Tackle Bonefish Tournament consists of two legs – one in January, the other in February. Phone 800-327-4149 for more information and reservations.

The Penny Turtle Billfish Tournament is held at the Great Abaco Beach Resort each May; Phone 800-468-4799. The Billfish Foundation's Tag Tournament is held in May at the Walker's Cay Hotel and Marina on Abaco; Phone 800-WALKERS. The Green Turtle Cay Yacht Club hosts a fishing tournament in May; Phone 242-365-4271. The What's Out There Tournament is held at Great

Harbour Cay in April; Phone 800-343-7256. The Boat Harbour Billfish Championship is held at the Marsh Harbour Resort in Abaco in June; Phone 305-920-7877.

The Bahamas Bonefish Annual Bash is held in February at the Club Peace and Plenty on Exuma; Phone 800-525-2210. The Andros Big Yard Bonefishing and Bottom Fishing Tournament is held in June; call the Bahamas Tourism Office at Phone 800-32-SPORT. There's also a bonefishing tournament held in mid-July at the Staniel Cay and Yacht Club on Exuma; Phone 242-355-2011. Bonefishing, as well as big game fishing, is a part of the Bahamian Outer Islands International Gamefish Tournament held in March; Phone 800-426-0466 for location, details and registration.

For a full listing and schedules, contact the Bahamas Tourism Office, Phone800-32-SPORT, or the Bahama Out Islands Promotion Board at Phone 800-688-4725.

Fishing Licenses & Permits

There are no restricted fishing seasons; it's open season throughout the year on whatever you want to catch. Licenses are not required if you're fishing from a Bahamian-registered boat. You will, however, need to obtain a sport-fishing permit if using your own craft. A single-visit permit costs $20 and is available at your legal port of entry into the Bahamas. An annual permit will cost you $250. You can also obtain your permit in advance by contacting the Department of Fisheries, PO Box N-3028, Nassau, Bahamas, Phone242-393-1777.

Only hook and line fishing is allowed in the Bahamas; use of a speargun is illegal. In fact, spearguns themselves are illegal in the Bahamas.

The number of lines per boat is limited to six in the water at any one time.

The bag limit per person per boat for dolphin, kingfish and wahoo, or any combination of the three species, is six.

Above that limit, fish should be released unharmed, as should all fish unless they are to be used for food.

Planning your fishing trip is easy. Many hotels offer packages of between three and eight days, with everything you need included in the rate: boat, bait, box lunches and gear. In some cases, even the use of a small sailboat is included (see specific chapters for package details).

Marine National Parks

More and more, the government of the Bahamas is concerned with protecting the fragile ecosystem and expanding the national park system, especially marine parks. At the time of writing, these included:

Peterson Cay National Park of Grand Bahama, a 1½-acre cay and its surrounding reef system.

Black Sound Cay National Reserve on Green Turtle Cay, Abaco, a two-acre mangrove reserve.

Tilloo Cay National Reserve, Abaco, 11 acres of exposed shoreline.

Pelican Cays Land Sea Park, Cherokee Sound, Great Abaco, a 2,100-acre undersea park with an extensive system of caves and reefs.

Exuma Cays Land & Sea Park, more than 112,640 acres of land and sea marine reserve of outstanding natural beauty.

Conception Island National Park, a 2,100-acre island bird and turtle sanctuary.

Union Creek Reserve, Great Inagua, a 4,940-acre enclosed reserve incorporating a tidal creek.

While you are welcome to visit these parks and reserves, preferably with a guide, it is an offense to remove anything from the parks, alive or dead. This includes seashells.

Sightseeing

On the Out Islands, sightseeing tours are provided by local taxi drivers, who can be hired by the hour, but come much cheaper if contracted for the full day.

Snorkeling & Diving

Scuba Diving

Diving off the Bahamas is excellent. Dive operators on most of the islands can take you on scheduled dives, or to locations of your own choosing.

For the most part, the waters off the Bahamas are very clear, shallow and offer an abundance of coral reefs and gardens for you to explore, as well as shipwrecks, modern and ancient.

Unless you are an experienced diver, it's probably best to work with an operator, especially if you want to go wreck or shark diving.

Dive Sites

The dive sites listed throughout this book are, for the most part, remote and difficult to get to without a qualified guide. The locations of most listed sites in the Out Islands are not marked in any way – on maps or in the ocean – and are the closely guarded secrets of the local dive operators who make their living taking divers out on guided tours. If you want to see a particular site, ask your operator. If there are enough people interested in the site to make a full boat, it will cost no more than the regular half-day or full-day tour. If not, you'll have to rent the boat and guide on your own, which can be expensive.

It is not recommended that you go off on your own. Local knowledge of the waters and currents is essential, and it's dangerous to dive without such knowledge, especially where shipwrecks are concerned.

Snorkeling

Snorkeling can be enjoyed almost anywhere with clear waters. The only place you need permission to swim is off private beaches.

You should seek professional advice before taking off into the deep. It matters little where you might be staying; even on the most remote of the Out Islands there will always be someone available to warn you about the currents or other dangers at any given spot.

Dangers

Sharks, predators of the deep, have gained an undeserved reputation. But sharks kill only when hungry. Shark attacks are extremely rare, especially in the Bahamas. They say you have more of a chance of being twice-struck by lightning than of being attacked by a shark.

Moray eels, on the whole, are nocturnal creatures and like to be left alone inside their chosen lair. There are a few that might have become accustomed to humans – and the handouts they have come to expect from them – but those that haven't can, if disturbed or threatened, give you a very nasty bite. Stay at a respectful distance.

Barracuda are not really dangerous, just scary-looking, especially with their rather frightening and ever-present grin. The sleek, silver tiger of the ocean is a curious creature, however, and will often follow you around, which can be a little unnerving. If you happen to be feeding the local reef fish, which you shouldn't do, you should always be on the lookout for something bigger. A barracuda after his share of the pie will attack like lightning and, although he's only after your hand-out, it might be your hand he takes.

Reef fish tend to be curious. They're not dangerous, but you might find them nipping at your fingers, toes and hair.

Rays, on the whole, are not dangerous. Tread on a stingray buried in the sand, however, and you're probably in for a trip to the local hospital. The ray's first reaction is self-preservation, and its natural instinct is to lash out with its murderous tail. Unless threatened or trodden on, however, it's pretty much harmless and fascinating to watch as it flaps over the sandy bottom. Just be careful where you're putting your feet.

Scorpionfish lie in wait for the unwary on coral heads or close to the ocean floor. They have a set of thick spines on their backs that can inflict a nasty sting. Keep your hands clear.

The stonefish, often hard to see due to its camouflage, can also give you a nasty sting. Look carefully before you touch anything.

Jellyfish, transparent and often difficult to see, are almost all harmless. There are, however, some that are not. It's best to avoid them all.

Coral is often sharp, and tiny pieces can become dislodged in cuts and abrasions. If this should happen, you'll be in for a painful couple of days. Fire coral should not be handled at all. Your best bet is not to touch any coral – not only because it can hurt you, but also because it's a delicate, living organism.

Sea urchins are spiky little black or red balls that lie on the sandy ocean floor or in nooks and crannies among coral heads in the shallow waters of the reef. Step on a sea urchin with bare feet at your peril. The spines are brittle, often barbed, and will give you a very nasty experience. Fortunately, urchins are easily seen and thus easily avoided. Keep a sharp lookout and don't touch.

If you do happen to get stung by coral, jellyfish, or an urchin, you can treat the sting first with vinegar. This will neutralize the poison. Then you should get some help from the local drugstore to ease the pain.

Wreck Diving

It is said that there are more than 500 shipwrecks in the Bahamas, and it's probably true. Some of these wrecks, especially those that allow access to their interiors, can be dangerous and even experienced divers should not go into them alone. There are plenty of guides and dive operators who do know their way around. Many wrecks are infested with fire coral. Many more are home to moray eels that are not dangerous if you give them space.

SAFETY

Take reasonable precautions and stay alert. You'll get into trouble only if you do something you shouldn't, are neglectful, or fail to take note of expert advice. Never dive alone.

Sun Seeking

There are literally thousands of beaches here – some crowded, some so deserted you won't see another human being for weeks at a time. Great expanses of sugar-white sand and the palest of green waters stretch for mile after sun-soaked mile. Almost every hotel is either on or close to a beach. Those that aren't provide free shuttle services back and forth to a carefully selected and monitored beach.

The Out Islands boast of some of the finest beaches in the world, including Fernandez Bay on Cat Island, Harbour Island off Eleuthera, Rolleville on Great Exuma, Great Harbour Cay on the Berry Islands, Staniard Creek on Andros, Stocking Island off George Town on Great Exuma, and the entire shoreline of Mayaguana Cay just east of Acklins Island.

Shopping

The Out Islands of the Bahamas have shopping with a difference. The prices are not always what you might hope for, but searching for a bargain is half the fun. From the tiny street market in George Town on Great Exuma to the three little stores on Mayaguana, there are thousands of opportunities to browse, argue and bargain. Haggling over price can be a fun experience.

Holidays

Bahamas Holiday Calendar

January: New Years' Day (Jan 1) is a public holiday.

April: Good Friday (1st Friday in April) and Easter Monday (Monday following Easter) are public holidays.

May: Whit-Monday. This public holiday follows Whitsunday (also known as Pentecost), the seventh Sunday after Easter.

June: Labor Day (June 1) is a public holiday.

July: Independence Day (July 10) is a public holiday that celebrates the Bahamas' independence from Britain. Parades and fireworks.

August: Emancipation Day, the first Monday in August, commemorates the end of slavery in the Bahamas in 1834.

September: Annual Bahamas Jazz Festival – an international event held the first week in September.

October: Discovery Day (Oct 12) is a public holiday celebrating Christopher Columbus' first landing in the Bahamas.

November: Guy Fawkes Festival (Nov 10) is celebrated on Eleuthera in honor of the capture of Guy Fawkes, who attempted to blow up the Houses of Parliament in England in 1605.

Central Banks Art Exhibition and Competition (Nov 16) is a national competition for artists under 26 years old, who showcase their works in a variety of media.

December: Christmas Day is a public holiday.

Boxing Day/Junkanoo Parade (Dec 26): The biggest public celebration on the islands, especially in Nassau. This is a traditional British holiday, when the wealthy boxed their Christmas dinner leftovers and presented them to their servants.

The Abacos

Getting Around

On Great Abaco a taxi is the most convenient mode of transportation. If you're headed on to the islands, it's the ferry.

By Ferry

To get to **Green Turtle Cay**, catch the ferry near Treasure Cay Airport. Taxi fare from the airport to the dock is $5. The ferry ride over to Green Turtle Cay will take about 50 minutes and cost $8; a same-day, round-trip ticket costs $15.

The taxi fare from Marsh Harbour Airport into town, or to Albury's Ferry Station, is about $12. Boats depart for **Man-O-War Cay** and **Elbow Cay** from Crossing Beach twice each day at 10:30 am and 4:30 pm. The one-way fare is $12; a same-day round-trip ticket costs $18. The ferry to **Great Guana Cay** leaves twice a day from the dock at the Conch Inn Marina at 9:30 am and 4:30 pm. The fare is $12 one-way and $18 for a same-day round-trip ticket. Children ride for half-fare.

*If you miss the ferry, either at Marsh Harbour or Treasure Cay, don't worry, you're not stranded. You can arrange a special charter by calling **Albury's Ferry Service** at 809-367-2306. A one-way ride will cost around $40. At Treasure Cay you can call the **Green Turtle Ferry** at 809-365-4166 or 4151.*

By Bicycle, Moped or Car

Bicycles are available to rent at many of the hotels and resorts throughout the Abacos and at **Brendal's Dive Shop** on Green Turtle Cay. Rental cars, bicycles and mopeds are also available in Marsh Harbour. At the time of this writing, the going rate for a rental car was negotiable, starting at about $60 per day. It's cheaper by the week. For a bicycle, you'll pay at least $10 per day or $50 per week. A moped will cost $40 for 24 hours, or $200 by the week – maybe less if you're prepared to haggle. 242-365-4411, www.brendal.com.

Donna's Cart Rentals Just up the road from the ferry dock, Donna's offer golf cart rentals at $45 per day or $270 for a full week. Carts are equipped with headlights for getting around in the evening. Definitely worth the investment if you are staying out of town and want the option of exploring the island or dining out. 242-365-5195, seansun@batelnet.bs.

Marsh Harbour

With a permanent population of just over 3,000 and a single traffic light (the only one on the Out Islands), the Bahamas' third largest city could be regarded as a major commercial center for the islands. It is, in addition, a major boating center, with craft of all shapes and sizes coming through for fuel, rest, food and water.

The little town has a shopping center of sorts, several small hotels, a couple of gift shops, and a number of restaurants.

Vacationers using Marsh Harbour as a center of operations will find the tiny community refreshingly quiet and well-equipped for most of your needs. From Marsh Harbour you can drive Great Abaco, or cruise the cays in a rental boat.

Walking

There are a number of good hikes. A leisurely half-hour stroll will take you to most of the sights and sounds of Marsh Harbour, while longer walks of up to three miles can provide a pleasant afternoon in the sunshine and some excellent views of the small off-shore cays and tiny outlying settlements.

A good place to begin is the **Conch Inn** (: 242-367-4000; see page 148). This is where the yachting fraternity congregates in - ever-increasing numbers. The water here is crystal clear, and you can watch the fish, crabs, and the boats as they come and go. You can even rent a boat yourself and take a leisurely cruise. Visit the Conch Inn for breakfast, lunch or dinner. The dockside bar and restaurant with its open-air dining is famous across the islands as a gathering spot and watering hole. There are several other restaurants close to the waterfront, including **Wally's** and **Mangoes**. The waterfront is also home to **Dive Abaco** (see page 172), one of the largest scuba and snorkeling centers in the Abacos. Along the way, bicycles can be rented at **Abaco Towns by the Sea**, a time-share apartment complex in downtown Marsh Harbour off Bay Street on the South Shore.

South from Town

A short walk from the old harbour to the south you will find Marsh Town and the **Abaco Beach Resort & Boat Harbour** (800-468-4799; www.abacoresort.com; see page 175), with its full-service marina and 160 slips. The hotel, set back a little from the water, is also the location of one of the most popular watering holes: the **Angler's Restaurant**. The Great Abaco Beach Resort is also home to **The Dive Shop**. On the waterfront in Marsh Harbour, **Seahorse Boat Rentals**, 242-367-2513, at Boat Harbour Marina on Bay Street, has boats, bicycles, windsurfers and snorkel equipment for rent. Follow Bay Street a little way to the east from Marsh Town and you'll pass through the tiny settlements of Pond Bay, Pelican Shores, Fanny Bay, and Upper Cut. The walk is a pleasant and leisurely way of spending an hour or two, and there are shady rest stops conveniently placed along the way.

North from Town

Go north from the waterfront in Marsh Harbour for an agreeable three-mile walk along Harbour Road to the quaint little fishing villages of **Dundas Town** and **Murphy Town**, two little communities with little churches and tiny clapboard houses. Be sure to drop in at **Mother Merle's Fishnet** in Dundas Town for conch salad, fresh fish, or a lobster plate that's excellent (take-out service only).

Driving

If you decide to drive, head out east or west where the country roads are something of an experience in themselves. Drive south to **Sandy Point** or **Hole in the Wall**, and you're in for a drive of about 100 miles, round-trip, with stops along the way at **Cherokee Sound** and **Casuarina Point**, where you'll find one of the island's most fascinating and not-to-be-missed characters, Nettie Symonette. Go north and a scenic drive of similar length will take you through Treasure Cay and on to the tiny villages of **Cooper's Town, Cedar Harbour, Mount Hope, Fox Town** and **Crown Haven**.

Man-O-War Cay

Man-O-War Cay is a small island community some three miles by boat from Marsh Harbour. It's the boat-building capital of the Abacos, and home to the Albury family, whose roots on the Abacos go back for many generations. They have something to do with almost everything that happens on the island – they operate the Albury ferry, the grocery store, the famous Albury's Sail Shop, the Harbour Store, Aunt Mady's Boutique, the Man-O-War Marina, Joe's Studio and many more of the island's prosperous businesses. Man-O-War Cay is a delightful place. There are no cars; the main mode of transport is either the golf cart or walking. There is just one hotel, **Schooner's Landing Resort** (see page 173 for details), and a few rental cottages and apartments.

Exploring

Along the **Queen's Highway**, a big name for such a narrow thoroughfare, is an assortment of quaint gift shops, stores, churches and the island's tiny post office. A few yards down one of the miniscule side roads is Man-O-War's magnificent beach, often deserted, but always inviting. If you enjoy walking, there's probably no nicer hike than the couple of hours it will take you to walk from one end of the island to the other. To visit Man-O-War, take the ferry from the Marsh Harbour dock. A same-day round-trip will cost you $12, and it's well worth the money.

Elbow Cay & Hope Town

Hope Town is a quaint little place reminiscent of old New England. The town is a labyrinth of tiny streets, of gaily painted blue, yellow, pink and white clapboard cottages, small-town stores, and old-fashioned churches. And the town is ablaze with flowers growing in tiny gardens and along the sidewalks: pink oleander, purple bougainvillea, and yellow and red hibiscus. Boats bob at anchor in the harbour, above which the famous candy-striped lighthouse dominates the land and seascape for miles around.

Hope Town's harbor is almost completely enclosed. Only when you've navigated its narrow entrance does the town heave into view. As with Man-O-War, you won't find any cars in the city.

Located on the narrow northern end of Elbow Cay, Hope Town faces the harbor to the west. To the east is the ocean and, only yards from the main highway at the end of a narrow street, a magnificent stretch of white sandy beach. Almost always, there's the irresistible smell of fresh-baked bread, cakes and pies that permeates the air.

Exploring

The town's two museums – the **Wyannie Malone Museum**,

off Bark Street at Hope Town Beach (open 10 am to 12:30, Monday-Saturday; entrance fee $1) and the **Hope Town Lighthouse**, across the harbour, close to Club Soleil – offer a peek into the town's and Elbow Cay's past.

You can stop for a cold drink at the **Hope Town Harbour Lodge Hotel** on Bay Street and enjoy lunch at **Captain Jack's**. From there, you might like to stroll up the hill to the **Bryle Patterson Memorial Garden**; a more peaceful or picturesque view would be hard to find. Hope Town is one of those storybook settings you may read about, but rarely find.

The Artist

While exploring Hope Town, you're sure to come across the **Jib**, one of the oldest residences on the island. If you're lucky enough to be there between October and March, be sure to visit **Dr. Hermann Schadt's**, a German artist. He and his wife, Ann, have been living between Frankfurt and Hope Town for the past 30 years. Locally, some just refer to him as "the artist" and after seeing his work you'll understand why. He works in watercolors. They burst with vibrant colors, yet are subtle enough to stare at endlessly. And they certainly manage to capture the radiance of Hope Town. The vast majority of his paintings are inspired by his local surroundings. It's likely that if you walked around town before visiting you'll recognize some of the buildings and beaches in his paintings. Although some of his work is for sale at local boutiques, you'll find a much larger selection at the Jib. You'll also find handbags and decorations designed by Ann Schadt. She uses only locally produced textiles and the designs are simple and fresh.

Green Turtle Cay & New Plymouth

Green Turtle Cay is perhaps the Abacos' most popular vacation destination. **New Plymouth**, the island's only town, is another quaint little colonial community. It was founded by English loyalists in 1783 after the close of the American War of Independence, making it one of the oldest settlements in the Abacos. Once the second largest city in the Bahamas after Nassau, the old town is a photo album of neat clapboard cottages, picket fences, and a profusion of flowers. Unlike Hope Town and Man-O-War Cay, however, New Plymouth is open to vehicular traffic.

Exploring

With the **Albert Lowe Museum** as the focal point of your tour, New Plymouth's narrow streets, galleries, quaint shops and restaurants are wonderful to explore. The museum, on Parliament Street among the bougainvillea, is in an old colonial building. It contains a fine collection of maritime memorabilia and will provide you with a unique peek into the life and times of the loyalist settlers. They are located at Parliament and King Streets. Open from 9 to 11:45 am and 1 to 4:30 pm, Monday through Saturday. Entrance fee is $1. Other places of interest include the **Loyalist Memorial Sculpture Garden**, the **New Plymouth Cemetery** with gravestones dating back to the 18th century, and the old **New Plymouth Jail**, unused now for more than two centuries.

But there's more to Green Turtle Cay than New Plymouth. The island boasts a number of **fine beaches**, some of the **best diving** locations in the Bahamas, and a network of roads that will take you on long hikes to **romantic bays and inlets**, quiet little harbors where boats sit at anchor, and a number of out-of-the-way restaurants and cafés where you can enjoy fish and lobster straight from the ocean.

Green Turtle Cay has three hotels, one in New Plymouth, the others on the harbor at White Sound (see pages 171-72 for details). The island can be reached only by private boat or by the ferry. The ferry service is good. You can leave for New Plymouth early in the morning from either Treasure Cay or the Green Turtle Club, returning to either dock in the mid-afternoon. There are also a couple of local tour operators who run trips to the island on a weekly basis.

Treasure Cay

Treasure Cay – the name is misleading, for it's not a cay at all – is on Great Abaco Island some 25 miles north of Marsh Harbour, and was the scene of the first major tourist development in the Abacos. During the 1950s, work began on the resort community. It has continued ever since. Today, the small town offers a variety of accommodations and facilities. There are luxury villas, condos, and time-share units. There's also a hotel, a 150-slip marina, several shops, a post office, grocery store, health clinic, dive shop and more. Best of all, Treasure Cay boasts one of the best beaches in the Bahamas. The four-mile crescent of sugar-white sand and waving palms, offset against a background of shallow, pale green sea, is the sort of stuff you see on the quintessential vacation poster. A major attraction is the golf course at Treasure Cay Hotel Resort & Marina, the only one in the Out Islands. There is also a dive shop at the resort, Treasure Divers.

Treasure Cay is close to the site where the first settlers of the Abacos built their homes in Charleton, near the northern end of Treasure Cay. It lasted only a year or two before its population moved on to what would eventually become modern-day Marsh Harbour.

Great Guana Cay

Great Guana is one of the largest of the outer Abaco cays. It's also the location of one of the smallest settlements on the Abacos, **Guana Harbour**. The community is set at about the midway point on the seven-mile-long island, and you won't find it until you've navigated the tiny harbour entrance. Guana Harbour has a permanent population of only 80. Most of the men make their living either by farming or fishing. Those that don't are employed at the Guana Beach Resort and Marina.

Like most of the cays in the Abacos, Great Guana is accessible only by private boat or ferry. The ferry runs a scheduled service from Marsh Harbour. The tiny village with its clapboard cottages, café, gift shop, liquor store, and grocery store, is a quiet retreat with narrow streets and waving palms. So, for the most part, Great Guana remains an unspoiled tropical paradise with more than seven miles of pristine white beaches, grassy dunes, and emerald waters, all set against a deep blue sky.

The Guana Resort & Marina and Seaside Villas, the only hotel on the island, sits amid the palms, seagrapes and casuarina trees on a tiny peninsula. The resort is a sportsman's dream. Here you can windsurf, snorkel, water-ski, sail, and go deep-sea fishing. See page 169-70 for details.

Walker's Cay

Far away at the northern tip of the archipelago, two tiny islands, Walker's Cay and Grand Cay, represent the end of the world, at least as far as the Abacos are concerned. Walker's Cay, reached only by private plane or boat, is the last stop in the Bahamas – a mecca for sport fishermen from around the world. It's a lonely place, with only one hotel, a marina, and a population of marine life that will delight angler and diver alike. Walker's Cay, protected and unspoiled, was once a refuge for pirates and ne'er-do-wells. Today it's a haven for anglers, divers, and sailors. It's also a sanctuary for those who want to spend a few days in total seclusion – where the air is sweet, the beaches deserted, the sea clear, and the sunsets spectacular.

Bird Watching & Nature Tours

These tours, operated by **Bahamas Naturalists Expeditions, Ltd.**, give you the opportunity to explore the nature trails in the Caribbean pine forests of the **Abaco National Park** with an experienced naturalist guide, who will explain everything of interest. You'll go in search of the endangered Bahama parrot, see a variety of orchids and bromeliads, and enjoy a catered picnic lunch on a deserted beach in southern Abaco. You'll also be able to snorkel in a freshwater, inland blue hole and see colossal stalagmites and stalactites that were formed more than 10,000 years ago.

Tours depart Marsh Harbour at 10 am and return at 4 pm. They cost $75 per person, including lunch and beverages. Snorkeling equipment is not included (you must bring your own). 809-359-6783 for reservations, or inquire at Sapodilly's Restaurant & Bar on Bay Street in Marsh Harbour, or at Sea Horse Boat Rentals, either in Hope Town or Marsh Harbour at Boat Harbour Marina.

The Different of Abaco

This is at **Casuarina Point**, Abaco. Also the home of the Great Abaco Bonefishing Club, the Different of Abaco is the dream of Nettie Symonette. The natural resort, a small, rustic hotel in the wilds of southern Abaco off Cherokee Sound, is an on-going development of naturally landscaped gardens, rock gardens, freshwater ponds, and saltwater inlets, where bougainvillea, hibiscus, croton, oleander, star of Bethlehem and native orchids provide a riot of color and greenery. The rock gardens are a natural home for a variety of land and marine life that includes crabs, curly tailed lizards and snakes, while Nettie's personal collection of wildlife includes the Exuma iguana, the Abaco wild boar, dozens of friendly ducks, local chickens, and a lovable old donkey – all living happily together in a habitat that closely emulates their own natural environments.

To visit The Different of Abaco you must take either a taxi or rent a moped or bicycle. Once there, you can enjoy a home-cooked meal, wander the grounds, spend hours watching the more than 50 species of wild birds that inhabit the area and, before you leave, enjoy a cup of Nettie's famous Bush Tea. Hike a mile or two south on Great Abaco Highway and you can see hundreds of Abaco parrots. A little farther on, about five miles from The Different, is the village of **Cherokee**, a picturesque colonial town at the edge of Cherokee Sound. If you're interested in staying for a few days, call Nettie at : 242-366-2150 or 327-7921. If you want to try some bonefishing, there's no better place than here (see *Fishing Packages*, page 147).

On The Water

Sport Fishing

The waters off the Abacos offer some great sport fishing. The flats around Cherokee Sound and Casuarina Point teem with bonefish. Boats are available for rent from a number of operators and the hotels on the islands offer a wide variety of sport and bonefishing packages. There are also several deep-sea charter fishing outfits that will take you right to the best waters to catch marlin, sailfish, wahoo, kingfish and barracuda.

Boat Rentals

Rich's Rentals, Marsh Harbour. 17- and 21-foot Paramounts, daily, three-day, weekly and monthly rates. From $95 to $140 per day. 242-367-2742.

Conch Inn Resort & Marina, operated by The Moorings. Charter sailboats, bareboat and crewed. Expensive – call for rates. 242-367-4000.

Island Marine. Boston Whalers and Aquasports, Rates start at $40 per day for a 15-foot Boston Whaler. 242-366-0181.

Sea Horse Boat Rentals, Great Abaco Beach Resort. 18- to 21-foot Boston Whalers, $85-$140 per day, depending on size. 242-367-2513.

Rainbow Rentals, 17-foot Paramounts and 21-foot Chris Craft. 242-367-2452.

Donny's Boat Rentals, Green Turtle Cay. 14- to 17-foot Boston Whalers and 19- to 23-foot Makos. Daily, three-day and weekly rates. 242-365-4119.

Dames Rentals, Green Turtle Cay. 14- to 23-foot boats available at daily and weekly rates. 242-365-4247.

Hope Town Dive Shop & Boat Rentals, Hope Town. Boats from 13 to 23 feet available, with daily, three-day, and weekly rates. 242-366-0029.

Fishing Tournaments

One of the first two legs of the **Bahamas Billfish Championship Tournament**, which takes place during the spring and early summer each year at five different locations, is held in April at Walker's Cay. The third and fourth legs are at Treasure Cay and Boat Harbour. For details and registration, 305-923-8022 or 242-367-2158.

The **Penny Turtle Billfish Tournament** is held at the Great Abaco Beach Resort in May. 800-468-4799 or 242-367-2158.

The **Billfish Foundation's Tag Tournament** is held in May at the Walker's Cay Hotel and Marina. 800-WALKERS.

The **Annual Treasure Cay International Billfish Tournament** is held in June. 800-327-1584.

The **Green Turtle Cay Yacht Club** hosts its annual fishing tournament in May. 242-365-4271.

The **Boat Harbour Billfish Championship** is held in June at the Marsh Harbour Resort. 305-920-7877 or 242-367-2158.

Fishing/Accommodation Packages

Important Note: All of the packages listed below were active and correctly priced at the time they were researched. You should be aware, however, that all are subject to change without notice. Please check with the provider at the Phone numbers listed for up-to-date packages, rates, and information.

Sport fishing packages are offered by several hotels on the Abacos, including those listed here. The rates quoted below are, unless otherwise stated, per person, double occupancy. For a full list of package operators, call either the **Bahamas Tourism Office** at 800-32-SPORT, or the **Bahama Out Islands**

Promotion Board at 800-688-4725.

The Tangelo Hotel: Wood Cay, Abaco. 242-365-2222 for reservations. http://oii.net/tangelo. This hotel specializes in bonefishing. Their basic package is a four-day/three-night stay that includes breakfast, lunch, and dinner, round-trip ground transfers, and two full days of fishing. The basic four-day package costs $778 for two persons based on double occupancy – a significant saving over the single rate of $686 per person. The package rate does not include airfare, taxes, or gratuities. An additional day of fishing will cost $200. Fly to Treasure Cay and take a taxi to the hotel or call for a pick-up.

Sea Spray Resort & Villas: Elbow Cay, Abaco, 242-366-0065, www.seasprayresort.com. Fly into Marsh Harbour, then take the ferry to Elbow Cay. This operator offers two options:

The basic four-day, three-night package is based on a group of four people and includes stay in an oceanfront villa with maid service and dinner each day. It also includes use of a 22-foot boat for three days, with bait and a boxed lunch each day, and 2½ days fishing with a local guide. $1,450.

The seven-night package includes use of the boat for six days, 3½ days fishing with a local guide, bait, and boxed lunches on fishing days. Four people: $2,450.

Both packages also include use of a Sunfish sailboat, freezer space, ice, local charts, gratuities, and the 8: hotel tax. Airfare, breakfast, and fuel for the boat are not included.

Schooner's Landing Resort: Man-O-War Cay, Abaco, 242-365-6143, www.schoonerslanding.com. Fly into Marsh Harbour then take the ferry over to Man-O-War Cay. A resort representative will meet you at the ferry dock. Schooner's Landing offers two packages:

The basic four-day, three-night package includes a beachfront, two-bedroom townhouse, fully equipped; maid service; use of a 20-foot boat for three days, including ice and bait; a local fishing guide for 2½ days; a box lunch on fishing days and evening meals. $275 per day.

The extended eight-day, seven-night package includes all the above, with the boat for six days and the guide for 3½ days, boxed lunches for three days and evening meals for three nights.

$1,850. Both packages include freezer space, private dock, local charts, gratuities and the 8: hotel tax. Airfare, fuel for the boat, tackle, taxi and ferry transportation are not included in the rates.

Note: Visa/Mastercard and American Express charges are subject to a 5: surcharge.

The Conch Inn: Marsh Harbour, Abaco, 242-367-4000, www.theconchinn.com. Fly into Marsh Harbour Airport and take a taxi to the hotel. The Conch Inn offers a basic four-day, as well as an extended eight-day, package. Included in the rate is transportation to and from the Marsh Harbour Airport; accommodations; use of the private pool and beach; daily maid service; a half-day of bonefishing, including bait, tackle and ice; and one full day of deep-sea fishing, including bait, tackle and ice. Meals, beverages, taxes and gratuities are extra. Call for rates.

Guana Beach Resort: Guana Cay, Abaco, 800-227-3366, wwwguanabeach.com. Fly into Marsh Harbour Airport, take a taxi to the ferry dock, and then take the ferry to Guana Cay. Guana Beach Resort's package includes five days (four nights) of deluxe accommodations; a welcome "Guana Grabber" cocktail; use of a Sunfish sailboat and beach boat; and three half-day fishing trips for $550. Airfare and meals are not included, but breakfast and dinner are available for an extra $32 per person, per day.

The Great Abaco Bonefishing Club: Located at The Different of Abaco, Casuarina Point, Abaco, 242-366-2150 or 327-7921. The Different of Abaco is a small, naturally developed retreat/resort with 10 guest rooms located just off Cherokee Sound. If you are looking for something different, want to get back to basics and away from it all for some fine bonefishing, this is the place. The Different offers four days of bonefishing and seclusion for $1,000 per person. The rate includes accommodations, meals, and three days of fishing with an expert local guide. More than that, though, you'll be taken to virgin flats where, rather than the elusive, skittish quarry you might expect, the bonefish have never seen a fly and will fight each other to take your bait. The bonefish here, from the tales of those who stalk them, fight harder and longer than anywhere else. The Different operates 10 boats, all with expert local guides, for fishing the flats of the Cherokee Sound or the flats at the Marls, some 18 miles down water.

Fishing Guides

Important Note: All of the guides listed below were active and the rates were correct at the time they were researched. You should be aware, however, that all are subject to change without notice. Please check with the provider at the Phone numbers listed for up-to-date packages, rates, and information.

Rates shown are per boat. Where no rates are given, they will be comparable to those that are shown. For more information, go to http://oii.net.

Will Key is available all year. He can take up to four people fishing on his 21-foot offshore boat, *Day's Catch*. Will specializes in bonefishing, reef and deep-sea fishing, snorkeling, sightseeing and shelling. Rates: $150 for a half-day; $250 for a full day. 242-266-0059.

Robert Lowe runs charters April through August. His 30-foot Stapleton, *Sea Gull*, has a capacity of six persons for deep-sea fishing. Rates: $220 for a half-day; $440 for a full day. 242-366-0266.

Maitland Lowe, an expert bonefisherman as well as deep-sea fisherman, takes anglers out in his 19-foot boat and charges $200 for a day's bonefishing; $150 for a half-day deep-sea fishing; and $250 for a full day. 242-366-0004.

Truman Major is a guide for all types of fishing, except bonefishing, year-round. Truman takes anglers out in his 30-foot Sea Hawk, *Lucky Strike*, and supplies all tackle, bait and ice. Rates: $220 for a half-day; $320 for a full day. 242-366-0101.

Captain Creswell Archer is available for deep-sea fishing and sightseeing out of Marsh Harbour. 242-367-4000 for reservations.

Orthnell Russell, the "Bonefish King," is in Treasure Cay. Contact the Treasure Cay Marina, 242-367-2570, or in Copper's Town, 242-365-0125.

The King Fish II, Treasure Cay. Sportfishing daily. 242-367-2570.

Lincoln Jones, Green Turtle Cay, 242-365-4223.

Joe Sawyer, Green Turtle Cay, 242-365-4173.

Trevor Sawyer, Cherokee, 242-366-2065.

Diving & Snorkeling

The Abacos have plenty of coral reefs and ancient shipwrecks to explore. Or just float around close to the surface and watch the thousands of brightly colored fish, crabs and other marine life.

From Walker's Cay to Sandy Point, the shoreline of the Abacos offers a huge and varied assortment of shallow flats, sand banks, patch reefs, and fringe and barrier reefs. Diving is mostly done in shallow waters, six to 15 feet deep, easily within the scope of inexperienced snorkelers. Visibility ranges, according to depth, up to a couple of hundred feet. The coral structures, which include everything from sea fans to brain coral, and from antlers to tubes, are often fissured, undercut and dotted with mysterious blue holes. Everywhere there is a never-ending parade of reef and pelagic (deep-sea) fish of every color imaginable. Add to that a dozen or so wreck sites and you have an underwater enthusiast's dream come true.

Photo: The Bahamas Ministry of Tourism

Abaco's Best Dive Sites

It's generally acknowledged that the best diving in the Abacos is between its eastern shores and the long line of cays on the 150-mile eastern barrier reef. For snorkelers, almost every beach throughout the archipelago offers something special.

Marsh Harbour:

The Towers. Huge coral pinnacles extend upward some 60 feet from the ocean floor and are riddled with spectacular tunnels and caverns.

The Cathedral, a huge cavern where shafts of sunlight filter through, splashing the seabed with color.

Grouper Alley, where, in 40 feet of unclouded water, great coral heads are honeycombed with tunnels.

Wayne's World, where the water approaches 70 feet in depth, and you can take a thrilling excursion along the outer wall of the barrier reef.

Pelican Cays National Land & Sea Park

Located just north of Cherokee Sound, this is a 2,100-acre undersea wildlife refuge where you'll swim among coral heads, dive into undersea caves, and visit with gaily colored fish and other reef dwellers. Pelican Cays incorporates the only inshore fringed reef in the Abacos and is home to some 170 different species of marine life, including green turtles and spotted eagle rays.

Green Turtle Cay

Green Turtle Cay is located some three miles off the northeast coast of Great Abaco, , a tiny island that measures no more than three and a half miles long by a half-mile wide. It has a coastline of small bays, inlets and sandy beaches, along with excellent diving.

Coral Canyons is a series of great canyons with an overhang that goes back into the reef some 60 to 80 feet. Often filled with huge schools of silver fish, the site provides great opportunities for underwater photography.

The Catacombs, another great site for underwater photography, is a shallow, sunlit cavern.

Coral Condos, in 60 to 70 feet of clear water, are a series of huge coral heads that provide homes for dozens of brilliantly colored reef fish.

Tarpon Reef, another magnificent series of coral formations, is home to a school of tarpon from which it gets its name, as well as a large green moray eel. The wrecks of the *Viceroy* and the *San Jacinto* (see *Shipwrecks*, below) lie in some 30 to 50 feet of water and, although scattered over a wide area, present some unique photographic opportunities.

Walker's Cay

Accessible only by private plane or boat or through the services offered by the Walker's Cay Hotel and Marina, this is the northernmost of the chain of islands that makes up the Abacos. Because of its splendid isolation and inaccessibility, the island enjoys a reputation for fine diving and there's no shortage of facilities, guides, or support. Walker's Cay Undersea Adventures (see *Dive Operators*, page 157-58) will provide expert guides, rental gear, and instruction. The diving off Walker's Cay features bank, fringe and patch reefs, as well as drop-offs. It's dense with coral formations in shallow waters, crowded with marine life and, because of its isolation, is a world unspoiled and now well protected.

Spectacular dive sites can be found throughout the area.

These include:

Spiral Caverns, a dramatic series of caverns in less than 50 feet of water that meander through vast coral formations filled with clouds of silver minnows.

Pirates' Cathedral is a magnificent reef cavern with a series of chambers and openings filled with fish and other marine life.

Barracuda Alley, the home of Charlie, a scary-looking, six-foot barracuda, provides a dive through 45 feet of water into a canyon-like coral reef formation.

Shark Canyon. A dive through almost 100 feet of crystalline water and coral formations into a canyon, where sleeping sharks can often be found on the sandy bottom.

Shipwrecks

Dozens of shipwrecks lie off the Abacos. Some of the wreck sites are spectacular; some are barely recognizable. Some are accessible only by private boat; others can be explored through the dive operators working out of Marsh Harbour, Hope Town, and Green Turtle Cay. Following is a list of some of the better known wrecks in the Abacos:

The USS Adirondack

The *USS Adirondack*, an Ossipee class, wooden, steam- and sail-driven sloop of 1,240 tons and 207 feet in length, was launched on February 22, 1862. Hers was a short life. She was a Federal gunboat, operating as a part of the South Atlantic Blockading Squadron, that went down on August 23, 1862 after running aground on the Little Bahama Bank during a voyage from Port Royal to Nassau. Every member of her crew was rescued, but attempts to salvage the ship failed. The wind and surf soon smashed her into pieces and she sank.

Today, there's not much left of her. What remains lies scattered in 10-30 feet of water over a wide area between No Name Cay and Man-O-War Cay. Two of her 11-inch guns, as well as several other smaller guns, can still be seen, but that's about all. The wreck can be reached via either Dive Abaco or Dave Malone at the Hope Town Dive Shop (see page 158). Dave will tell you that it's hardly worth the effort. Even so, if you're a Civil War buff, the *Adirondack* offers at least some historic significance.

The USS San Jacinto

The *USS San Jacinto* was also a Civil War gunboat. Launched on April 16, 1850, she was an experimental ship – one of the first to be powered by steam and sail. Unfortunately, her engines were not as reliable as those used in later ships and were a problem throughout her service. At the time of her demise she was employed as a part of the blockade against the Confederate ports on the east coast of the US. She ran aground off Chub Rocks on New Year's Day, 1865. In her time, although plagued by her unreliable machinery, she was credited with the capture of such Confederate blockade runners as the *Lizzie Davis*, the *Roebuck*, the *Fox* and others.

Today, what little remains of the *San Jacinto* lies scattered over a wide area in some 40 feet of water. Her superstructure is all gone, smashed to pieces by 145 years of pounding surf. She can be explored with Brendal's Dive International Shop of Green Turtle Cay (800-780-9941).

The Viceroy

The *Viceroy*, a turn-of-the-century steamship, lies in about 50 feet of water close to Chub Rocks, not far from the wreck of the *San Jacinto*. The ship's engines and props are still intact and make for some great close-up photography. The *Viceroy* is also the home of "Pickles," a seven-foot green moray eel who likes to be fed tidbits.

The H.M.S. Mermaid

The *H.M.S. Mermaid* set sail from Charleston, South Carolina on December 1, 1759, bound for New Providence; she never made it. On the morning of December 4th, fighting gale force winds and heavy seas, she found herself driven relentlessly toward the breakers. In a futile attempt to save his ship, Captain James Hackman tried three times to anchor her, and each time the ropes snapped under the force of the storm. For hours, the captain and crew fought to save the ship. The heavy guns were thrown overboard in a last-ditch attempt to lighten the ship and float it over the reef; it was not enough. The *Mermaid* finally ran aground about a half-mile offshore. For almost a month, the ship lay on the rocks, the surf pounding at her hull. Finally, on

January 6, 1760, she broke up and sank; her remains were to lie undiscovered for 227 years until 1987, when Carl Fismer of the Spanish Main Treasure Company found her resting in only 10 feet of water. Fismer, using a magnetometer, first found one of her anchors, then another. Then, one by one, he found her long-abandoned guns and, finally, what was left of her hull among the rocks and sand off Mermaid Beach.

The wreck is easily accessible to both divers and snorkelers, and can be reached via a guided tour by Gary Adkinson and Barry Albury at the Walker's Cay Hotel and Marina Dive Shop. 800-327-8150.

The Bonita

The *Bonita,* an English World War II transport vessel, was sunk in a location known only to Brendal Stevens of Brendal's Dive Shop, is now a grouper feeding station in 60 feet of water and is included in Brendal's schedule of dive sites.

The Barge

This wreck consists of the scattered remains of an old landing craft in 40 feet of water off Fiddle Cay.

The Demira

A 411-foot steel-hulled freighter that sank during a hurricane in 1928, she lies in 30 feet of water and is accessible to both scuba divers and snorkelers.

Best Snorkeling Sites

Nine hotels in the Abacos participate in the Jean Michel Cousteau "Snorkeling Adventures" program (see page 41). All are featured at the http://oii.net website.

Abaco Inn, Elbow Cay, 800-468-8799

Bluff House Club, Green Turtle Cay, 800-688-4752

Great Abaco Beach Resort, Marsh Harbour, 800-468-4799

Green Turtle Club, Green Turtle Cay, 800-688-4752

Guana Beach Resort, 800-227-3366

Hope Town Harbour Lodge, Elbow Cay, 800-316-7844

Pelican Beach Villas, Marsh Harbour, 800-642-7268

Spanish Cay Inn, Cooperstown, 800-688-4752

Walker's Cay Hotel, 800-WALKERS

sites are as follows:

...a Reef

...of the reef where angelfish school in large numbers. ...ere is less than 20 feet deep; it's ideal for beginners.

Blue Strip Reef

Spawning grounds for a variety of reef fish. Lots of colorful underwater formations. Large schools of blue striped grunts.

Crawfish Shallows

A fun place to visit, great for lobsters and the occasional sleeping nurse shark.

Elkhorn Park

A vast area of reef with acres of elk and staghorn corals. Lots of colorful reef fish, and lots of octopus. Coral heads are close to the surface.

Fowl Cay Reef

A large expanse of coral reef just a few minutes swim from the beach. Many interesting formations, and a large friendly grouper named "Gillie."

Hope Town Reef

An area of reef with lots of soft and hard corals, multitudes of colorful reef fish. Great for beginners.

Jeanette's Reef

Lots of small invertebrates, schools of colorful fish, and the occasional marauding barracuda.

Meghan's Mesa

An area where you can see a variety of soft and hard corals, all sorts of little critters, and lots of plume worms.

Pirates Cathedral

A labyrinth of caverns and underwater arches, all safe to swim through. Great for experienced snorkelers.

Pelican Park

This is a great site to observe sea turtles and eagle rays, along with a wide variety of other marine life.

Smugglers Rest

Lots of fun to be had here. The remains of a plane wreck, now home to all sorts of marine life.

Spanish Cannon

Very little is left of the Spanish galleon that sank here on the reef. Look for the cannon scattered among the ballast stones.

Sandy Cay Reef

A great place to observe some of the larger inhabitants of the coral reef: southern stingrays, spotted eagle rays, etc.

Dive Operators

Dive Abaco

Marsh Harbour, Abaco, Bahamas. 800-247-5338, fax 242-367-2787, www.diveabaco.com. Dive Abaco, a small operation catering to divers and snorkelers, has been in business for more than 15 years and operates out of a wooden building on the waterfront at the Conch Inn, East Bay Street.. They have a staff of four, including two instructors, and their boat can carry up to 12 divers. Dive Abaco's retail store sells snorkel gear, accessories, and carries 35 sets of rental gear. The company is affiliated with NAUI, PADI, and CMAS.

Brendal's Dive Center International

Green Turtle Cay, Abaco, Bahamas. 800-780-9941, www.brendal.com. Brendal Stevens, in business now for more than 10 years, offers instruction and a variety of specialized and individual tours. There is an all-day dive, snorkel, and glass-bottom boat tour, plus a sailing trip to a secluded island with a seafood cookout. The shop offers two-tank morning dives, one-tank afternoon dives, and night dives (by special arrangement). The operation has two boats: a new custom dive boat with capacity of up to 24 passengers and a smaller boat with capacity of 12. There's a staff of three, including an instructor. The shop store sells a full range of gear and accessories, and it carries 30 sets of rental gear. Brendal's is affiliated with SSI, CMAS, and NAUI.

Dive Guana

The only dive operator on Guana Cay, Troy has been in business five years and has an extensive knowledge of the best spots on the reef. Both half-day and full-day dive/snorkel trips are available and free transportation is provided to/from your property. The full-day trips include a combination of diving/snorkeling and a guided tour of one of the local islands. The full-service dive center offers instruction as well as equipment, underwater camera and boat rentals. In addition, they offer bicycle, kayak and fishing pole rentals. They can also arrange private villa or hotel accommodations. Dive/snorkel packages are available if staying at the Dolphin Beach Resort or Ocean frontier Hideaways. 242-365-5178, www.diveguana.com.

Froggies Dive Shop

For over six years, Lambert and Teresa Albury have been satisfying divers/snorkelers with their wide-ranging reef knowledge and top-quality service. They offer both half- and full-day scuba and snorkeling options. Full-day tours include a combination of snorkeling/diving and island-hopping. They are happy to arrange specialty trips such as night dives and shark dives. They have three boats at their disposal so large groups can be easily accommodated. A full-service dive center has everything you might need for purchase or rental. Although they are PADI-affiliated they accept SSI and NAUI as well. ☐242-366-0431, froggies @batelnet.bs.

Walker's Cay Undersea Adventures

PO Box 21766, Ft. Lauderdale, FL 33335. 800-327-8150, www.nealwatson.com. With more than 21 years in business, they offer a wide range of diving options: two-tank dives in the morning and afternoon, two night dives each week, and shark dives three times a week. The outfit has a staff of six, including four instructors, and two boats with capacities of 16-25 passengers. The company store sells gear and accessories and keeps 15 sets of rental gear on hand. Walker's Cay Undersea is affiliated with PADI, SSI, NAUI, and YMCA.

The Dive Shop

Great Abaco Beach Resort, Marsh Harbour, Abaco, Bahamas. 800-468-4799, wwwabacoresort.com. This is operated by Doug Laurie, who offers diving and snorkeling excursions for novice and experienced divers.

The Hope Town Dive Shop

Hope Town, Abaco, Bahamas. 242-366-0029. A fully equipped shop: B/Cs, regulators, masks, fins, belts, and boat rentals.

Dive/Accommodation Packages

Important Note: All of the packages listed below were active and correctly priced at the time they were researched. You should be aware, however, that all are subject to change without notice. Please check with the provider at the Phone numbers listed for up-to-date packages, rates, and information.

Dive packages are offered by several hotels on the Abacos, including those listed below. The rates quoted are, unless otherwise stated, per person, double occupancy, and were current at the time of writing. Credit cards are accepted unless otherwise stated.

The Conch Inn

Marsh Harbour, Abaco, Bahamas. 800-247-5338, fax 242-367-4004. This package includes professionally guided scuba diving trips from Dive Abaco's full-service dive shop, tank and weights, two dives per day, hotel accommodations, and use of the fresh-water pool. The package does not include airfare, meals, taxes, or gratuities.

1   5 days/4 nights (includes 3 days of diving): call for rates.
2   8 days/7 nights (includes 4 days of diving): call for rates.

H A special airfare is available, either from Miami or Fort Lauderdale, for $150 per person, plus $15 tax. Airlines serving Marsh Harbour are US Air Express, American Eagle, Gulfstream, and Bahamasair (see page 330-32).

Schooner's Landing Resort

Man-O-War Cay, Abaco, Bahamas. 242-365-6072, fax 242-365-6285, e-mail info@schoonerslanding.com. Fly into Marsh Harbour, take a taxi to the ferry dock and ride the ferry to Man-O-War Cay, where you will be met by a Schooner's Landing Resort representative. They offer two packages based upon a four-person occupancy. The four-day package includes a fully equipped beachfront, two-bedroom townhouse with maid service; a 20-foot boat for two days to explore the surrounding islands or dive the national parks; a one-day professionally guided dive trip (two-tank dive); one full tank per person each day for two days; boxed lunches for three days; evening meals; use of a private dock; gratuities, and hotel taxes. The eight-day package includes all the above plus use of the 20-foot boat for five days and one full tank per person for five days. Packages do not include air fare, fuel for the boat, taxi and ferry transportation, snorkel gear, regulator, and B/C. Visa/Mastercard and American Express charges are subject to a 5: surcharge.

3   4 days/3 nights: $1,650
4   8 days/7 nights: $2,525

The Green Turtle Club

Green Turtle Cay, Abaco, Bahamas. 800-780-9941, www.greenturtleclub.com. Fly into Treasure Cay Airport, take the ferry to Green Turtle Cay and disembark at the Green Turtle Club. The lobby is just a few yards in front of you. Airlines serving Treasure Cay are USAir Express, American Eagle, Gulfstream, Island Express, and Bahamasair (see pages 330-32 for contacts). The club offers a wide variety of dive package options for all seasons. Included in all rates are luxury accommodations at the Green Turtle Yacht Club, use of the freshwater swimming pool, windsurfing, beach chairs, tennis, two daily dive trips to the reefs or wrecks, tanks, back pack, weight belts, and a welcome drink. Not included are air fares, meals, transfers, the ferry from and to Treasure Cay, and airport departure taxes. Diving is with Brendal's Dive Shop on Green Turtle Cay, close to the Green Turtle Yacht Club. Call the toll-free number for rates.

Walker's Cay Hotel and Marina

Walker's Cay, Abaco, Bahamas. 800-327-8150. Walker's Cay Hotel and Marina operates its own plane service out of Fort Lauderdale. Dive packages include round-trip airfare from Fort Lauderdale; transfers to and from the hotel; deluxe air-conditioned accommodations; breakfast and dinner daily; three dives per day (two in the morning and one in the afternoon); tank, weights and belt; room taxes, maid, and MAP meal gratuities. Not included are bar charges, incidentals, US and Bahamian departure taxes. Non-divers may deduct $40 per night from the above. Private pilots may deduct $150 from the packages rate. Call the toll-free number for rates.

Dive packages are also offered by the following:

Marsh Harbour
Lofty Fig Villas (242-367-2681)

Abaco Towns by the Sea (242-367-2227)
Green Turtle Cay, Bluff House (242-365-4246)
Coco Bay Cottages (800-752-0166)
Hope Town, Hope Town Hideaways (242-366-0030)
Where to Stay & Eat
$ - less than $20 per person
$$ - $20-$50 per person
$$$ - $50+ per person

Dining

Elbow Cay

$$ The Abaco Inn Restaurant on White Sound is open to the public for breakfast, lunch and dinner. Free transportation is provided to and from Hope Town, so give them a call to get the ferry times – you'll need to make a reservation anyway. Conch fritters, conch salad, lobster, dolphin, grouper and rack of lamb are a few of the items you're likely to find on the evening menu. 242-366-0133.

$$ Club Soleil is at Hope Town Marina across the water from the Hope Town itself, so you'll need a boat to get there. If you don't have one, the restaurant will provide transportation. Located under the famous candy striped lighthouse, Club Soleil specializes in continental cuisine and fresh fish, with a champagne brunch on Sundays. 242-366-0224.

$-$$ Captain Jack's is a great little waterfront café next to Hope Town Harbour. They serve breakfast, lunch, and dinner on the veranda in an easy-going atmosphere. Specialties include seafood of all sorts, home-made bread, and even turtle burgers. 242-366-0247.

$-$$ The Harbour's Edge, as its name indicates, is right on the waterfront in Hope Town where you can enjoy a fine view. The restaurant, with its inside bar, is a popular watering hole for nautical types and locals alike. The food is always good, and the specialties include crawfish salad, conch chowder, and gullywings (chicken wings). Happy Hour is 5 pm until 6 pm. The restaurant is open for lunch and dinner only. 242-366-0087.

$$ Hope Town Harbour Lodge in Hope Town is a good spot for a quiet breakfast on the veranda, lunch by the pool, or candlelight dining in an intimate atmosphere. There is also a

Sunday champagne brunch with fresh seafood, roast beef, and chicken. 242-366-0095.

On Da Beach Restaurant/Bar. They weren't lying when they named this restaurant. It sits, perched on a dune no more than 50 feet from the ocean. Their motto, "no shirts, no shoes, no problem," holds true, so feel free to go barefoot. All of the grilled seafood options are excellent and on certain nights they serve specially prepared Bahamian dishes. On Sundays, they offer the local favorite, chicken souse, served with grits and Johnny cakes, alleged to be the perfect cure for a hangover – something you'll probably need if you make it for their monthly full moon party where generous pours, bustling crowds, and festive music will keep you up socializing into the wee-hours of the morning.

$$ **Rudy's Place** is about a mile from Hope Town and is open for dinner only. They do provide free transportation from the town and from many of the hotels, so you'll need to make a reservation. The atmosphere is simple but the food is always good and you can expect to find lamb, steak, turtle, and fresh fish on the menu, all complemented by excellent home-made bread. 242-366-0062.

Great Abaco & Marsh Harbour

$-$$ **The Conch Inn Restaurant** at the marina is a popular gathering place for all sorts of interesting people, many of them sailors. Some are locals; others are visitors. The semi-outdoor, harbour-view dining room and bar, with its rustic décor and yachting memorabilia, has a beachcomber, waterfront atmosphere. It's relaxed and easy going – canvas shorts, colored shirts, and sandals are the standard dress. The restaurant is open for breakfast, lunch, and dinner. The menu offers a wide variety, mostly Bahamian, of ocean-fresh seafood, including conch salad, cracked conch, and lobster; or you can have steak or chops. 242-367-4000.

$$ **Angler's Restaurant**, at the Boat Harbour Marina, specializes both in Bahamian and American cuisine. If you want to enjoy a quiet drink at the poolside you can drop in at the Sand Bar, or go indoors for a little mother's ruin (gin) at Penny's Pub. Both are close by. 242-367-2158.

$$ Café La Florence. Located on Queen Elizabeth Drive, just across from Memorial Plaza, La Florence is open for breakfast, lunch and dinner, Monday through Saturday. Specialties include a variety of Bahamian dishes, lots of fresh seafood, including lobster and grouper, and a wide selection of fresh-baked goodies.

$$ The Castle Café is a charming little restaurant set high on a hill overlooking Marsh Harbour and the ocean. Unfortunately, they are open only for lunch, which is served daily from 11 am until 5 pm on the terrace. The house itself is a large, old-world mansion. It's a gathering spot for the locals and for the sailing fraternity. Home-made specialties, including wonderful soups, seafood salads, and sandwiches, are all prepared by the owner.

$ The Golden Grouper is in Dove Plaza. Open Monday through Saturday from 7 am until 3 pm daily for breakfast and lunch. It serves Cuban, Chinese, and Bahamian dishes.

$ The Main Street Grill at Royal Harbour specializes in fried chicken, home-made burgers, and gourmet potatoes. Open daily from 11 am until 10 pm. This is a great place to take the kids for a quiet family meal.

$ Kool Scoops is *the* ice cream parlor in the Abacos. Located in downtown Marsh Harbour, next to the Canadian Imperial Bank, Kool Scoops offers a wide selection of flavors and an air-conditioned dining room. Open from 11 am until 10 pm, Monday through Saturday, and from 1 pm until 10 pm on Sunday.

$$ The Bayview Restaurant is on the water in Marsh Harbour, a mile west of the traffic light. Specialties include seafood and prime rib. Open daily for lunch and dinner from 11 am until 11 pm; champagne brunch is served on Sunday from 11:30 am until 3:30 pm. The restaurant has an all-tide dinghy dock.

$ The Sand Bar is a popular gathering spot at the Abaco Beach Resort. There's a pool with a swim-up bar. Snacks are available from 11 am until late, but you can also choose from a full bar menu. The specialty is frozen tropical drinks.

$$ The Jib Room is just across the water from the Conch Inn and is open for lunch daily and for dinner Wednesday through Sunday. You'll enjoy your meal on the waterfront at an umbrella-covered table in a Bahamian, rustic-garden atmosphere.

$$ Mangoes on the waterfront, just across the road from the Lofty Fig, is another of Marsh Harbour's institutions. The restaurant is open for lunch and dinner every day except Sunday, specializing in burgers and fresh seafood at lunchtime and candlelight dinners in the evening. The bar on the waterside veranda is the ideal spot for an evening drink while watching the sun go down.

$ The Tiki Hut on Bay Street near the Conch Inn is the place to go for American sandwiches, burgers and Bahamian dishes.

$$ Wally's, across the road from and facing the harbour, is the most famous restaurant in Marsh Harbour. The colonial-style, two-story building is reminiscent of a pink-and-white Southern mansion. Dine inside or outside on the veranda, but first sit at the bar and enjoy one of Marine's or Barbara's special island drinks. The Bahamian cooks specialize in local cuisine and, so they say, "you can't get fish any fresher anywhere in the Bahamas. It comes straight from the boat and into the kitchen." Try the fried grouper or, better yet, the coconut curried wahoo. If you don't like seafood, they also offer a number of beef and poultry dishes.

$ Mother Merle's, on Dundas Road about two miles north of the stoplight, is open for dinner only. Bahamian specialties include conch salad, cracked conch, chicken, home-made pies, and fresh fish. No credit cards.

Great Guana Cay

$$ The Guana Beach Resort Restaurant serves breakfast to hotel guests only, but opens up to everyone for lunch and dinner. Lunch can be eaten on the pool deck or inside. The dinner menu includes an assortment of Bahamian dishes, as well as fish, chicken, and steak. 242-365-5133.

$$ Nippers Beach Bar & Grill. This is the kind of place to sit and stay a while. And that's exactly what hundreds of islanders and tourists do every Sunday for the famous afternoon pig-roast. But on any day of the week, the multicolored picnic tables and the cast of local characters make this a fun place to hang out. When in season, be sure to try the grilled wahoo. It's seasoned to perfection and accompanied by the local Bahamian rice, a truly addictive dish. Thirsty? Give the famous Nipper's punch a try; it packs a wallop and goes down easy. If in the mood for graffiti, scribble a message on a dollar bill and post it along with the hundreds of other bills tacked to the walls. Menu includes a large selection of Bahamian seafood. Prices range from $9 to $16 for lunch and $18-$30 for dinner. 242-365-5143, www.nippersbar.com.

$$ Blue Water Grill. The opening of Blue Water Grill in 2003 introduced casual gourmet dining to this island. Request a table on the outdoor deck and catch a spectacular sunset over the Sea of Abaco and then be treated to a masterfully crafted meal with Bahamian flavor and flair. Although the taste of the food is likely to have you feeling good physically, the fact that much of the produce is organically grown will leave your karmic side feeling satisfied as well. They serve both lunch and dinner, along with a charming selection of wines. Appetizer prices range from $9 to $16, entrées range from $24-$32. 242-365-5230, www.bluewatergrillredskylounge.com.

Art Café & Bakery. Just opened in 2005, Shawna Sands' fresh-baked goods have already become a staple in many residents' diets. The treats include cookies, cakes and pies. But her real specialty is bread. Cinnamon-raisin, coconut and plain white top the list. If you have something special in mind, just ask and she's likely to whip one up the next day. Choose from a selection of international coffee and take a seat on the outdoor deck to enjoy views of the harbor. Large ceiling fans keep the place cool, even in the midday sun. In the evenings, locals congregate for ice cream and homemade desserts. They serve breakfast (one of the only places on the island), lunch and dinner. Wireless Internet access. Located in the bright periwinkle building adjacent to the ferry dock.

Green Turtle Cay

$$ The Bluff House Restaurant sits on a hill overlooking White Sound and is a romantic spot for a candlelight dinner with breathtaking views of the ocean and the lights of New Plymouth in the distance. Your dinner includes complimentary wine and the menu offers a range of dishes such as fresh lobster, prime rib and roast duck. The restaurant provides free transportation to and from New Plymouth, and from hotels and boats. 242-365-4247.

$$ The Green Turtle Club is also on White Sound. Breakfast and lunch are served outdoors on the patio. Dinner is served at a single sitting at 7 pm in the opulent dining room. Reservations must be made before 5 pm. The menu offers a choice of three entrées each evening, which might include lobster, duck, chicken, veal, or prime rib. 242-365-4271.

$ Laura's Kitchen is on King Street in New Plymouth. You can eat inside or take out your order. The restaurant serves conch, fish, chicken, conch burgers, and ice cream. 242-365-4287.

$$ The New Plymouth Inn Restaurant is just across the way from the Sculpture Garden, right in the center of Hope Town. It is one of Hope Town's popular gathering places. You'll need to make a reservation, as the dining room is small and intimate. Dinner is served in a single sitting at 7:30 pm, and the menu will include a choice of three entrées. 242-365-4161.

$ Plymouth Rock Café is at the end of Parliament Street on the main government dock. The café is open only from 9 am until 3 pm, serving sandwiches and burgers at the counter. 242-365-4234.

$$ The Wrecking Tree, on New Plymouth Harbour, is open for breakfast, lunch and dinner. This is the place to enjoy a beer, or any one of a range of exotic tropical drinks. Specialties include Bahamian pastries, conch salad, and chicken. 242-365-4263.

McIntosh Restaurant and Bakery. In business 10 years and for good reason. The fresh-baked pies, cakes, and pastries draw a regular crowd. Local favorites include the key lime pie, coconut cream pie and bread pudding. Breakfast, lunch and dinner are also an option from a menu that includes local Bahamian favorites, conch and grouper, as well as more standard American fare. If you need to cool down, they also have an ice cream shop where you can sample both traditional and more creative options.

$ Harvey's Restaurant. Open for just over a year, they have already developed a very loyal following. If you go for lunch try one of the sandwiches served on locally baked Bahamian bread. The blackened grouper is a flavorful option and the seafood sampler gives you a great overview of some of the island's most popular culinary delights. Bahamian and American fare. They serve lunch and dinner and offer a kids' menu. Prices range run $6-$10 for lunch and average around $14 for dinner entrées.

Man-O-War Cay

Albury's Bakery is in a private home just across the way from the Man-O-War Grocery on Queen's Highway. They sell some of the best bread, home-made pies, and conch fritters on the islands. Call ahead to place your order. 242-367-3147.

$$ The Man-O-War Pavillion is an open-air restaurant at the harbour. The menu is mostly Bahamian and includes a variety of seafood dishes – conch, grouper, dolphin, and shrimp – along with chicken, burgers and an assortment of side orders. On a fine day, this can be a very relaxing dining experience. 242-365-6185.

Accommodations

Hotel Meal Plans

CP (Continental Plan) includes a continental breakfast.

EP (European Plan) denotes no meals, although restaurant facilities are available either on the property or nearby.

MAP (Modified American Plan) denotes breakfast and dinner.

FAP (Full American Plan) includes all meals.

All-Inc. (All-Inclusive Plan) includes all meals, beverages (alcoholic and soft), water-sports, tennis and golf, if available.

Elbow Cay

Hope Town Harbour Lodge sits on top of a bluff and, though still "in town," is just as close to the harbour as it is to the beach. The view from the Lodge is one of the best on the island. Some of the rooms are in the main building, some in quaint little cottages by the water, and some in the Butterfly House, one of the oldest buildings in Hope Town. Some rooms are air-conditioned. The others are cooled by soft breezes blowing in from the ocean and, except on the hottest days, remain comfortable throughout the year. The rate is $100 per night for one person, $115-135 for two, and $125-$145 for three people.

MAP is $33 extra per night. 800-316-7844, or write Hope Town Harbour Lodge, Hope Town, Abaco, Bahamas. www.hopetownlodge.com.

The Club Soleil at the Hope Town Marina is just across the harbour from Hope Town itself, so you'll need a boat or the ferry to get back and forth, but that's half the fun. From its romantic spot beneath Hope Town's famous candy-striped lighthouse, you have a fine view of the harbour and the town itself. Lunch is served on a deck that surrounds the pool. There's also a great place to eat, the Club Soleil Restaurant, close by, or you can take the ferry over to town for your evening meal. The rate per night for up to two persons is $115, and for three persons it's $125. MAP will cost $32 per night extra. 242-366-0003, or write Club Soleil Resort, Hope Town, Abaco, Bahamas.

The Abaco Inn is two miles south of Hope Town on Queen's Highway. It lies on a narrow ridge with the ocean at one side and White Sound at the other. This small hotel offers 12 guest units, six on the ocean side and six with harbour views. Some units are air-conditioned. There is a pool built right into the coral rock, hammocks for two, and a fleet of bicycles for guests to use free of charge. Complimentary transportation is provided into Hope Town. The rate is $120 per night for one person, $135 for two, and $155 for three. MAP is $33 extra per night. 800-468-8799 or write Abaco Inn, Hope Town, Abaco, Bahamas. www.abacoinn.com.

Hope Town Hideaways is one of the newest and most luxurious accommodations on the island. Each of the four large, air-conditioned villas has a modern kitchen, breakfast bar, dining room, living room, and wrap-around deck so you can follow the sun – or stay in the shade – all day long if you wish. The villas are set on 11 landscaped acres across the water from Hope Town. The views of the town, harbour, and lighthouse are spectacular and, although Hope Town is a short boat ride away, you are within easy reach of shops, restaurants, and beaches. Rates start at around $140 per night, per person, and go up to $220 per night, EP only. 242-366-0224, or write Hope Town Hideaways, One Purple Porpoise Place, Hope Town, Abaco, Bahamas. www.hopetown.com.

The Sea Spray Resort & Villas is at the south end of the island about three miles from town on White Sound. The resort offers a selection of one- and two-bedroom ocean-view cottages and villas, all with air-conditioning and daily maid service. Each unit has a deck and a barbecue pit. The beach is a bit rocky, but has lots of character. You'll have the use of a Sunfish sailboat or windsurfer, free of charge, and you can rent a bike just down the road at the Abaco Inn. The resort is a great place for hiking, too. Hope Town is just an hour away on foot, and Tahiti Beach less than 30 minutes. Fly into Marsh Harbour and take the ferry over to Elbow Cay; transfer from the dock to the resort is free. The daily rate per person is $150; EP only, but you can arrange to have your meals catered. 242-366-0065, or write the Sea Spray Resort, White Sound, Elbow Cay, Abaco, Bahamas. www.sea-sprayresort.com.

Turtle Hill Villas. Located a short-ride away from the ferry dock, Turtle Hill offers both two- and three-bedroom villas, each with a large deck looking out to the ocean. Inside, the villas have a spacious and airy feel with large, fully equipped kitchens. Air conditioning and ceiling fans adorn each villa. If you need to cool off, you can choose from two freshwater pools or the ocean. If you choose the ocean, a short boardwalk takes you to a pristine expanse of soft sand. The sandy bottom invites you to spend plenty of time frolicking in the waves. If you want to explore the charming streets and shops of Hope Town, a walk to town will take 20 minutes on foot. Feeling more adventurous? It's very common to simply wave down a passing vehicle for the two-minute ride into town. **On Da Beach Restaurant & Bar** is on the premises (see page 161) and is perched just above the beach. It's a great place to laze away with a drink in one hand and a book in the other. A minimum three-night stay is required. Depending on the number of guests and the villa you choose, rates range from $340 to $550 per night and include a golf cart rental. 800-339-2124, 242-366-0557, www.turtlehillvillas.com.

Great Guana Cay

Oceanfrontier Hideaways. Although you may be more accustomed to log cabins in the mountains or woods, these six three-bedroom log cabins nestled among the palm trees will shatter any preconceived notions you have. In fact, the cozy cabins actually enhance the laid-back feel on Guana Cay. Half-refrigerators, coffee makers, microwaves, toasters, hot plates, and air conditioners are standard. The barbecue on the private deck gives you another cooking option. Everything is located on the main floor of the cabin except for the third bedroom, which requires a steep climb up a secure ladder. A walkway winds its way through the small property to a deck overlooking a magnificent beach. Take 17 steps down a private stairway and you're in the stunning beach landscape. The sturdy cabins eliminate outside noise, a good thing considering that directly adjacent sits **Nippers Beach Bar & Grill** (see page 164), one of the most popular bars in all of the Abacos. Noise probably won't be an issue, however, as you'll likely find yourself there most evenings sharing drinks and swapping stories with the locals. EP only. Rates range from $225 daily to $1500 weekly. 519-389-4846, 888-541-1616, www.oceanfrontier.com.

Dolphin Beach Resort. Peeking out from the dense tropical landscape, the lodge and cottages are painted in a kaleidoscope of colors. The Colors of Junkanoo, an annual Bahamian festival, reflect the festive feel of the resort. If you're in the mood for a dip, you can head out to the swimming pool or saunter along the short walkway to a five-mile sweep of coral-colored sand with great swimming, beachcombing, snorkeling and kayaking. On a lazy, hazy afternoon, grab a book from the library, a soft drink from the cooler, and while away the hours on your own private deck.

While the lodge offers four spacious rooms and a somewhat luxurious level of living, the tiny one-, two- and three-bedroom cottages offer a more self-contained experience. Ceiling fans and the ocean breezes keep things cool in most of the cottages, but a few do offer air conditioners. There is no restaurant on the premises but a few good options are close by. The office doubles as a gift shop in case you need to stock up on gifts. Rates range from $200 per night in the Lodge to $440 per night for a three-bedroom cottage, with discounted weekly rates. EP only. 800-222-2646, 242-365-5137, www.dolphinbeachresort.com.

The Guana Beach Resort is the place where you can get away from life in the fast lane. There are no teles or television sets in the guest rooms, but all are air-conditioned and some even have kitchens. There's also a bar and a restaurant that specializes in exceptional seafood. You can eat outside on the deck if you wish. Set back among the palms, the hotel is on a small peninsula with the marina on one side and the bay on the other. There are seven miles of deserted beaches, the crystal waters of the ocean, a fleet of Sunfish sailboats for guests to use free of charge, and an abundance of opportunities for snorkeling, fishing, shelling or exploring. The ferry makes pickups twice each day in Marsh Harbour, which is only a few minutes ride from the airport. The rate for up to two persons per night is $140 and $150 for three persons. MAP is $35 per night extra. 242-365-5133 or write to Guana Beach Resort, PO Box 474, Marsh Harbour, Abaco, Bahamas. www.guanabeach.com.

Green Turtle Cay

Coco Bay Cottages, Green Turtle Cay. The five-minute ride on the "highway" is a bumpy affair but once you arrive you'll understand why 80: of their guests are repeat visitors. Six cottages sit a literal stone's throw away from both the ocean and the bay. Walk the popular bone-fishing flats on the bayside or grab your beach blanket and snorkeling gear and head to the deserted beach on the oceanside. The two- and three-bedroom cottages are clean and well-tended. Although each cottage has air-conditioning and ceiling fans, you'll find the trade winds that blow regularly are just as effective at keeping you cool. Don't be surprised if you get an invite for a cocktail or a bite to eat. The owners, Nicole and Larry Fleming, treat guests more like family. For those traveling with children or in large groups, the 'rec' cottage is stocked with games, books, beach equipment and a satellite television. All units are fully equipped for cooking. If you prefer to eat out, a quick scamper in a golf cart opens up various dining options on the southern end of the island. Daily rates range run $250-$300, with discounted weekly rates on all cottages. EP only. 800-753-0166 or 242-365-5464, www.cocobaycottages.com.

The New Plymouth Inn is in the heart of New Plymouth on Parliament Street among the shops and galleries and only a short walk away from the beach. Once the home of sea Captain Billy Roberts, the restored 150-year-old building has 10 comfortable guest rooms, each with private bath, some with canopied beds and some with twin beds. The hotel also has a bar and dining room, a saltwater pool, and a landscaped garden entrance with a wrought-iron table and chairs. The room rate is $85 per night for one person, $120 for two, and $180 for three persons MAP. 242-365-4161 for reservations, or write New Plymouth Inn, Green Turtle Cay, Abaco, Bahamas.

The Green Turtle Club & Marina is at the end of White Sound, north of New Plymouth. It's a place known around the world in yachting circles. The walls of the tiny bar and lounge are papered with autographed dollar bills – thousands of them – and the ceiling is hung with yacht club pennants of all shapes and sizes. Dinner at the Green Turtle Club is an experience in itself. Guests are escorted into an elegant, formal dining room for the single-sitting meal, and are served a series of delicious courses in candlelit splendor. Outside, the club's tiny strip of private beach faces the sun and the harbour where dozens of boats, large and small, bob at anchor. The guest rooms are devoid of s and television sets, but all are air-conditioned and all have private decks with views of the harbour or sound. At night, you'll wend your way along a dimly lighted path from your room to the lounge or dining room. From Treasure Cay, take a taxi to the dock and then the ferry over to Green Turtle Cay. The rate for one or two persons per night is $145 and for three, $165. MAP is an extra $36 per night. 242-365-4271, or write The Green Turtle Club, PO Box 270, Green Turtle Cay, Abaco, Bahamas. www.greenturtleclub.com.

The Bluff House Beach Hotel & Yacht Club is up on a hill overlooking White Sound and offers fine views of the island and the town of New Plymouth in the distance. The hotel has 30 guest accommodations, including rooms, suites and villas. All are air-conditioned, have private porches, and views of the water. The clubhouse, overlooking the pool and the ocean, is decorated with original paintings and framed posters. Guests can use the tennis courts free of charge, and the staff will arrange diving and fishing trips. Daytime boat rides to New Plymouth are also free for guests. The daily room rate is $90 for up to two persons, and $125 for three people. MAP is $34 extra per day. 242-365-4247, or write Bluff House, Green Turtle Cay, Abaco, Bahamas. e-mail info@bluffhouse.com, www.bluffhouse.com.

Man-O-War Cay

Schooner's Landing sits on the water's edge a short walk from the marina. Each of the resort's two-story units has two bedrooms, two baths, and comes fully equipped with all the amenities you expect to find at a luxury resort, including a beach far away from the crowds and smell of the city. With no motor vehicles on the island except for those of the utilities, you must walk everywhere, but that's a large part of the resort's appeal. Nowhere is more than a mile away and the fresh air and splendid views, not to mention the exercise you'll get, are food for the soul. To get to Man-O-War, fly into Marsh Harbour, take a taxi to the ferry dock and then ride over to the island, where a representative from the resort will meet you. The rate per person per night is $150, EP only. 242-365-6072, or write Schooner's Landing, Man-O-War Cay, Abaco, Bahamas. http://oii.net/schooners.

Marsh Harbour

The Conch Inn at Marsh Harbour is on the waterfront, East Bay Street, less than 10 minutes from the airport, and only five minutes from the ferry dock. There are 10 rooms, each with a view of the water, twin beds, private baths, televisions, and air-conditioning, but no teles. The hotel restaurant, open for breakfast, lunch and dinner, is something of an institution and watering hole for locals and visitors. The room rate is $85 per night for one or two persons, and $95 for three persons, EP only. 242-367-4000 for reservations, or write to The Conch Inn, PO Box 434, Marsh Harbour, Abaco, Bahamas. www.go-abacos.com/conchinn.

Pelican Beach Villas, a small resort on Pelican Shores across from Marsh Harbour Marina, offers five comfortable, two-bedroom, two-bathroom villas, each with a full kitchen, living room, and private deck on the beachfront. With all the amenities of Marsh Harbour and its marina close by, you'll always have plenty to see and do, from deep-sea fishing to scuba diving, and from boating to hiking. The resort is only minutes away from the airport and ferry dock, where you can take a sightseeing trip around the islands. The rate is $145 per night for one person, $160 for two, and $175 for three; EP only. The weekly rate is $975, with an additional $75 per extra person. To make reservations, 800-642-7268, or write Pelican Beach Villas, PO Box AB20304, Marsh Harbour, Abaco, Bahamas. www.pelicanbeachvillas.com.

Abaco Beach Resort & Boat Harbour in Marsh Harbour adjoins Boat Harbour Marina. It's a modern hotel with an extensive range of facilities. The opulent rooms and two-bedroom villas, all facing the pool, beach and/or the marina, have air-conditioning, satellite television, teles (a real luxury in the Abacos), balconies and well-lit dressing areas. You'll find there's lots to see and do. You can rent a boat at the marina and go exploring by yourself, take a guided boat trip around the nearby islands, or go deep-sea fishing or scuba diving. You can stroll the waterfront and pristine beaches, go shelling in front of the hotel, or grab a bike and head off into town or down the road for a day of sightseeing. There is also a fine restaurant with a five-star chef in charge of the cuisine. The daily rate, depending upon the season, varies from a low of $95 per person for an ocean-view room to a high of $350 for what they call a "Grand Villa." Fly into Marsh Harbour and take a taxi to the resort. 800-468-4799, or write the Great Abaco Beach Hotel, PO Box 511, Marsh Harbour, Abaco, Bahamas. www.abacoresort.com.

Spanish Cay

Spanish Cay Resort & Marina. If you're looking for something really different, this is it. Spanish Cay is a private island, a world away from civilization. Privacy is the essence of a vacation here. With more than 180 acres of tropical forests and mangroves, miles and miles of secluded beaches where the water is the palest jade, and the reef at the ocean's edge only a mile away, you'll find seclusion easily. That's not to say that you'll have to give up all those little luxuries that make for an enjoyable vacation. With its five luxury suites and seven apartments, the Inn is a small, self-contained resort with two restaurants, four tennis courts, and the outgoing atmosphere of a local yacht club. While on the island, you'll have the use of a golf cart and a set of snorkeling gear. You can hike around the island, go fishing, or rent a boat and spend your days on the water. To get there, fly into Treasure Cay and take a taxi to the ferry dock, where you'll find a boat waiting to take you over to Spanish Cay. The rate per night per person is $180; EP only. 800-688-4725, 242-365-0083, www.spanishcay.com, or write the Inn at Spanish Cay, PO Box AB22504, Cooper's Town, Abaco, Bahamas.

Treasure Cay

Treasure Cay Hotel Resort & Marina. Located some 17 miles north of Marsh Harbour, Treasure Cay is home to one of the largest resorts in the Out Islands. It caters to a wide cross-section of adventurers: golfers, boaters, divers, bone fishermen and -women, and blue water anglers. The resort is a diverse complex of hotel rooms, cottages and condos – some 95 units in all. All guest units are air-conditioned and come with mini-fridges, hair dryers, coffeemakers, and ironing gear; the larger, deluxe units have microwave ovens too. The villas, recently renovated, have full kitchens and washers and dryers. Some of the suites have loft bedrooms, some have marina views, all are nicely furnished and tastefully decorated. Perhaps the most unusual facility on the property is its 18-hole golf course, the only one in the Abacos. Golfers take note: if you're looking for something really different, give this one a try. Also of note to blue water anglers is the resort's Annual Treasure Cay International Billfish Tournament held in June each year (call 800-224-2627 or visit www.treasurecayfishing.com for details). As to the rest of the property: the gardens are a riot of tropical color, the beach is spectacular, the restaurant menu includes cuisine from Europe and America, the bars serve just about any concoction you might be able to imagine. There's also a full service dive shop, six tennis courts, a 150-slip marina, and you can hire fishing guides and dive guides on the property. Treasure Cay, Abaco. 800-327-1584; fax 242-365-8847; www.treasurecay.com. Rates from $180 through $395. MAP available.

Walker's Cay

Walker's Cay Hotel & Marina provides the only

accommodation on Walker's Cay. The 62 rooms and four villas make for a comfortable stay, although there are no teles or televisions. The main house has a dining room, a shop, an indoor game room, and an indoor-outdoor bar. The island itself is a sportsman's paradise, and the hotel staff will be pleased to make arrangements for custom excursions to scuba dive, deep-sea fish, or shark dive. The nightly rate for two persons is $100, for three persons it's $120. MAP costs $32-50 extra per night. 800-925-5377; e-mail info@walkerscay@com, www.walkerscay.com.

Wood Cay

The Tangelo Hotel, on the main highway in Wood Cay, has 12 rooms with private baths, air-conditioning, ceiling fans, satellite TV, and complimentary pick-up for boaters in Fox Town, or from the airport. The restaurant, with its bar, is open for breakfast, lunch and dinner, specializing in Bahamian food such as stewed fish, conch salad, fresh grouper, and peas and rice. Fishing trips and guides can be arranged. The room rate is $66 per night, EP only. 242-367-2222 for reservations, or write to The Tangelo Hotel, PO Box 830, Cooper's Town, Abaco, Bahamas. http://oii.net/tangelo.

Andros

Geography & Wildlife

The geography of Andros is both varied and interesting. The central portion of the island, known locally as the "The Big Yard," is densely forested with mahogany and pine. More than 50 varieties of orchids bloom in the undergrowth of The Big Yard. The west coast of the island, "The Mud," – actually part of the Great Bahama bank – is mostly marsh and scrub. The east coast flanks the Great Barrier Reef. Southern Andros is where you'll find one of nature's last great mangrove forests in the Bahamas. The 40-square-mile tract is home to a variety of wild birds and animals, including the endangered Bahamian parrot, herons, egrets, lizards of every shape and size, iguanas that grow to more than six feet in length, and the Bahamian boa-constrictor – non-poisonous, but scary nonetheless. In the late spring each year, visitors are treated to a rare performance when the Andros land crabs migrate by the thousands from the forest to the sea.

In April of 2002 the Andros Conservancy and Trust (ANCAT) was successful in getting the Bahamas National Trust and the Bahamian government to declare a national park on the island of Andros – **The Central Andros National Park**. It encompasses the highest concentration of blue holes in the Bahamas, two portions of Andros Barrier Reef, a land crab management area, and North Bight mangrove/wetland nursery. Approximate size: 288,000 acres.

Andros is guarded by one of the world's longest and best-preserved barrier reefs and houses the highest known density of blue holes in the world. Its extensive wetlands are of national, regional, and international importance and it boasts the "best bonefishing in the world." It provides critical habitat for endangered birds, crabs, and iguanas. It is also the country's largest reservoir of freshwater.

This first phase of park designation focuses on Central Andros – North Bight, Fresh Creek, Blanket Sound, Young Sound, and Staniard Creek – protecting forests, blue holes, coral reefs, wetlands, and mangroves, and paves the way for additional protection in the north and south. This park system will be co-managed by the Bahamas National Trust and the Andros

Conservancy and Trust (ANCAT – www.ancat.org).

CHICKCHARNIES: Andros is the place where, so they say, you'll find those funny little Bahamian gremlins known affectionately as Chickcharnies. These strange little creatures, with three toes and red eyes, are said to hang upside-down in the trees casting down good- or bad-luck spells upon passers-by, depending upon their mood.

History

As with most of the islands in the Bahamas, Andros once was populated by the native **Lucayan Indians** and here, as elsewhere, the Indians became extinct not long after the **Europeans** landed.

For most of its history, little of note happened on Andros. It became a center for wrecking and a one-time base of operations for Captain Morgan, but it wasn't until 1845 that industry of any sort came to the island. That year, the **Andros Fibre Company** was established to manufacture sisal for use in the making of rope. The industry was short-lived, however. The poor quality of the soil contributed to the company's demise and, by the late 1920s, it had departed.

Next came timber production, but that too eventually died out, leaving the island with a serious unemployment problem and a system of roads almost beyond repair.

Then tourism arrived on the islands and things began to look up. Today, the tourist industry on Andros, while still in its infancy, is flourishing as more and more people discover the quiet beauty of this almost-deserted tropical paradise.

Getting There

By Air

Andros has four airports: to the north, **San Andros**; in the middle, **Andros Town**; and to the south, **Mangrove Cay** and **Congo Town**. All but Mangrove Cay are international ports of entry served by Bahamasair from Nassau, and several carriers from the mainland. The one-way fare from Nassau on Bahamasair to all airports on Andros is $45.

Visitors from Europe can travel from London and other major

continental cities to make connections in the US through Miami, Atlanta, Orlando, and other cities. Also, your travel agent can hook you up with one of several package operators serving the United States and the Bahamas, such as British Airways Holidays, Thomas Cook, American Express Holidays (see pages 49-50 for contacts).

To Andros Town From:	Airline
Nassau	**Bahamasair** operates regular daily schedules, 800-222-4262. Round-trip fare, $65.
Freeport	**Major Air**, 242-352-5778. Round-trip fare, $85.
Fort Lauderdale	**Island Express**, 954-359-0380. Round-trip fare, $230.
Miami	**Bahamasair** operates a daily schedule from Miami to Andros Town. Round-trip fare, $165.

To Congo Town/South Andros Airport from:	Airline
Nassau	**Bahamasair** operates regular daily schedules,

	800-222-4262. Round-trip fare, $96.
Freeport	**Major Air**, 242-352-5778. Round-trip fare, $99.
Fort Lauderdale	**Island Express**, 954-359-0380. **Lynx Air**, 954-491-7576.
Miami	**Bahamasair** operates a daily schedule from Miami to Andros Town. Round-trip fare, $165.

To San Andros Airport with Access to Nichol's Town from:	Airline
Nassau	**Bahamasair** operates regular daily schedules, 800-222-4262. Round-trip fare, $65.
Freeport	**Major Air**, 242-352-5778. .
Fort Lauderdale	**Island Express**, 954-359-0380. Round-trip fare, $230.

By Mail Boat

Mail boats sailing from Potter's Cay make regularly scheduled stops at North, Central and South Andros. Schedules are listed below, and in the *At a Glance* section at the back of the book. Mail boat schedules depend on the weather so they don't always leave on time. It's best to call ahead and make sure. 423-339-1064.

Lisa J. II leaves Potter's Cay, Nassau, for North Andros – Nicholl's Town, Mastic Point, and Morgan's Bluff – on Wednesday at 3:30 pm, returning on Tuesday at 12 noon. Sailing time is five hours. The fare, one way, is $30.

Mangrove Cay Express sails for Mangrove Cay and Lisbon Creek on Wednesday at 6 pm, returning on Monday at 4 pm. Sailing time is 5½ hours. The one-way fare is $30.

The Captain Moxey sails for South Andros – Kemp's Bay, Bluff, Long Bay Cay, Driggs Hill, and Congo Town – on Mondays at 11 pm, and returns on Wednesday at 11 pm. Sailing time is 7½ hours. The one-way fare is $30.

Lady Gloria sails for Mangrove Cay, Sandy Point, Moore's Landing, and Bullock Harbour on Tuesday at 8 pm, and returns on Sunday (time varies). Sailing time is five hours. The one-way fare is $30.

There are several other sailings weekly with varying schedules on Wednesdays, Tuesdays and Thursdays. Call the dock master, 242-393-1064, for details.

By Private Boat

Andros is the largest of the Out Islands. It's a strange, sparsely populated, remote land of endless shoreline, and inland lakes intertwined with canals. Ports of entry are Nicholl's Town, San Andros, Congo Cay, Mangrove Cay and Fresh Creek, all on the east coast. The east coast is also the location of the world's third largest barrier reef, making it something of a mecca for scuba divers, as well as yachtsmen. Unfortunately, docking facilities around the island are still somewhat limited, although several new marinas are in the planning stage.

Andros Lighthouse Yacht Club & Marina at Andros Town offers 20 slips and most basic services and facilities: showers, fuel, water, ice, and electricity. Accommodations are available nearby, and there are a couple of nice restaurants. Maximum depth at high water is 12 feet. VHF 16. 242-368-2305, fax 242-368-2300.

Getting Around

On Andros most of the main roads are paved and in varying stages of repair from fair to quite good. Get off the beaten path, however, and it's a different story.

*All four airports and the docks are served by independently owned **taxis**. Fares are reasonable, starting around $8 for two people.*

By Bicycle

If you have the time to ride, you can see an awful lot of the island. There's very little local traffic here, so you can peddle off down the highways and byways without a care in the world; just be sure to ride on the left side of the road. Bikes can be rented at **Small Hope Bay Lodge** in Andros Town (242-368-2013; $15 per day), and at many of the hotels on the island. From Andros Town you can head out to visit such places as Small Hope Bay, Calabash Bay, Coakley Town, and Fresh Creek. All are only a short distance from each other and easily reached by bicycle.

By Car

This way you can see it all. The main roads are often deserted and, whichever direction you take, you can drive for miles without passing a single person along the way.

You can make arrangements to rent a car – often somebody's private one – through your hotel when you arrive, but there are also two rental agencies: one at Fresh Creek, called **Amklco**, 368-2056; the other at Calabash Bay, called **Berth Rent-A-Car,** 368-2102. The rates are $65 per day, with a $100 deposit.

When you head out northward for the deserted beaches and shallow water flats off the east side of the island, be prepared for a sometimes bumpy ride. The drive from Andros Town to **Nicholl's Town** in the north will take you along more than 40 miles of a dusty, deserted road; yes, it's paved and in relatively good condition.

Fresh Creek is the home of the **Androsia Batik Factory**. Since 1973 Androsia has been coloring the Bahamas with unique hand-waxed and hand-dyed fabrics and garments that are inspired by the beauty of the islands. Androsia is located on Androsia Street, a right turn after you make the turn onto Light House Club Drive from Queens Highway. Self-guided tours of the factory are available Monday-Friday from 8 am to 4 pm. Their outlet store is open Monday-Wednesday, 8 am-4 pm, Thursday and Friday, 8 am-5:30 pm, and Saturday, 8 am-1 pm. Worth a visit. 368-2020 or 2080; www.androsia.com; info@androsia.com.

A little further on you'll find the lovely beaches at **Small Hope Bay** and, eight miles further on, is **Staniard Creek**. It's a tiny settlement with neat little churches and a beach where, at **Jolly Boy's Enterprises**, you can hire a boat and go out cruising the bonefish flats.

From Staniard Creek, the road takes you past the **Forfar Field Station Marine Science Center** to **Stafford Creek**, and then on to **Owen's Town** and **San Andros Airport**. Continue northward to **Nicholl's Town, Morgan's Bluff** or **Red Bays**, whichever takes your fancy.

Go south from Andros Town along the coast road and you'll find a road leading off left to the **Atlantic Undersea Test and Evaluation Center**, one of several top secret British and American bases on the island. Take the road to the right, however, and you'll find yourself in **Bowen Sound**, and then **Man-O-War Sound**, **Cargill Creek**, and **Behring Point**, tiny settlements almost forgotten by the faraway world, where the beaches are great and the fishing is even better.

Fishing Camps

Cargill Creek is home to two of Andros' finest fishing camps: **Cargill Creek Lodge** (241-368-5129) and **Andros Island Bone Fishing Club** (**242**-368-5167). At Behring Point you'll find another popular fishing lodge: **Nottages Cottages** (242-368-4293).

The villages to the south of Behring Point, where the Northern Bight separates North and South Andros, are not accessible by private car. **Mangrove Cay** and **South Andros** can be reached by water taxi; the service runs twice each day in the morning and afternoon. Drive to Behring Point Dock and leave your car in the parking lot. You'll also need to take the water taxi to **Lisbon Creek**, and the ferry to **Drigg's Hill**. From there you can take a regular taxi to **Congo Town** and the other small settlements further south where you'll find some remote, unspoiled beaches.

Sightseeing

Andros Lighthouse

The Andros Lighthouse was built in 1892 to mark the southern entrance to the Fresh Creek Channel. In 1952, three old cannons were added in front of the Lighthouse and a tower built on the top. The cannons came from the *Cottsac* schooner, which wrecked on Stanyard Rock in the 1800s.

Late Bahamian singing artist, Blind Blake immortalized the Lighthouse through a tragic tale expressed in the song, *Run Come See Jerusalem*, and it has become part of Bahamian culture and folklore. The song tells of four sloops sinking at the mouth of the creek, trying to make it to the safety of the Fresh Creek Harbor during the 1929 Hurricane. The entire community stood on the shoreline and watched as 20-plus locals drowned under the glow of the Lighthouse, as the seas swallowed the sloops and passengers.

The Lighthouse is now a local landmark and the logo for the Andros Town Development Company as well as the Lighthouse Yacht Club & Marina.

On The Water

Sport Fishing

The fishing off Andros is as good as anywhere else in the Bahamas – if not better. Andros is rapidly becoming known as the bonefishing capital of the world. The waters south of Behring Point consistently yield bonefish weighing in at more than 10 pounds. Offshore, marlin, tarpon, and sailfish can reach majestic proportions. On the barrier reef, huge groupers of 40 and 50 pounds are not unusual and are regularly taken, along with amberjack, snapper, and yellowtail.

There are three major fishing camps on Andros, any of which will be pleased to arrange whatever you might fancy: **Cargill Creek Lodge**, 368-5129; **Andros Island Bone Fishing Club**, 368-5167; and, at Behring Point, **Nottages Cottages**, 368-4293.

Boat Rentals

Andros Island Bone Fishing Club. Bone fishing charters from $350 per half-day, $600 per full day. 242-368-5167.

Diving

Andros' barrier reef – third largest in the world after Australia's Great Barrier Reef and the reef off the coast of Belize – is one of the planet's outstanding natural wonders. From the outer edge of the 120-mile reef that parallels the eastern shore, the ocean drops off more than 6,000 feet into a trench known as "The Tongue of the Ocean." To dive off the edge of the reef over the "Tongue" is to experience a feeling of insecurity like none you've ever known. Imagining the great depth below you will send you hurrying back to the security of the shallower waters. In addition to the wonders of the barrier reef, the flats around Andros are riddled with blue holes: mysterious circular depressions caused by the collapse of limestone caves far beneath the surface. These blue holes are home to thousands of species of fish and marine life. Blue holes come in all shapes and sizes, from small depressions inside the reef, to great tidal caverns in the bights and bays.

There are a number of shipwrecks for you to explore as well.

Perhaps you don't dive, but you do like to snorkel. Well, along the entire length of the eastern shore, bay after bay, beach after beach, and reef garden after reef garden await you. The shallow waters of the flats and inner reefs will provide myriad snorkeling opportunities.

Best Dive Sites

The Underwater Caverns at Lisbon Cay

The Underwater Caverns at Lisbon Cay provide an unusual diving adventure. The caverns, a network of limestone structures thought to have formed when the island was much larger and when more of its surface was above the ocean, make for a formidable and exciting dive. You'll need an experienced guide to take you. There are also underwater caverns to explore off Morgan's Bluff at the northern end of the island.

Blue Holes

There are at least 100 blue holes around Andros, of which the most famous may be **Uncle Charlie's Blue Hole**, which was featured in Jacques Cousteau's television series.

The Giant Staircase

The Giant Staircase is a spectacular series of coral steps descending steadily downward toward the drop-off, where you can swim among coral of every shape and size.

The Garden

The Garden is another wonderful coral formation. To name but a few, there are seafans, elkhorn, brain, and tube formations, and all the life-forms that inhabit the great reef are represented: snappers, sergeant majors, groupers, rays, eels, angels, and even the giant parrotfish.

Shipwrecks

Although there are many wrecks off Andros, most of them still await discovery. Only the two below are regularly visited.

The *Marion*

The *Marion* was a fairly large barge that capsized in the late 1980s. There were attempts to raise her, but all failed and she still lies in some 70 feet of water. The hulk, 100 feet long and 40 feet wide, has been gutted and permits easy access for divers.

The *Potomac*

This British tanker built in 1893, 345 feet long and 44 feet wide, ran aground in a hurricane off the north end of the island on September 26, 1929. She broke in half and went down in shallow water, 18 to 20 feet, where she lies today. The action of the ocean has smashed her to pieces and there's not much left for you to explore except the remains of the bow section and her boilers.

Best Snorkeling Sites

Remembering that Andros is home to the world's third largest barrier reef, it's no wonder that the island has more than its fair share of suitable snorkeling sites. As you can imagine, it would be impossible to list all of them here.

Central Park

Central Park is an area of the reef where you can see a great many unique coral formations, among them three major stands of elkhorn coral, all in less than 15 feet of water. It's an excellent site for beginners.

China Point

This is a great place to observe a grand variety of colorful reef fish: sergeant majors, blue tangs and trigger fish.

The Compressor

The Compressor is just that, an old compressor that has turned into a tiny reef. Lots of fun, and a highly unusual snorkeling experience.

Davis Creek

Not a creek at all, but a large tidal flat fringed by mangroves. A unique snorkeling adventure.

Goat Cay

Goat Cay is a great place to hunt sea biscuits and sand dollars.

Lisben's Point

Lisben's Point is a large area of reef with many unusual coral formations, including elk and staghorn, brain, seafan and star coral.

North Beach

Lots of small shoals and patchy areas that are home to all sorts of colorful fish and other species of marine life. Lots of fun, and easy, too.

Red Shoal

A patch of reef encrusted with elk and staghorn corals. Large schools of fish moving this way and that make this an unusual spot.

Trumpet Reef

A great place to watch the small invertebrates scurry about the ocean floor tending to their daily business.

Dive Operators

Small Hope Bay Lodge

They have been in the diving business for more than 42 years and they know the island waters well. The staff includes three instructors and four dive masters. They conduct two-tank morning dives, one-tank afternoon dives, and night dives, provided they have a minimum of six participants. Their professional affiliations include PADI, NAUI, SDI/TDI, and Universal Referrals. They offer comprehensive instruction for beginners and specialize in blue hole and wall diving. They offer several specialty dives with either one or two participants and the dive master. These are usually to inland blue holes, deeper exploration of the Ocean Blue Hole, and deeper wall dives, or you can plan your own dive with your dive master. They also offer a relaxed shark observation dive. Costs average $85 per dive. 800-223-6961. www.smallhope.com.

Dive/Accommodation Packages

Important Note: All of the packages listed below were active and correctly priced at the time they were researched. You should be aware, however, that all are subject to change without notice. Please check with the provider at the Phone numbers listed for up-to-date packages, rates, and information.

Small Hope Bay Lodge

At Fresh Creek, they offer a flexible package based on double occupancy at a rate of $259-$289 per night, per person, depending on the season. Singles pay a $45 surcharge for a private room, or they can have a private room with a shared bath in a family cabin and then they pay no surcharge. Dive package discounts are offered for stays of seven days or more. Included in the rate is the round-trip transfer to and from the hotel; beachfront accommodations; three dives per day; breakfast, lunch and dinner daily; conch fritters and hors d'oeuvres every evening, all bar drinks and beverages (!); all hotel and food taxes; service charges; intro scuba diving lessons; hot tub, bicycles, sailboat and windsurfer. Complimentary baby-sitting services are provided during the cocktail hour. 800-223-6961. www.smallhope.com.

Where to Stay & Eat

Dining

$$ **The Beacon**, 242-368-2305, at the Andros Lighthouse Yacht Club, is open for breakfast, lunch and dinner. Fresh seafood and local cuisine. Reservations suggested.

$$ **Small Hope Bay Lodge**, 242-368-2014. Open for breakfast, lunch and dinner, the restaurant serves a full American-style breakfast, a hot buffet at midday and dinner in the evening, with a variety of fresh seafood, including lobster, as well as beef, pork and chicken. Reservations required.

Accommodations

Hotel Meal Plans

1 **CP** (Continental Plan) includes a continental breakfast.
2 **EP** (European Plan) denotes no meals, although restaurant facilities are available either on the property or nearby.
3 **MAP** (Modified American Plan) denotes breakfast and

dinner.

4 **FAP** (Full American Plan) includes all meals.

5 **All-Inc.** (All-Inclusive Plan) includes all meals, beverages (alcoholic and soft), water-sports, tennis and golf, if available.

Andros Lighthouse Yacht Club and Marina, in Andros Town, 242-368-2300, www.androslighthouse.com. The hotel is a five-minute walk from the beach, near the lighthouse from which it takes its name. The 20 guest rooms are all nicely furnished, with marbled tile, reproduction furniture, and all are cooled by ceiling fans. There's a swimming pool and a fine dining room where you can enjoy traditional Bahamian fare and great views of the marina. Fresh Creek is a short walk across the bridge. Rates start at around $130 per person, per night; MAP is $40 extra.

Small Hope Bay Lodge, at Fresh Creek in North Andros, 800-223-6961. The Lodge is pretty much dedicated to divers, but offers those who are looking for a real getaway something special. This resort has just 20 guest rooms in small cabins along the beach under the shade of the palm trees. All have ceiling fans, are tastefully decorated, and furnished with bed linens made from batik cloth manufactured at the nearby Androsia plant. Most rooms have private baths; others share one between two rooms. The atmosphere is definitely casual, as you'll find if you decide to wear a tie to dinner – you'll lose it quite quickly to one of the staff brandishing a pair of scissors. The resort is closed for four weeks during September and October (exact time varies). Rates are $189-$209 per night per person, meals, drinks, taxes and activities included. www.smallhope.com.

Coakley House, 800-223-6961, 242-368-2013, is also at Fresh Creek and is a good choice for independent travelers looking for a villa rental. It offers three air-conditioned bedrooms, 3½ baths, large living room, dining room, fully equipped kitchen and laundry room. The house takes full advantage of magnificent water views and breezes from any direction. Outside it has a lovely patio overlooking the sea and its own private dock. Boat or car rentals, fishing, diving, and maid/cook service can all be arranged through Small Hope Bay Lodge. Call for rates. www.coakleyhouse.com; coakleyhouse@smallhope.com.

Andros Island Bone Fishing Club, at Cargill Creek, 242-368-5176. As the name implies, bonefishing is the essence of this community. The atmosphere is very relaxed, the accommodation rustic, but comfortable, with all sorts of amenities, and the lounge has a large, open, ocean-front deck with lots of heavy wooden chairs for relaxing. On the beach among the palms you'll find hammocks and more beach chairs free of charge. Rates per boat are $275 per half-day; from $450 per full day. EP only. Contact through Andros Island Bonefishing Club, www.androsbonefishing.com.

Creekside Lodge, at Cargill Creek/Behring Point, 242-368-5176. The Lodge is expensive, but when you consider that the rate includes everything but your beverages, and when compared to what a day's fishing can cost you at the hands of a local operator, it's a very good value. Most people who stay at the Lodge are avid anglers. There is no beach to speak of, but there is a small pool. The hotel's 15 guest cottages are all well-furnished and have television sets. Each has a private bath – very nice too – and ceiling fans to complement the air-conditioning. The restaurant is right at the water, and the lounge is one of the island's popular gathering places. Behring Point is about 35 miles south of the airport and 12 miles from Andros Town. The rate is $275 per night, per person. It includes all meals and unlimited fishing.

Bimini

Just 50 miles off the east coast of Florida, Bimini is one of the best known of the Bahamas. It's most popular with fishermen, and is within easy reach of amateur sailors from the American mainland. Bimini is actually two distinct islands separated by a narrow ocean passage and a number of minor cays. It has a total land mass of less than 10 square miles, a rich history and a wealth of natural resources.

Most of the community's population, about 1,600, lives on North Bimini in **Bailey Town**, while **Alice Town**, also on North Bimini, is the main tourist center where most of the hotels, restaurants, and fishing operations can be found. There's an airport on South Bimini, although most visitors arrive on the islands at North Bimini Harbour via sea plane from Miami.

The Biminis are perhaps the best-known of the Bahamian Out Islands thanks to the publicity provided by such famous fishermen as Ernest Hemingway, Adam Clayton Powell, Jr., and Zane Grey. Today, they are widely accepted as a sport fishing mecca. Beyond that, the Biminis are an excellent yachting and cruising center and an exciting destination for divers.

Most of Bimini's visitors come to fish. The seas off the tiny islands abound with white and blue marlin, tarpon, sailfish, swordfish, amberjack, wahoo, barracuda and shark. Bonefish, too, are plentiful on the flats off the coast of Alice Town. More than 20 fishing tournaments each year draw anglers from around the world in search of the great billfish and a place in angling history.

History

Some say these islands were once part of the road system of the Lost Continent of Atlantis. Ponce de Leon visited Bimini in his search for the Fountain of Youth. Did he find it here? The locals will tell you that he did and, with tongue in cheek, will point out its precise location.

Bimini's modern history centers around the two people who made it famous. **The Compleat Angler**, a hotel and bar in Alice Town is where **Ernest Hemingway** spent most of his time when he wasn't writing or fishing. Its lobby is jam-packed with Hemingway memorabilia. His cottage, now a part of the **Bimini**

Blue Water Resort, is thought to be the place where he wrote most of *To Have and Have Not*.

Adam Clayton Powell, a New York Congressman, spent a great deal of his time on the island fishing, as well as socializing in The End of the World Bar in Alice Town, a hole-in-the-wall with a sandy floor.

Alice Town, the home of the **Bimini Big Game Fishing Club**, is the fishing capital of the little island group. It's in Alice Town that you'll find the best restaurants and bars – such local institutions as **Captain Bob's**, where you can eat breakfast and buy a packed lunch for the day's fishing; **Fisherman's Paradise**, where you can eat excellent Bahamian fare for lunch and dinner; **The Bimini Breeze, The Wee Hours Club,** and **The End of the World Bar**.

Getting There

By Air

The Biminis are not as well-served as other Out Islands. Several airlines offer scheduled service to South Bimini out of Fort Lauderdale, and there is regular sea plane service into Alice Town from Fort Lauderdale.

To North Bimini from	Airline
Fort Lauderdale	**Pan Am Air Bridge**, 800-424-2557.
Miami	**Pan Am Air Bridge**, 800-424-2557.
Paradise Island	**Pan Am Air Bridge**, 800-424-2557.

To South Bimini from:	Airline
Fort	**Island Air Charters**, 800-444-9904, fax

Lauderdale	954-760-9157; **Bel Air Transport**, 954-524-9814, fax 954-524-0115.
Freeport	**Major Air**, 242-352-5778, fax 242-352-5788.

By Mail Boat

Mail boats sail regular schedules from Potter's Cay, Nassau. Call ahead to make sure of departure times and arrivals. 242-393-1064.

Bimini Mack makes a weekly stop at Cat Cay and North Bimini. Call the dock master for schedules, 242-393-1064. Sailing time is 12 hours. The one-way fare is $45.

By Sailboat

The Biminis are the most popular sailing destination from mainland Florida. Less than 50 miles from the coast, they are well within reach of most sea-going sailors. While I was visiting the east end of Grand Bahama a couple of years ago, I ran into two adventurous types who had made the crossing from Florida on Hobe Cats. It took them almost 10 hours. Not something I would recommend, but it shows what can be done.

The Flings:

If you'll be crossing to the Biminis for the first time, the **Bahamas Boating Flings** might be the way to go. Sponsored jointly by the Bahamas Ministry of Tourism and the South Florida Marine Industries Association, the flings are organized fleets of not more than 30 vessels brought together to make the crossing from either Miami or Fort Lauderdale for boats of at least 22 feet, and from Palm Beach in boats at least 24 feet. Each boat pays a fee of $65 to participate. Flings are organized throughout the summer, when sailing conditions are best. For more information, call the Bahamas Tourist office in Miami at 800-327-7678 or 305-932-0051.

For seasoned sailors, the official port of entry is Alice Town on North Bimini. The **Bimini Big Game Fishing Club**, with 100 slips, is the premier marina on the islands. It can accommodate boats up to 100 feet, and offers services that include showers, fuel, groceries, engine repair, water, ice, and electricity. There's also a restaurant, accommodations and a swimming pool. You can radio ahead on VHF 9/16. 800-737-1007, fax 242-347-3392.

Bimini Blue Water Marina is a smaller, but no less popular, base of operations. It offers 32 slips, along with showers, fuel, groceries, engine repair, water, ice, electricity and much more. Restaurants and accommodations are available nearby. Call ahead on VHF 16/68. 242-347-3166, fax 242-347-3293.

The airport and the docks are served by independently owned taxis. Fares are reasonable, starting around $10.

On The Water

Fishing

If you don't have your own boat, you'll need to charter one. Costs average $200-$300 per person for a half-day; $350-$400 per person for a full day. For more information, call the Bahamas Tourism Office at 800-32-SPORT.

1 **The Bimini Big Game Fishing Club**, Alice Town, 242-347-2391 or 800-327-4149.
2 **The Bimini Blue Water Resort & Marina**, Alice Town, 242-347-3166.
3 **The Bimini Reef Club & Marina**, South Bimini, 305-359-9449.
4 **The Sea Crest Hotel & Marina**, Alice Town, 242-347-3071, www.seacrestbimini.com.
5 **Weech's Dock**, 242-347-2028.

Fishing/Accommodation Packages

Important Note: All of the packages listed below were active and correctly priced at the time they were researched. You should be aware, however, that all are subject to change without notice. Please check with the provider at the Phone numbers listed for up-to-date packages, rates, and information.

The Bimini Big Game Fishing Club

On North Bimini, they offer two three-day, two-night packages. The deep-sea fishing package includes deluxe accommodations and a full day fishing from a 28-foot Bertram with a captain and mate for $372 per person (double occupancy).

The Backwater Fishing package includes deluxe accommodations and a full day of bonefishing with a guide for $225 per person (double occupancy). 800-737-1007, www.biminibiggame.com.

The Bimini Blue Water Resort & Marina

They also offer two packages; you decide the length of each. The daily rate for a bonefishing package, including hotel accommodations and a half-day of fishing with a guide, is $250 for two persons. The daily rate for the deep-sea fishing package, including hotel accommodations and a half-day aboard the 46-foot *Sir Tones*, is $465 for two persons. 242-347-3166.

Fishing Tournaments

Listed below are the major tournaments conducted off Bimini throughout the year. There are also a number of smaller tournaments in the area. For more information call the Bahamas Tourism Office at : 800-32-SPORT.

JANUARY: The **Bimini Light Tackle Bonefish Tournament**, 1st leg, Bimini Big Game Fishing Club, 242-347-3391.

FEBRUARY: The **Bimini Light Tackle Bonefish Tournament**, 2nd leg, Bimini Big Game Fishing Club, 242-347-3391.

MARCH: The **Annual Bacardi Rum Billfish Tournament**, Bimini Big Game Fishing Club, 242-347-3391.

MAY: The **Bimini Festival Tournament**, Bimini Big Game Fishing Club, 242-347-3391.

JUNE: The **Big 5 Tournament**, Bimini Big Game Fishing Club, 242-347-3391.

JUNE: The **South Florida Fishing Club Tournament**, Bimini Big Game Fishing Club, 242-347-3391.

AUGUST: The **Bimini Native Fishing Tournament**, Bimini Big Game Fishing Club, 242-347-3391.

SEPTEMBER: The **Small B.O.A.T. Tournament**, 1st and 2nd legs, Bimini Big Game Fishing Club, 242-347-3391.

NOVEMBER: The **Wahoo Tournament**, Bimini Big Game Fishing Club, 242-347-3391.

Diving

Diving off the Biminis is excellent and most of the popular dive sites can be reached quite quickly by boat. The main attraction of underwater Bimini is the abundance of fish and marine life, although the reefs are not quite as extensive or as spectacular as they are off Andros or Abaco. Expect to see huge schools of grunts, snapper, and goatfish. Groups of spotted eagle rays congregate in the channel between the two main islands, and the ever-present groupers grow to record-breaking proportions.

Best Dive Sites

The reefs off Bimini vary in depths from a shallow 15 feet to more than 100 feet.

Tuna Alley & the Victories

To the south you'll visit Tuna Alley and the Victories, where miles of coral reef and drop-offs are populated by almost every type of tropical marine life you can imagine. The area is riddled with caverns, channels and tunnels at depths varying from 30 to 90 feet.

Rainbow Reef

Rainbow Reef lies in an easy 25 to 35 feet of water and offers divers spectacular coral formations and lots of schooling fish, along with nurse sharks of varying sizes, turtles, groupers, and even barracuda.

The Bimini Barge

This is the wreck of an ocean-going barge now sitting on the bottom in some 100 feet of water. Its superstructure, however, is only 60 feet from the surface.

The *Sapona*

The *Sapona* is the wreck of a 350-foot concrete transport that was originally named the *Lone Star*. She ran aground in 1926 during a hurricane and broke in half under the relentless action of the sea. During World War II, the hulk was used as an aerial target by the US Navy and Air Force. Today, the *Sapona* sits in a mere 20 feet of water with her superstructure showing above the water like the bones of some motionless leviathan. The wreck lies in shallow waters and is accessible to both divers and snorkelers. She's a wonderland of dead machinery, ship's propellers, and interior locations, all lit by the rays of sunlight filtering down from the deck areas above.

Dive Operators

Bill and Nowdla Keefe's Bimini Undersea Adventures has been in business for more than 14 years and has a well-deserved reputation for good service and an in-depth knowledge of the undersea Biminis. The company has a staff of seven, including four instructors, and conducts a regular schedule of dives that includes two-tank morning dives, one-tank afternoon dives, and night dives on Wednesdays and Saturdays. The newest attraction is a program called "Swim With The Wild Dolphin." A pod of wild spotted dolphins has taken up residence off Bimini. The Keefes offer Dolphin Excursions two-three times weekly aboard their dive boats *Destiny* and *Adventurer*. Trips are done both in the morning and afternoon and can be anywhere from three-four hours in length. In most cases, once the pod has come to the boat, the dolphins allow you to swim and interact with them. It takes approximately an hour to reach the "Dolphin Grounds." The company's professional affiliations include PADI and NAUI. Pre-booked rates: adults, $109; children (eight-12), $69; guests, $89; children (under eight), no charge. On-island rates: adults, $119; children (eight-12), $79; guests, $99. 800-348-4644, 242-347-3089, dolphins@biminiundersea.com., www.biminiundersea.com.

Spotted Dolphins

Spotted dolphins are different in many ways from the more well-known grey bottle nosed dolphins that you see in captivity. In the wild, spotted dolphins actually seek out human interaction. In contrast, the bottle nosed dolphins tend to be curious but tentative, more often than not shying away from swimmers. In captivity, their roles are reversed. Spotted dolphins are virtually un-trainable and do not do well in a captive environment. Bottle nosed dolphins are very trainable and adapt well to captivity.

Dive/Accommodation Packages

Important Note: All of the packages listed below were active and correctly priced at the time they were researched. You should be aware, however, that all are subject to change without notice. Please check with the provider at the Phone numbers listed for up-to-date packages, rates, and information.

Bill & Nowdla Keefe's Undersea Adventures at Bimini Big Game Fishing Club offers a series of all-inclusive dive packages. Off-season rates (September 15th to May 14th) for two nights, $350; three nights, $490; four nights, $629; five nights, $769; six nights, $908; seven nights, $1,048. From May 15th through September 14th, the rates are increased by some $80 to $280, depending upon the length of stay.

All rates are per person, per night, and are based on double occupancy. Each package includes three dives per day (two on arrival and departure days), one night dive, transfers to and from the hotel, deluxe air-conditioned accommodations, breakfast and dinner each day, all service charges, use of tanks, weights and belts, and use of tennis courts. 242-347-3391.

Best Snorkeling Spots

Bimini Shoreline

Bimini Shoreline is an area of the reef with lots of coral formations, colorful reef fishes, and a bird's eye view of everyday life on the reef.

Bimini Road

This is the most interesting snorkeling site in the Out Islands. A number of stone structures are believed by some to be part of the lost continent of Atlantis.

Eagle Ray Run

You'll see dozens of eagle rays swimming in formation. It's a rare experience.

Healing Hole

Thought to be the site of the fabled Fountain of Youth.

LaChance Rocks

A group of huge rocks on the ocean floor, inhabited by dozens of species of small marine life, including invertebrates.

Rainbow Reef

One of the most densely populated sections of reef in the Bahamas. Here you'll have the chance to observe many species of reef-dweller.

Rock Sound

A shallow water snorkeling experience over a rock and coral field.

Sapona

An unusual snorkel over a sunken concrete ship.

Stingray Hole

The place to observe lots of stingrays. You can feed them, too.

Where to Stay & Eat

Dining:

$$ Bimini Bay, 242-347-2174, located in a mansion on North Bimini overlooking Paradise Point, is open from 3 pm until 6 pm for an early afternoon tea.

$$ The Gulfstream Restaurant and Bar, 242-347-3393, at the Bimini Game Fishing Club in Alice Town, offers an extensive menu of fresh seafood dishes, beef, chicken and a selection of fine wines. Open daily for breakfast, lunch and dinner. Reservations a must.

$-$$ The Red Lion, 242-347-3259, in Alice Town, is open Tuesday through Sunday for bar meals and dinner from 6 pm to 11 pm. The bar is open until 2 am.

Accommodations

Hotel Meal Plans

CP (Continental Plan) includes a continental breakfast.

EP (European Plan) denotes no meals, although restaurant facilities are available either on the property or nearby.

MAP (Modified American Plan) denotes breakfast and dinner.

FAP (Full American Plan) includes all meals.

All-Inc. (All-Inclusive Plan) includes all meals, beverages (alcoholic and soft), water-sports, tennis and golf, if available.

Bimini Big Game Fishing Club, Alice Town, 800-737-1007, www.biminibiggame.com, $150 EP. The hotel, with its 50 guest rooms, including cottages and suites, and 100 boat slips, is headquarters of the Bimini sport fishing industry. The guest rooms are all luxuriously appointed and have TVs, tiled floors, rattan furniture, and are decorated in pastel shades of green and white to make for a cool, tropical atmosphere. The hotel has three bars, two dining rooms, a swimming pool, and a tennis court. The beach is nearby.

Bimini Blue Water Resort, Alice Town, 242-347-3166, $100 EP. Most of the hotel's 12 guest rooms overlook the beach, all are comfortably appointed, and sit adjacent to the private beach. Of special interest is the cottage once owned by Ernest Hemingway, now part of the hotel complex. If you make arrangements far enough in advance, you can stay here, surrounded by an atmosphere unlike anywhere else. The cottage, next door to Hemingway's other watering hole, The Compleat Angler, has a blue marlin hanging over the living room fireplace, a kitchen, three bedrooms, and a large patio.

The Compleat Angler Hotel, Alice Town, 242-347-3122, $85 EP. A cozy hotel with 13 guest rooms, huge shade trees, balconies, and courtyards reminiscent of New Orleans' French Quarter than on the islands. This was once the haunt of Ernest Hemingway, and his presence can still be felt among the memorabilia. In the bar, the walls are hung with nautical flags, pennants and old photographs. One of the photographs shows Hemingway with the remains of a 500-pound blue marlin, the victim of a shark attack, that might have been the inspiration for his famous 1952 work, *The Old Man and the Sea.*

Sea Crest Hotel, Alice Town, 242-347-3071, www.seacrestbimini.com, $90 EP. The Sea Crest is a small, comfortable hotel, though it lacks both a pool and a restaurant. The 10 guest rooms are neatly furnished, have TVs and either double or single beds. The beach is just across the road and a number of good restaurants are within walking distance.

Eleuthera

Eleuthera, playground to many of the rich and famous, is one of the longest islands in the Bahamian archipelago. More than 110 miles long, but less than two miles wide, the island is home to about 10,500 residents. It lies some 60 miles to the west of Nassau and, with three airports – Governor's Harbour, North Eleuthera and Rock Sound – and daily flights from Miami, Fort Lauderdale and Nassau, it's one of the most accessible of the Out Islands.

History

Founded by English settlers in the mid-1700s, and named for the Greek word meaning "Freedom," the island is a combination of white picket fences and pastel-painted cottages, with a wild and secluded landscape of stark cliffs, deserted beaches, rolling hills and bluffs, dusty roads, pine, casuarina, palms, seagrape and scrub undergrowth. It has miles and miles of scenic coastline and emerald waters of the northern Caribbean Sea.

Getting There

H Be sure to ask your carrier which airport is the correct one for your hotel. Get it wrong, and you could find yourself facing a taxi ride of 90 miles or more.

Eleuthera and its nearby islands are served by three tiny international airports: **North Eleuthera**, **Governor's Harbour** at the center of the island, and **Rock Sound** to the south. All enjoy scheduled service from Nassau and, to a lesser extent, from the mainland. The main ports of entry for sailors are Cape Eleuthera, Governor's Harbour, Harbour Island, Hatchet Bay, North Eleuthera, and Rock Sound. And, the island is well served by mail boats out of Potter's Cay, Nassau.

By Air

To Governor's Harbour, Gregory Town, Hachet Bay, and	Airline:

Palmetto Point from:	
Nassau	**Bahamasair**, daily. 800-222-4262. Round-trip fare, $74.
Freeport	**Major Air**, daily. 242-352-5778.
Fort Lauderdale	**USAirways Express**, 800-622-1015, **Twin Air**, 954-359-8266, **Bel Air Transport**, 954-524-9814. All operate a daily schedule. The round-trip fare starts at $264.
Miami	**American Eagle**, daily. 800-433-7300. Round-trip fare, $175. **Bahamasair**, daily. 800-222-4262. Round-trip fare, $170.

To North Eleuthera, Gregory Town, Harbour Island, and Spanish Wells from:	Airline
Nassau	**Bahamasair**, 800-222-4262, and **Sandpiper**, 242-328-7591, offer a daily schedule.
Fort Lauderdale	**Gulfstream** (Continental Airways Connection), **Twin Air**, 954-359-8266, and **USAirways Express**, 800-622-1015.
Freeport	**Major Air**, 242-352-5778.
Miami	**Gulfstream** (Continental Airways Connection), 800-231-0856, **Bahamasair**, 800-222-4262.

To Rock Sound and Tarpum Bay from:	Airline:
Nassau	**Bahamasair**, daily. 800-222-4262.
Fort Lauderdale	**Island Express**, daily. 954-359-0380.
Freeport	**Major Air**, 242-352-5778.

By Fast Ferry

Accommodating 177 passengers, the ***Bohengy*** is the only full service fast ferry in the Bahamas offering round-trip high-speed transportation from Nassau to Spanish Wells and Harbour Island, as well as twice weekly from Nassau to Governor's Harbour, Eleuthera. The huge, 115-foot catamaran is powered by two jet engines and travels at a cruising speed of 35 knots/40 mph. With a draught of only 3½ feet, she is easily able to navigate the shallow waters and reefs of the islands. Notwithstanding the sometimes bumpy ride, especially when the sea is running a little high, passengers cruise in fully air-conditioned comfort in an enclosed cabin or on the open top deck. There's a snack bar offering light refreshments and the ferry is fully accessible to the physically challenged.

The *Bohengy* is one of Bahamas Ferries' fleet of three vessels. The **Sea Link** provides round-trip service from Nassau to Exuma, Abaco, Andros and Eleuthera, while the **Sea Wind** operates between Nassau, Andros, Eleuthera and Abaco. The *Sea Wind* can carry up to 400 passengers with luggage, 35 vehicles, and freight.

The Bohengy Fast Ferry departs from Potters Cay in Nassau, Mon-Sat, 8 am, arriving 10:15 am. Return is at 3:55 pm, arriving at 6:15 pm. On Sun, it departs at 8 am, arriving at 10:15 am. Return is at 2 pm, arriving at 4:15 pm.

On Fridays at 7 pm the *Bohengy* sails to Governor's Harbour, a popular weekend vacation spot. Arrival at 9 pm.

Fare To Harbour Island, Spanish Wells and Governor's Harbour is $110 round-trip (adult), $70 (child); $65 one way (adult), $45 (child). Bahamas Fast Ferries, 242-323-2166, www.bahamasferries.com,

By Mail Boat

Bahama Daybreak III sails from Potter's Cay, Nassau, on Mondays at 5 pm, stopping at Rock Sound, Davis Harbour, and South Eleuthera. She returns on Tuesday at 10 pm. Sailing time is five hours. The one-way fare is $20.

Eleuthera Express sails from Potter's Cay, Nassau, on Mondays at 7 pm for Governor's Harbour and Spanish Wells. She returns on Tuesday at 8 pm. Sailing time is five hours. The one-way fare is $20.

Captain Fox sails from Potter's Cay, Nassau, on Fridays at noon for Hatchet Bay, and returns on Wednesday at 4 pm. Sailing time is six hours. The one-way fare is $25.

Spanish Rose sails from Potter's Cay on Thursdays at 7 am for Spanish Wells. Sailing time is five hours. The one-way fare is $20.

Eleuthera Express sails from Potter's Cay on Thursdays at 7 am for Rock Sound, Davis Harbour and South Eleuthera. Sailing time is five hours. The one-way fare is $25.

By Private Plane

All three airports are accessible to private pilots. Eleuthera's remote FSS frequency is 124.2.

By Private Boat

Eleuthera is one of the most popular cruising destinations in the Bahamian archipelago. Full-service marinas are available from one end of the 90-mile long island to the other. All marinas monitor VHF 16.

Spanish Wells

Spanish Wells Yacht Haven offers 30 full-service slips with access to fuel, water, ice, etc. There are several boat yards nearby where boats can be hauled out of the water for repairs.

Harbour Island

Valentine's Resort and Marina offers 39 full-service slips along with access to all of the restaurants in Dunsmore Town.

Harbour Island Club and Marina is a full-service operation with showers, a Laundromat, fuel, water and ice. The 32 slips have 30- and 50-amp hookups.

Hatchet Bay Marine Services of Eleuthera offers 20 full-service slips and their own Harbour View Restaurant and Bar.

Palmetto Shores

The **Palmetto Shores Vacation Villa** offers eight slips.

Governor's Harbour

The harbor itself is a large, protected bay where you can drop anchor for just about as long as you like. A dock allows you to tie up and take a short walk into town for provisions.

Rock Sound

Rock Sound, at the southern end of the island, is Eleuthera's largest community. The town offers a large, well-protected bay where you can drop anchor and come ashore to replenish supplies.

Package Vacations

Several major operators offer air-inclusive vacations to Eleuthera. Unfortunately, the hotel options are limited to the Cove Eleuthera, which is a great place to stay, and a couple of other smaller hotels, but there's nothing available on Harbour Island. A creative travel agent could build a custom package for you, not a difficult proposition. Other than that I recommend the following:

American FlyAAWay Vacations

They offers air-inclusive vacation packages to the Cove Eleuthera from most major US cities, connecting to American Eagle in Miami. Typically, a five-night package for two – no meal plan – from Atlanta will cost about $1,200 for two persons, maybe a little less, depending on the time of year. Break that down and you see that you're paying around $600 per person, including airfare, which represents great value for money. Rates from other gateway cities are comparable. Facilities include tennis courts, a fresh-water swimming pool, and ocean fishing. Accommodations are in duplex-style cabins surrounded by tropical gardens. These are comfortably furnished, and enjoy either a garden or ocean view. There are no teles or televisions in the rooms; these are available in the main building. If you're looking for a real getaway you'll enjoy the feeling of being beyond reach. You can book through your travel agent, or call American FlyAAWay, 800-321-2121, www.aavacations.com.

Apple Vacations

Apple Vacations offers packages to Eleuthera using scheduled air carriers which, in this case, means American Airlines. They offer several hotel options, including the Cove Eleuthera, Unique Village and, to the south, Palmetto Shores Vacation Villas. Rates run just a little higher than those offered by American FlyAAWay Vacations, but departure options are more extensive – they will provide connection flights from most cities with an airport. www.applevacations.com.

Getting Around

Transfers from any of the three airports to your hotel must be by private **taxi**. Even package vacations do not include transfers. If you're visiting Harbour Island, you'll find taxis waiting for incoming aircraft just outside the main building. They will transfer you to the ferry dock. It's not far – you could easily walk it in five minutes – and the fare should be just a couple of dollars. If you decide to walk, turn right out of the main building; it's all downhill from there. **Ferry boats** also meet in-coming aircraft. If you're visiting one of the hotels in the Governor's Harbour area – the Cove, Unique Village, etc. – your taxi fare will be about $40, one-way, for two persons. Once you've checked into your hotel, you can rent a car or bicycle to do your sightseeing.

The several towns on the island are separated by many miles of almost deserted beaches. Want to swim or snorkel? Simply leave the road, park your car – there are several rental agents on the island – and walk right into the water. You're in one of the finest reef locations in the world.

Island Driving Tour

There are two towns of interest on the north end of the island: **Spanish Wells** and **Harbour Island**.

Due to its thriving crawfish industry, Spanish Wells – named for the Spanish explorers who put ashore in search of fresh water and provisions – is one of the wealthiest communities in the Bahamas. Harbour Island, just off Eleuthera's northern coast, is a resort island where the beach is tinged with pink and the water is clear.

Farther south is **Gregory Town**, the pineapple capital of the island. This fruit is responsible for the tiny village's prosperity and is honored each June during the **Pineapple Festival**. The festival includes a Miss Teen Pineapple Pageant, a pineapple-eating contest, dancing in the streets, a basketball shootout, music and a street party on Saturday night. Along the way from Spanish Wells to Gregory Town, you'll pass through the Bluff, Upper and Lower Bogue, and then over a natural bridge called **Glass Window Bridge**. The narrowest point on the island, the bridge, with its spectacular views to the north and south, is the result of millions of years of erosion by wind and sea.

From Gregory Town, the road heads southward through Alice Town, past Hatchet Bay, James Cistern, on into Governor's Harbour at the center of Eleuthera.

Governor's Harbour is typical of the tropical towns you'll find dotted around the Out Islands. It's fairly remote, but has a charm all its own: a tiny church loaded with history, shops where you can buy local souvenirs and crafts, boats bobbing at anchor in the bay and, here and there, restaurants where you can sample real Bahamian food. It's not as upscale as other resort areas at Harbour Island and Spanish Wells, but it is interesting and enjoyable. Said to be the earliest settlement on the island,

Governor's Harbour offers several places to stay, including a Club Med, and there's even a bank. If you really want a getaway vacation, Governor's Harbour might be just the place.

Continue south along the road from Governor's Harbour through Palmetto Point, Savannah Sound, past Windermere Island and on through Tarpum Bay. You'll then reach Rock Sound, the largest settlement on the island.

A Windermere Island was once the favorite getaway haunt of Prince Charles and Princess Diana.

Tarpum Bay is an artist's community. It was here that Mal Flanders, an American, came to paint the island life and scenery. His work is well known, and you might want to drop by the studio. Another good place to visit at Tarpum belongs to another artist. Scotsman MacMillan Hughes built the strange-looking structure he likes to call **The Castle** with his own hands. Take a moment to visit, view his work, and enjoy a tour of his home. Both are on Queen's Highway.

Rock Sound, along Queen's Highway, south of Tarpum Bay and north of Greencastle, boasts a number of attractions, including **Ocean Hole**, a large inland lake connected to the ocean by a labyrinth of subterranean tunnels. Some say the hole is bottomless. Its depth has been measured to more than 100 feet. Either way, it has become home to a variety of fish and marine animals, many of which are accustomed to being fed by hand. Steps cut into the coral make for easy access to the hole, the water, and the fish, providing a rare photographic opportunity.

If you're a golfer or tennis player, stop by **The Club**, on Queen's Highway at Rock Sound. The club's magnificent 18-hole golf course, designed by Robert Trent Jones, is considered one of the finest golfing challenges in the Bahamas. Greens fees are $70 for 18 holes; $45 for nine holes. Club rental, $15. No need to book tee times in advance.

Walking and bicycling are both popular pastimes on Eleuthera. The miles of deserted roads, vast stretches of pristine sand, tiny bays and coves, side tracks, pathways and trails all make for endless hours of peddling or hoofing. You can rent bicycles at almost all of the island's hotels for about $15 per day.

Bicycling or walking

Yes, you can do it by bicycle, just be sure to take something to drink. Once you leave your resort, rest stops and country stores are few and far between.

Day Trips to Harbour Island

If you are staying in Nassau or Paradise Island, you'll want to make the relatively short trip to Harbour Island and its famous pink sand beach – voted the #1 island in the region (Bermuda/Bahamas/Caribbean) in 2005 by *Travel & Leisure* magazine. Your feet will relish the powder-soft sand, your body will relax in the warm turquoise water, and your soul will welcome the laid-back pace of the island. Be sure to bring sunscreen, hat, bathing suit, towel, snorkel gear, camera, and a ready smile. You can easily enjoy a full-day trip, including four hours on Harbour Island, for less than $200 (ferry $110, golf cart $40-50, lunch $10, dessert $3 = $173). Here's how.

Take the 2½-hour **Fast Ferry** ride to Harbour Island (roundtrip $110 adults; $70 children). You need to arrive at the ferry dock at least 45 minutes ahead of departure. The ferry departs Potter Cay, Nassau at 8 am and arrives around 10:30 am. You'll want to return to the ferry dock by 3:10 pm for a 3:55 pm departure. Call for reservations and to verify fare and times (242-323-2166; www.bahamasferries.com)

Once you arrive, your golf cart will be waiting for you. Reserve ahead – www.harbourislandguide.com/golf-cart-rentals.htm; www.baretasseashellinn.com; $40-50 for a four-seater). Just hop on and remember to drive on the left side. Golf carts and walking are the main forms of transportation, so you can't get in too much trouble. Be sure to grab an island map as you leave the ferry. Take an hour to cruise around the island, check out the ice cream-colored New England-style houses, and browse the shops in Dunmore Town. You'll find the locals quick to smile and wave, or offer advice if needed.

Next, head north from the Ferry Terminal on Bay Street for lunch at **Wade's Seaside Takeaway**, a hole-in-the-wall eatery frequented by the locals. Lunch will cost you up to $10 for a main dish plus three sides. Try the cracked conch – it is lightly battered and fried, non-greasy, tender and sweet. Wade's is popular so you may have to wait for your food. No problem. Just sit at one of the simple tables under the shade of an ancient banyan tree and take in the view of the bay. Listen to the roosters crowing, your conch being chopped, and the hum of golf carts down the street. You may even get to watch your conch being selected from the pen close to the shore.

If you are in the mood for dessert, head up to **Ma Ruby's Restaurant** at the Tingum Village Hotel on Colebrooke Street for her famous coconut tart or key lime pie (a steal at $3). One of the "Top 10 Cheeseburgers in Paradise" can be ordered here as well.

Allow an hour for the best part – the pink sand beach for walking, sunning, swimming, or snorkeling. The beach can be accessed via several public access points – check the map. Alice Street public beach access is close to Ma Ruby's. Stop for a moment just to take in the stunning view of the three-mile-long pink sand beach and turquoise water with few, if any, people. The gentle waves and warm water will softly caress your body. For snorkeling, check with a local first for the best spot to access the semicircle-shaped reef. You'll want to stay here awhile – guaranteed.

Be sure to check your watch so you make it back to the ferry in time. Once aboard, you'll likely be napping with a contented smile on your face.

On The Water

Fishing

Deep-sea and bonefishing expeditions can be arranged through many of the hotels – just ask at the front desk. Rates average $150-$250 per person for a half-day; $325-$425 for a full day. The hotels listed below are particularly helpful at making advance arrangements for you. See www.eleu.net/marina-e.html for details on the marinas of Eleuthera.

Coral Sands Hotel, Romora Bay on Harbour Island, 800-333-2368., www.coralsands.com.

Valentines Inn & Yacht Club, Harbour Island, 242-333-2142.

Spanish Wells Yacht Haven, Spanish Wells, 242-333-4255.
Spanish Wells Marina, Spanish Wells, 242-333-4122.
Hatchet Bay Marina, Hatchet Bay, 242-332-0186.
Harbour Island Club & Marina, Harbour Island, 242-333-2427, www.harbourislandmarina.com.

Boat Rentals

Buccaneer Club. Guided boat rentals can be arranged from $200 per day and small boats from $65 per day. 242-332-2000, www.buccaneerclub.com.

Diving

Most of the major dive sites are located around Harbour Island. Along the eastern coast of Harbour Island and Eleuthera, a long fringed reef guards the shoreline. It's a vast undersea continent of sand and coral, where ocean creatures congregate. Stop off at any of the tiny bays and inlets, put on your mask and snorkel, walk a few yards out from the beach, and you'll discover all the wonders of the inner reef at your feet. Take to a boat and venture a little further out toward the edge of the reef, strap on your scuba gear, and you'll enter a crystal world of color, marine life, coral cathedrals, and shipwrecks. See www.eleu.net/diving.html for details on diving on Eleuthera.

Best Dive Sites

Stingray Hole

Just to the north of Spanish Wells, this is a long stretch of fringed reef that has spelled disaster for dozens of ships over almost three centuries. In one spot, three wrecks lie one atop the other. The reef itself has a variety of reef and deep-sea fish, along with crustaceans, urchins, and anemones at depths varying from 10 to 80 feet.

The Plateau

Just off Harbour Island, this is a huge underwater plain of rolling coral, sandy crevices, ledges, cuts and channels at depths that vary from 45 to 100 feet, all densely populated with marine life.

The Arch

Also off Harbour Island, the Arch is a giant coral grotto with schools of gaily colored fish swimming back and forth, ever-changing their direction like some underwater flock of birds.

The Current Cut

An exciting adventure for experienced divers. Located between Eleuthera and Current Island, the 100-yard-wide channel is subject to the changing tides that send a mighty current eddying through the corridor. Divers enter the channel at one end and come tumbling out the other in a flurry of bubbles and churning water. You'll need to wear a wet suit to ride the Cut.

The Pinnacles

The Pinnacles represent part of a mountain of coral heads rising upward from the ocean floor and covered with giant sponges, elkhorn, seafans, plate, brain and tube corals. You'll need to go deep to explore this one.

Shipwrecks

The *Arimoroa*

The *Arimoroa*, often called the Freighter Wreck, is a 260-foot Lebanese freighter that ran aground in 1970. Apparently, the ship caught fire at sea and the captain decided to ground her on Egg Island to save the crew. The crew made it safely ashore and the fire continued to burn. Today, the hulk sits on the rocks in 20 feet of water. The burned-out shell is a haven for fish and other marine life. The wreck provides a wonderful photographic opportunity.

The *Carnarvon*

The *Carnarvon* is another old freighter that ran aground in 1919 and sank off North Eleuthera. She now sits on the sandy bottom in about 30 feet of water. The site is littered with wreckage, including the ship's anchors, boilers, engines, and propeller. It's an easy dive and, once again, a great photo opportunity.

The *Cienfuegos*

A 90-foot passenger liner launched in Pennsylvania in 1883, the *Cienfuegos* ran aground on February 5, 1895 in heavy seas north of Harbour Island. All the passengers and crew survived.

Today, battered to pieces by the persistent action of the sea, what's left of the liner is scattered over a wide area in 30 to 40 feet of water. There's still plenty to see.

The Train Wreck

Not far from the *Carnarvon* wreck, this is what's left (wheels, etc.) of a steam locomotive from the Civil War submerged in 20 feet of water. It was lost when the barge carrying it went down in 1865 during a storm on the Devil's Backbone reef.

Best Snorkeling Sites

Bird Cay

Bird Cay has lots of fish, conch, and other small marine life.

Blue Hole

This area of reef around an old blue hole offers lots of corals and colorful marine fish.

Current Cut

Not for the fainthearted, this is a "roller-coaster ride through a tidal cut that attracts all sorts of marine critters."

Gaulding's Cay

One of the most beautiful reef gardens on the island. Lots of corals of every description, sea anemones and bonefish.

Glass Window Bridge

Once the bridge between north and south Eleuthera, the structure has now taken on new life as a sunken reef.

Muttonfish Point

This is home to large numbers of mutton snapper, from which the site gets its name, and many colorful reef fish.

Oleander Reef

Just a short swim from the beach, this is one of the island's most densely populated underwater areas, with plenty of reef fish.

Paradise Beach

Not far from the beach, the barrier reef here is home to a huge parrot fish, schools of jacks, and lots of other reef dwellers.

Pineapple Dock

This old wreck now hosts a multitude of colorful fish, invertebrates, and many other species of small marine life. **Sea**

Fan Gardens

If you're looking for a thrill, this is the site for you. The gardens are the home of "Baron," a large barracuda.

Cousteau Snorkeling Adventures

Five hotels on Eleuthera participate in the Jean Michel Cousteau "Snorkeling Adventures" program (see page 41): **Cambridge Villas**, in Governor's Harbour, 800-688-4752; **Palmetto Shores Villas**, Governor's Harbour, 800-688-4752; **Rainbow Inn**, Governor's Harbour, 800-688-4752; **The Cove Eleuthera**, Gregory Town, 800-552-5960; and **Unique Village**, Governor's Harbour, 800-688-4752. All of these hotels include most of the following popular snorkeling locations in their itineraries.

Dive Operators

Romora Bay Club Dive Shop

On Harbour Island, with a staff of four, including two instructors, they have been in business for more than 20 years. Regular daily dives are conducted in the mornings and afternoons. The staff will be pleased to organize custom trips to suit individual interests. The company's professional affiliations include PADI. Packages are available through most of the hotels on Harbour Island. One-tank dives cost $35; two-tank dives, $60. 242-333-2325. www.romorabay.com.

Valentine's Dive Center

In business for 17 years, the center has a staff of six, including three instructors. They conduct daily dives in the mornings and afternoons, and night dives once a week. The company operates two boats, with capacities of 10 to 28 persons. One-tank dives cost $35; two-tank dives, $60. A dive at the Current Cut is $125. Professional affiliations include PADI and SSI. Valentine's can cater to individual site requests and conducts excursions to many of the most popular dive sites. Packages are offered through Valentine's Yacht Club & Marina. 800-383-6480. www.valentinesdive.com.

Where to Stay & Eat

Dining:

Gregory Town

$$ Cove Eleuthera, 242-335-5142, www.thecove-eleuthera.com. Open for breakfast, lunch and dinner, the restaurant has a view of the waterfront, poolside dining, and a menu that offers American and Bahamian cuisine.

Hatchet Bay

$$ Hatchet Bay Yacht Club, 242-335-0396. Open for breakfast, lunch and dinner, the Yacht Club has a nautical atmosphere, along with a casual Bahamian menu featuring burgers, conch, grouper and lobster.

$$ The Rainbow Inn, 242-335-0294, www.rainbowinn.com, is open for dinner. It's a popular local watering hole and you'd be well advised to make reservations for dinner. The menu includes a large selection of Bahamian and continental dishes, including conch, lobster and escargots. Closed on Sunday and Monday during the summer, and on Sunday only in the winter.

Palmetto Point

$$ Unique Village Restaurant & Lounge, 242-332-1830, is open for lunch and dinner, specializing in local dishes, steak and seafood, peas and rice, and conch served several different ways.

Harbour Island

$ Coral Sands Beach Bar, Sundeck and Lounge, 242-333-2320, is open from 11 am until dark. No reservations are required. It overlooks the three-mile Pink Beach and serves lunch until 3 pm.

$$-$$$ Romora Bay Club, 242-333-2325. The restaurant features indoor or outdoor dining for breakfast, lunch and dinner. Fixed menu, with alternative choices. Dinner is served at one 7:30 sitting. An elegant dining experience. Reservation and proper dress required for dinner.

$$ Runaway Hill Club, 242-333-2150, is open to the public for dinner only. You need a reservation. A set menu is served at 8 pm in an elegant dining room. Cost is $40 per person.

$$ Angela's Starfish Restaurant, 242-333-2253, is open

daily from 8:30 am until 8:30 pm for breakfast, lunch and dinner. The menu features authentic Bahamian cuisine.

Wade's Seaside Takeaway, 242-333-2066 north from the Ferry Terminal on Bay Street, Wade's operates out of a small bay-side hut. Try them for lunch, an excellent, casual choice for tasty local fare. With a steady stream of locals stopping here for lunch, you may wait a little for your food, but it will be worth it. Sit under the shade at one of the wooden tables in back and enjoy the view of the bay, with small boats and conch shells piled in the turquoise water. The cracked conch, lightly breaded and fried, tender and slightly sweet, comes with three sides and costs $10. Lunch ranges from $7 to $10; choices include chicken, pork chop, conch, fish, and lobster. Ask any local where it is.

$ The Bahama Bayside Café, 242-333-2174, is on the waterfront north of the Straw Market. Open from 7:30 am until 9 pm for breakfast, lunch, dinner and snacks.

$$ The Landing, 242-333-2707, a harbor-front restaurant, is open daily for breakfast, lunch and dinner. The menu is extensive and features Bahamian and Mediterranean dishes. Open until 10 pm.

$$ The Reach, 242-333-2142, is on the waterfront at Valentine's Resort and Marina. The atmosphere is casual, the service pleasant and fast, and the food is as good as it gets. Popular with yachting fraternity. Open from 7:30 am until 10 pm for breakfast, lunch, dinner and snacks.

Hotel Meal Plans

CP (Continental Plan) includes a continental breakfast.

EP (European Plan) denotes no meals, although restaurant facilities are available either on the property or nearby.

MAP (Modified American Plan) denotes breakfast and dinner.

FAP (Full American Plan) includes all meals.

All-Inc. (All-Inclusive Plan) includes all meals, beverages (alcoholic and soft), water-sports, tennis and golf, if available.

Accommodations

Hilton's Haven on Queen's Highway at Tarpum Bay, 242-

334-4231. This is a 10-room guest house without all the facilities of the larger hotels and resorts. Don't let that put you off, though. The lack of facilities is more than made up for by the close personal attention you'll receive at the hands of the owner. Rates start at around $55 per person, per night; MAP is $30 extra.

Bahama House Inn, 242-333-2201, www.bahamahouseinn.com Located right in Dunmore Town on Dunmore Street, it is a five-minute walk from the ferry landing or the famous pink sand beach. John and Joni Hersh have paid loving attention to the details of their B&B. The rooms are colored in Caribbean crisp whites, warm yellows, ocean blues, tropical pinkish-reds, and pale greens. There are ceiling fans and air conditioning; tiled private baths; verandas with ocean views; a lush garden; a library filled with books; a living room with TV; and a large open kitchen. Full breakfasts include omelets, banana rum pancakes, French toast, and fruit. The historic main house was built in 1798 by the island's first justice of the peace, Dr. Johnson. Favorite rooms may be booked months in advance by returning guests. There are seven rooms. $125 to $160 per night; $15 more in the high season. Closed August-October. No kids under 12 or college students.

The Cove Eleuthera, Gregory Town, 800-552-5960, www.thecoveeleuthera.com. The Cove sits on 28 acres with its own secluded beach, swimming pool, and tennis courts. The 24 guest rooms are all nicely furnished, air-conditioned, and have covered porches. Bicycles are available for rent, and hikers can wander the grounds, the beaches, and the island roads. Call for rates.

The Romora Bay Club, Harbour Island, 800-327-8286, www.romorabay.com. The Club is a luxury resort surrounded by lush greenery and secluded trails. All guest rooms are tastefully decorated; each has several pieces of original art. Some have kitchens; most have rattan furniture, and all have air-conditioning, patios, and ceiling fans. The pool is new and there's plenty of room for relaxing. The bar overlooks the harbor and the beach is only a short walk away. The restaurant features an international menu prepared by a world-class chef. Rates are in the region of $280 per night; MAP is $50 extra per person, per day.

Coral Sands Hotel, Romora Bay, Harbour Island, 242-333-2350, www.coralsands.com. The guest rooms and suites, some in the main building and some in an annex, are all well-appointed and have patios, large closets, and living areas. There's a lighted tennis court, indoor games, and bikes, motor scooters and boats available for rent. Meals are served on the patio overlooking the ocean. There's live music on weekends. Rooms start at $260 per person, per night; MAP plans are available.

Cambridge Villas, Gregory Town, 242-335-5080. This is a retreat for those who like to get away from it all to fish, snorkel, dive or simply sit back and do nothing at all. You can stroll the beach in search of shells by day and dance to the seductive sounds of the steel band by night. Accommodations include apartments with living room, bath, air-conditioning and fully equipped kitchenette; standard, superior double, triple, and quad rooms all feature private baths. The staff is happy to arrange fishing, diving, snorkeling, and sightseeing excursions. The resort even has its own five-passenger airplane on hand for island-hopping charters. There's a pleasant dining room, with great food, swimming pool, and complimentary transportation to the beach. Car rentals are available. Rates start at around $110 per person, per night. MAP plans are available.

Tingum Village Hotel & Ma Ruby's Restaurant, Colebrooke Street, PO Box 61, Harbour Island, 242-333-2161 Ma Ruby is known for her cooking and as one of the "women who molded the modern Bahamas." Posted articles and write-ups in more than one book attest to that. Lunch ranges from $3 to $18. Try the coconut tarts or key lime pie and, of course, the Cheeseburger in Paradise, one of the 10 best according to Jimmy Buffet. Hotel and restaurant staff proudly "go beyond the norm to treat guests one-on-one." The hotel, a five-minute walk to the famous pink sand beach, boasts that it is the first family-owned, fully operated hotel on Harbour Island, operating year-round since it started. The pleasant, clean rooms with private baths, currently undergoing renovation, sit scattered throughout the lush green property. Nineteen rooms. From $95 for single rooms to $150 for suites.

The Exumas

From a point just 35 miles southeast of New Providence, the Exumas – a chain of 365 islands and cays – lie strung out across some 95 miles of ocean almost to Long Island. The total population is about 3,550.

It's an area of great natural beauty with tiny cays, secluded inlets, isolated beaches, and great fishing, an ideal vacation spot for boaters, fishermen, and beachcombers.

Most of the islands' inhabitants live on **Great Exuma** or **Little Exuma**, both of which are in the southern part of the island chain. **George Town** is the population center of Great Exuma, while **Williams Town** is the main town on Little Exuma. The Exumas are easily reached by air from Miami or Nassau on daily flights to Exuma's International Airport at **Moss Town**, just a few miles north of George Town.

Exuma Cays Land & Sea Park

To the north on Great Exuma and Staniel Cay lies the Exuma Cays Land & Sea Park. The park, administered by the Bahamas National Trust, is a 177-square-mile tract of islands, cays, and reefs where the underwater world can easily be seen through 10 feet or so of water. Accessible only by boat, this is a conservation area where you can observe the wildlife and marine life in its natural surroundings, unspoiled and beautiful. The park – specifically Allens Cays – is home to the **Bahamian Dragons**, rock iguanas that can grow to more than two feet long. Undersea are reefs, blue holes and shipwrecks. **Ocean Rock** features an underwater valley known locally as the **Iron Curtain**, with huge caves full of black coral.

History

The Lucayan Indians, the first inhabitants of the Exumas, were followed in the 1600s by the **Spanish** explorers, who virtually wiped out the Indians. About the same time, the discovery of salt sparked the Exumas' first prosperous industry. This prosperity, however, brought its own problems. The salt merchants' ships made easy pickings for pirates, and the islands were a natural haven for the corsairs.

In 1783, a group of loyalists fleeing from the aftermath of the American Revolution settled on the islands and, for a while at least, cotton brought new industry to the islands. Both the salt and the cotton plantations were manned by slaves, most of whom were imported from the former British colonies in America. This new prosperity didn't last, however. Insects destroyed the cotton, and it was found that salt could be produced more profitably on other islands in the Bahamas.

Rolle Town on Great Exuma is the direct result of the influx of the Loyalists in 1783. John Rolle settled in the area with his slaves, more than 300 of them, and soon acquired a great deal of land granted to him by a grateful English king. Rolle was later knighted for his services.

Rolle's Heirs

After the slaves were freed by England's 1834 Act of Emancipation, most of those belonging to Lord Rolle took his name – and his land. Today, many of the inhabitants of the Exumas are named Rolle and it's not clear whether they were given the land by a philanthropic master or simply took it along with his name and their freedom. Today the land cannot be sold, but must be passed down from generation to generation.

Rolle Town sits on top of a hill. The houses are painted in bright colors of blue, pink and yellow. The view from the little town is spectacular.

The descendants of John Rolle's slaves are mostly **farmers** or **fishermen**, selling the day's catch, along with tomatoes, onions, mangoes, and avocados to hotels. Those who aren't farmers or fishermen earn their livelihood as a part of the burgeoning **tourist industry**, working at the hotels and marinas.

Getting There

By Air

Two international airports serve the Exumas, **George Town** and **Staniel Cay**, neither as grand as the designation "international" implies.

To George Town Airport from:	Airline
Nassau	**Bahamasair** operates two daily schedules, morning and afternoon, 800-222-4262. Round-trip fare, $120
Fort Lauderdale	**Island Express**, 954-359-0380; **Air Sunshine**, 800-327-8900. Round-trip fare, $170.
Miami	**American Eagle**, 800-433-7300; **Bahamasair**, 800-222-4262. Both operate regular daily schedules. Round-trip fare, $175.

To Staniel Cay Airport from:	Airline
Nassau	**Bahamasair** operates regular daily trips, 800-222-4262. Round-trip fare, $120.
Fort Lauderdale	**Island Express**, 954-359-0380. Round-trip fare, $170.

By Mail Boat

Mail boats operate weekly between Nassau (Potter's Cay Dock) and, as always, schedules depend on the weather so they can be erratic. The dock master can be reached at 423-339-1064.

Grand Master sails from Potter's Cay, Nassau, for George Town on Tuesdays at 2 pm, and returns on Fridays at 7 am. Sailing time is 12 hours. The fare, one way, is $55.

By Private Boat

The waters around these islands make sailing a great pleasure. To the north, **Allen's Cay** and **Leaf Cay** represent the northern extremity of the archipelago and, less than 40 miles from Nassau, they are easily accessible from the island's capital. There's a protected anchorage between the two.

*If you're interested in the local wildlife, you'll want to visit **Leaf Cay**; it's the home of the rare Bahamian iguana. The iguana is a protected species. So, if you have a dog on board, you are requested not to take it ashore because of the threat it will pose to the iguanas.*

From the south end of **Norman's Cay**, the **Exuma Cays Land & Sea Trust** extends some 22 miles to the north and seven miles to the east and west on either side of the islands. Since commercial fishing is banned within the boundaries of the Trust, the waters there are teeming with fish. And, as the average depth of the water is only eight feet, it represents one of the finest snorkeling grounds in the Bahamas.

Sampson Cay is just south of the Trust. Here, boaters have a choice of a 500-foot dock in the outer harbor, or the 30 full-service slips at the **Sampson Cay Club and Marina**. The VHF frequency is 16.

Staniel Cay Yacht Club is also just south of the Trust. They offer 15 full-service slips, along with showers, fuel service, water, ice, groceries and other sea-going necessities. The VHF frequency is 16. 242-355-2024, fax 242-355-2044.

Moving farther south, **Elizabeth Harbour**, at **George Town**, offers a sheltered anchorage within easy reach of the shops and stores.

Exuma Fantasea Marina is also at George Town. There you'll have access to 36 full-service slips, water, and fuel. There's a restaurant and shops nearby in George Town. The VHF frequency is 16. 242-336-3483, fax 242-336-3483.

George Town is the Exumas' official port of entry.

Getting Around

Most of the cays that make up the Exumas are accessible only by boat. **Staniel Cay**, north of George Town, is famous for its beaches, diving, and fishing, and for its great underwater grotto, where the James Bond movie, *Thunderball,* was filmed. Staniel Cay is the jumping-off point for the **Exuma Cays Land & Sea Park**; there are no organized trips. To reach Staniel Cay, charter a small plane at George Town and fly in, or rent a sailboat and crew and travel by sea. The sea voyage will take about a day and a half.

To see George Town and the surrounding area, you have two or three different options. You can take in the sights slowly on foot; you can rent a bicycle, motor scooter, or car and head out on your own; or you can hire a taxi and do it in relative style and comfort.

By Taxi

Your taxi driver will give you a running commentary and you'll soon know almost as much about the Exumas' principal town as he does. A taxi for a day will cost about $120, depending upon how good you are at bargaining. The easiest place to find a cab is at the airport.

George Town On Foot

To do the sights of George Town on foot – it won't take long – start in the center of town on the Queen's Highway. There you'll find the **Club Peace and Plenty**, named for the ship that brought John Rolle to the islands. The hotel was opened in 1955 and encompasses the remains of an old warehouse on Harbourfront. You can take a ferry from the Club to **Stocking Island**, where you might spend an afternoon on the beach or snorkeling in the clear green waters.

Walk a short distance north along Queen's Highway and you'll come to **St. Andrews**, a little church with a gabled roof and arched doorways. To the south is the **Government Administration Building**, which houses the local police station and post office. There's a small park opposite with a straw market offering locally made gifts and trinkets. A bit farther on to the north is the **Town Café**, a good little restaurant for breakfast or lunch. Nearby **Exumas Transport**, 336-2101, has cars for rent. **Sam's Place**, a great seafood restaurant with the best conch salad on the island, is just a few steps farther. From there, it's back to Club Peace and Plenty.

Touring by Bus

Christine Rolle's Island Tours (242-336-4016) has a nice new air-conditioned bus, and the price of her three- to four-hour tours is $20 per person. There's an Eastern Tour (Little Exuma, Shark Lady, Hermitage Plantation Ruins, and many secluded beaches), and Western Tour (Loyalist tombs, Emerald Bay, Barra Terre, and bush medicine. Contact Christine through your hotel.

Touring by Motor Scooter

You can see a lot of Great Exuma this way, and at a pace to suit yourself. You can rent a motor scooter at **Dive Exuma**, 242-336-2893. Rates are $35 per day; $240 per week. Once again, the place to start is right in the center of George Town at the Club Peace and Plenty on Harbourfront. Head out northward along the east coast via the Queen's Highway for about eight miles, past Hooper's Bay, Moss Town to the left, then Ramsey and Jimmy's Hill, until you come to **Ocean Bight**, a tiny, picturesque fishing village where you can spend a quiet afternoon swimming and walking before returning to George Town.

Touring by Bike

Starfish – The Exuma Activity Center, 242-336-3033, rents 21-speed specialized mountain and cruiser bikes for $15-$25 per day. Downtown George Town; e-mail starfishexuma@pocketmail.com.

Touring by Car

This is the way to do the island in style. It will take about four hours – longer if you stop for a snack or a swim – to see all the sights along the Queen's Highway from George Town to Barraterre at the northern tip of Great Exuma, a journey of only 30 miles or so. Follow the road along the coast to Hooper's Bay and then head into **Moss Town**, a tiny farming community with brightly painted houses and two little churches. From there, the road winds on and rejoins the coast road.

As you proceed from Moss Town to **Rolleville** – be sure to take in the tiny bays, inlets and beaches along the way – you'll pass through Farmer's Hill and Steventon, the remains of two of Lord Rolle's once-great plantations. The great houses are long gone, but the descendants of the slaves that once worked the cotton fields still live in and around the area.

Rolleville, one of the largest settlements here, is in fact a tiny community of a few small houses, a church, and **The Hilltop Tavern**, where you can enjoy a lunch of fresh grouper and an ice-cold drink.

From Rolleville, you must return the way you came for about a mile, where the road branches off to the west for **Alexander** – another old plantation settlement – and on to **Barraterre**, a quaint fishing village well worth the drive from George Town. Barraterre offers several stores where you can buy locally made handicrafts and gifts, an inn for something to eat and drink, and a beach where you can watch fishermen bringing in the day's catch.

If you drive south from George Town for about 15 miles on Queen's Highway, you'll cross a bridge to Little Exuma and the islands' southernmost community of Williams Town. Along the way you'll pass through **Rolle Town**. Turn left into the village, then head up the hill to the **old cemetery**, where you'll find several historic graves and tombs, including those of Captain Alexander McKay and his family. Alexander McKay arrived on the Exumas from Scotland in 1789 to farm 400 acres of land given to him by the English king, George III.

A little farther on you'll find the **Peace and Plenty Bonefish Lodge**, where you can arrange to go bonefishing with Captain Bob Hyde or one of his expert guides.

From Rolle Town, continue south and cross the bridge to **Little Exuma**. Just beyond the bridge you'll see a sign pointing the way to **Tara, Home of the Shark Lady**, and another sign proclaiming that the Tropic of Cancer runs right through the good lady's home. Be sure to visit Tara; it's an amazing experience.

The next and last stop on your drive south is **Williams Town**, a community at the end of the Exumas' world. Here you'll find the church of **St. Mary Magdalene** and the remains of yet another cotton plantation. Only the ruins of the great house and some of the slaves' quarters survive.

From Williams Town it's back to George Town. At the end of the day, you find it hard to believe that your round-trip, after all you saw and did, was less than 35 miles.

Nightlife

There's a **Fish Fry** every Wednesday evening at the Naval Docks just north of George Town. It's great fun and attracts both the locals and tourists. Fresh snapper, conch fritters, ribs, and plenty of Kalick beer, along with music of the islands, make this a unique experience.

On The Water
Sea Kayaking & Sailing

Important Note: All of the offerings listed below were active and correctly priced at the time they were researched. You should be aware, however, that all are subject to change without notice. Please check with the provider at the Phone numbers listed for up-to-date packages, rates, and information.

Sea kayaking is one of the few outdoor adventures that almost anyone, experienced or not, can enjoy. It's offered in several areas of the Bahamas, but nowhere is it as popular as in the Exumas. Here you can spend up to a couple of weeks paddling the open waters between the islands of the chain: long hot days, balmy nights spent under canvas, lots to see and do, good food, and fine company. True, you have to be fairly fit to handle the often strenuous exercise of paddling for several hours at a time. But the sheer vastness of the seascapes, the pristine beaches, and the crystal waters, make this type of experience one-of-a-kind.

There are several outfits that handle sea kayaking expeditions to the Exumas.

Starfish – The Exuma Activity Center, toll-free 877-398-6222, local 242-336-3033. This outfit offers a variety of outdoor adventures: full- and half-day guided sea kayak trips to caves, shipwrecks, smugglers' hideouts, mangrove rivers, blue holes, and the ruins of former Exuma Governor William Walker's mansion on Crab Cay. In addition, they have more than a dozen five- and seven-day kayak touring trips from November through May. The most popular is the Exuma Classic, with four days and three nights of island-to-island kayak touring, plus three nights lodging, transfers, sailing and bike day trips, for $895 to $995, depending upon your choice of lodging. The six-day, five-night kayak tour is $695, and the week-long "BahamaMamaShip" adventure offers a week of guided day adventures with all meals and houseboat lodging for a group of six people at $5,995. They also have three different eco-tours of the harbor and adjacent islands by motor boat for $25 per person. There's a fleet of Hobe Wave sailboats for rent and instruction is available, for a price, of course. Finally, they offer a day-long, private romantic getaway to a secluded island complete with boat driver, lounge chairs, table, snorkel gear, kayak, camera, mats and a gourmet picnic, all for just $95 per person. www.kayakbahamas.com; e-mail wise@carol.com. Late-breaking news: Starfish has just completed the purchase of Exuma Sailing Adventures. See the following listing.

Starfish/Exuma Sailing Adventures, 242-336-3033, www.exuma-bahamas.com, is offering five- and eight-night sailing expeditions up through the Exuma cays and the Exuma Land & Sea Park. Due to the prevailing winds, these tours are one-way. The boats are 21-foot Sea Pearls, twin sails, 12-inch draught, and they carry two to three people. The sailboats are accompanied by a powerboat, which carries all of the supplies and camping gear. Experienced guides and sailing instructors are on hand. This is a great new adventure opportunity. Check it out – availability and rates – on their website.

Ecosummer, 800-465-8884, www.ecosummer.com, operates a fleet of Klepper kayaks complete with sailing rigs, offering nine- and 15-day expeditions during February, March and April. The Heart of the Exumas is a nine-day expedition covering some 45 miles between Staniel Cay in the south to Norman's Cay in the north. Most of the trip is spent in the Exuma Land & Sea Park. The itinerary is designed to provide a more leisurely pace than the longer Complete Exumas itinerary. You can expect to paddle, and hopefully sail, an average of seven miles per day. But, as winds in the Bahamas are variable, and often blowing in the wrong direction, you'll get plenty of exercise. Still, the seven miles is usually covered quickly, leaving plenty of time for snorkeling, beachcombing, and exploring. The trip grade for the Heart of the Exumas expedition is level 3, meaning that it demands sustained physical activity. It is designed for those who have less vacation time available and who wish to sample tropical kayaking in the most protected part of the Bahamas.

The Complete Exumas expedition – 15 days – covers a distance of about 100 miles from George Town in the south to Allen's Cay in the north, passing through Exuma Land & Sea Park en route. Each day is a mixture of paddling or sailing between camps and exploring both on land and in the water. Daily distances average about 10 miles, which can take a half-day of paddling, less if the winds are helping you. The expedition also includes paddling in tidal creeks and lagoons, and in and out of the more intricate locations among the cays. Again, there will be plenty of time for snorkeling, beachcombing, and exploring some of the tiny settlements along the way. The trip grade for the Complete Exumas Expedition is level 4, with the potential for long paddling days under weather conditions that might include strong winds and high temperatures. The trip is for those who want to experience the entire Exuma Chain and gain the satisfaction of having completed a seldom-offered kayak opportunity.

You don't need previous experience to go on one of the expeditions, but you do need to be fit and in good physical shape. The kayaks are very seaworthy and easy to handle.

The climate during the three months the expeditions are offered sees daytime temperatures between the mid-70s and the low 80s, while the nights are almost always cool and balmy; rainfall averages less than two inches a month.

Take along your snorkeling mask and fins, casual and outdoor clothes, and a good pair of hiking shoes or boots.

The Heart of the Exumas Expedition is offered seven times between March 1st and April 12th (call for exact dates) and costs $1,595 per person, which includes the services of a fully qualified guide and assistant. All equipment is provided, including folding kayaks, paddles, life jackets, tents, and kitchen/cooking gear. Prices are based on shared occupancy on days one and eight, shuttle bus service between the airport and the hotel, charter flights between Nassau and the Exumas on days two and nine, and all meals from breakfast on day two to breakfast on day nine.

The Complete Exumas Expedition is offered twice during the second half of February each year, and costs $2,295 per person, which includes the services of a fully qualified guide and assistant. All equipment is provided, including folding kayaks, paddles, life jackets, tents, and kitchen/cooking gear. Prices are based on shared occupancy in George Town on day one and in Nassau on day 15, airport transfer in George Town, boat transfer to Nassau on day 14, and shuttle bus service to the airport on day 15, and all meals from breakfast on day two to dinner on day 14.

Ibis Tours of Boynton Beach, FL, 800-525-9411, e-mail info@ibistours.com, wwwibistours.com, runs trips in Florida's Everglades as well as the Bahamas. They offer an eight-day kayak trip, including snorkeling and swimming into sea caves. Folding kayaks with sails are used in the Bahamas. Most of this trip is within the Exuma Cays Land & Sea Park. Besides the normal amenities, the price for this tour includes a round-trip charter flight from Nassau to the Exumas, and hotel lodging for the first night plus two hotel meals. $1,595 per person. In 2003, there will be two trips in March and four in April.

Twelve persons is the limit on an Ibis trip, with an average guest-to-guide ratio of 5:1. You'll receive in advance a packing list that identifies what you should bring and what they supply; an itinerary of where and when to meet; a medical information form and an insurance form. The price of an Ibis Tour includes all the meals, the boats, all paddling equipment and all the camping equipment, including tents and sleeping bags. Waterproof storage bags are supplied for all personal gear. They "guarantee" great food on all Ibis Trips and they even have a cookbook in the works. Wine is served with dinner, plus rum punches in the Bahamas.

Fishing

As it is on most of the Out Islands, the fishing is spectacular. On the east side of the island chain lies the 6,000-foot drop-off of **Exuma Sound**. Big fish inhabit the waters here. Giant marlin, sailfish, and wahoo have been caught in the Sound in record numbers. On the reefs, the water is clear and shallow, providing a happy hunting ground for snapper, record-breaking grouper and even lobster. For the bonefisherman, there are more wadeable flats in the Exumas than anywhere else in the Out Islands, and there are no crowds to bother you. The bonefish average around four or five pounds, but 10-pounders are not uncommon and you might get lucky and hook something even bigger. Bonefishing guides, too, are plentiful. The **Peace and Plenty Bonefishing Lodge** has several on its staff and, if you simply ask around, there are plenty of locals who know the area and are willing to serve as guides.

Fishing Tournament

July 4th is the date for the **Annual Bonefish Tournament** at Staniel Cay & Yacht Club. 242-355-2044 for information and registration.

Fishing Packages

Important Note: All of the packages listed below were active and correctly priced at the time they were researched. You should be aware, however, that all are subject to change without notice. Please check with the provider at the Phone numbers listed for up-to-date packages, rates, and information.

Club Peace and Plenty

Club Peace and Plenty in George Town, 242-345-5555, www.peaceandplenty.com/resorts/resorts.htm, offers a series of bonefishing packages. The rates are per person, based on double occupancy.

Four days/three nights: $777

Five days/four nights: $1,036

Six day/five nights: $1,295

Seven days/six nights: $1,544

An extra night plus fishing is $259 per person

An extra night with no fishing is $200 per person

Each package includes the following: waterfront location, air-conditioned accommodations; Monday night cocktail party; full days of fishing with an experienced guide; expert instruction for first-timers; transportation to the flats, and to and from the airport; breakfast and dinner daily; boxed lunches on fishing days; boat service to Stocking Island; shuttle between the hotel and the Beach Inn; meal exchange between the hotel and the Beach Inn.

Boat Rentals

Staniel Cay Yacht Club, on Staniel Cay, north of Great Exuma, 242-355-2024, www.stanielcay.com. Fishing charters only from $250 to $650 per day.

Minns Water-sports, 242-336-3483. A 17-foot Boston Whaler rents for $70 per day, or $350 per week. Minns is in downtown George Town on Lake Victoria across from Club Peace & Plenty.

Powerboat Adventures

Island World Adventures, Nassau, 242-363-3333, offers a unique excursion to the northern Exumas. If you have a day to spare, take my advice and book this day-trip; you won't regret it. The adventure begins in Nassau in the early morning – you need to be at the dock by 8:30 am – when you board one of two state-of-the-art, high-speed powerboats. Then, together, the two boats speed across the clear waters more than 40 miles to **Saddleback Cay** in the northern Exumas. There you'll wade ashore to relax and unwind on one of the Exumas' many uninhabited islands. Be sure to take along your camera and snorkeling gear. The shallow waters of the coral reef are home to a multitude of colorful marine life, and it's all unspoiled. Here, you're likely to encounter rays, turtles, even dolphins. When lunchtime rolls around, you'll be treated to a meal under the palms and savor some authentic Bahamian cuisine. The palm-thatched roofs and gentle breezes make for a very pleasant dining experience. As the day wears on, you'll reboard the boats and begin the trip back to Paradise Island, stopping along the way at **Leaf Cay**, home to a colony of friendly iguanas. You'll arrive back at the dock around 5 pm. Although the outing is not recommended for children under three, people with acute health problems, or pregnant women, this is one adventure you really shouldn't miss. The cost of the day-trip includes the boat ride, lunch, sodas, water, beer, rum punch, snorkeling, guided tours and pick-up from your hotel.

Diving & Snorkeling

They say there are some 365 islands in the Exuma chain. But no one has ever bothered to count them properly. The reefs, blue holes, and drop-offs are teeming with reef and deep water fish and other marine life. With an island and its surrounding beaches and reefs for every day of the year, you'll never lack someplace new to explore. For snorkelers, the Exumas are a wonderland of flats, shallow reefs and beaches. You can snorkel almost anywhere. Just wade out a hundred yards or so, and plunge in.

Best Dive Sites
Pagoda Reef

Pagoda Reef is not far from George Town. The elkhorn coral, leaf and sheet corals here have evolved into a magnificent pagoda-like grotto. The whole formation is populated by a great underwater family of parrotfish, sergeant majors, snappers, angels and crustaceans.

Angelfish Blue Hole

Just outside Elizabeth Harbour, this hole is considered the number one dive site in the Exumas. It is tidal, which creates currents and vortexes in and out of the cave. The idea is to dive the hole at the quiet time between the tides. Never dive Angelfish without expert guidance.

Angelfish is a huge aquarium filled with thousands of fish.

Crab Cay Crevasse

Not far from Angelfish, this is another spectacular blue hole. The crescent-shaped opening is just 15 feet below the surface. Here, you can dive to the sandy bottom of the cave, where you'll see crabs, lobsters and anemones. I strongly recommend you dive with a guide.

Mystery Cave

Mystery Cave is a network of caverns extending for miles beneath Stocking Island and the surrounding ocean. Starting at a depth of only 15 feet, the cavern system soon drops off to a heart-stopping 100 feet. Never dive Mystery Cave without an expert guide.

Dive Operators

Exuma Scuba Adventures, 242-336-2893, www.exumascuba.com, opened in March of 2000 and is owned and operated by a highly qualified staff from the Small Hope Bay Resort on Andros. They operate out of Club Peace and Plenty in George Town, and fill the gap left when Exuma Fantasea went out business several years ago. They have one instructor and two dive masters, three boats and 20 sets of rental gear. One-tank dives are $45, snorkeling is $15.

Dive/Accommodation Packages

Important Note: All of the packages listed below were active and correctly priced at the time they were researched. You should be aware, however, that all are subject to change without notice. Please check with the provider at the Phone numbers listed for up-to-date packages, rates, and information.

Club Peace and Plenty

Club Peace and Plenty in George Town, 242-536-2551, offers an eight-day, seven-night package during the period of May 1st to December 15th for $1,099 per person, based on double occupancy; and again from December 16th to April 30th for $1,199 per person, double occupancy. See page 255 for details.

Where to Stay and Eat

Dining

$$ **Eddie's Edgewater**, on Charlotte Street in George Town, is the place for fresh fish. Famous for turtle steak, the restaurant also serves fresh grouper, fried snapper, pea soup and dumplings, and the inevitable peas and rice. 242-336-2050.

$ **The Town Café & Bakery**, on Main Street, is a great place for breakfast. The fresh-baked donuts and muffins are to die for. The pancakes are terrific and, if you'd like to try the local food, there's boil fish, chicken souse, and Johnny cake. 242-336-2194.

$$ **Sam's Place** features a magnificent view of the ocean from an elevated dining room. Great food and a pleasant atmosphere. 242-336-2579.

$ **Kermit's Hilltop Tavern** in Rolleville is a bar and restaurant serving lunch and dinner. Fresh fried grouper, minced lobster, conch, curried mutton, and fresh fruit from Kermit's own farm are on the menu. 242-345-0002.

$$ The Fisherman's Inn in Barraterre is both a night club and a restaurant, featuring an old-world nautical atmosphere. It can be extremely busy. 242-355-5017.

Accommodations

Important Note: Accommodation rates listed below were active and correctly priced at the time they were researched. You should be aware, however, that all are subject to change without notice. Please check with the provider at the Phone numbers listed for up-to-date packages, rates, and information.

The Four Seasons Resort on Great Exuma is on Emerald Bay, 15 miles northwest of the island's capital, George Town. It features a wealth of amenities, including two restaurants, three swimming pools, and a crescent-shaped white-sand beach, as well as a magnificent Greg Norman-designed golf course. Accommodations include 183 guestrooms, suites, and villas, all with stone floors, handcrafted furnishings, and premium bedding with duvets and down pillows. All have either a terrace or balcony with a view of the hotel's gardens or the ocean and Emerald Bay.

There is an Asian-inspired spa with 17 treatment rooms and four outdoor cabanas. The staff offers more than a dozen different treatments, many of which incorporate the use of local salts and indigenous herbs, oils, and flowers. The adjacent spa garden provides an opportunity for quiet times, relaxation and meditation. A full-service fitness center has a full range of exercise equipment, complimentary fitness classes, personal trainers, and steam rooms. Along with the golf course, there are on-site tennis courts, as well as a marina. A variety of water-sports activities are also available on-site.

Rates start at $400 per night for an ocean-view room and rise to more than $750 per night, depending upon the season. PO Box EX29005, Queen's Highway, Emerald Bay, Great Exuma; 800-921-2650, 242-336-6800, fax 242-336-6801, www.four-seasons.com/greatexuma.

Palm Bay Beach Club Hotel and Resort, overlooking

Elizabeth Harbour and Stocking Island on Great Exuma, is within walking distance of the island's capital, George Town, and is just seven miles from Exuma International Airport.

Amenities include a white, sandy beach, large swimming pool, full range of water sports, beach bar serving barbecued meals, a full-service, but casual, outdoor restaurant, and shuttle service to George Town. The resort has over 40 beachside cottages and hillside villas, and you have a choice of studio, one-bedroom, and two bedroom units.

If you're a golfer, you'll really enjoy the challenge of the new Four Seasons, Greg Norman Signature Golf Course at Emerald Bay, just a short drive away. Whether you love to snorkel, swim, wander along a deserted beach or relax in the sun, the Palm Bay Resort offers something for everyone: white sandy beaches, the island's largest freshwater pool, sea kayaks, and two Hobe Cats for the exclusive use of guests. The water is shallow and calm, making it safe for children.

There are several restaurants on-site, or you can enjoy an evening out at one of the nearby restaurants in George Town. The Pool Bar & Grill has calypso music and a great view.

Accommodations include 40 private, beachfront cottages, townhouses, and inland villas, most of which have panoramic views of the gardens, bay and the ocean. All are painted in bright, Bahamian-inspired colors. Choose from studio, one- or two-bedroom cottages all with ocean, garden or pool views. All of the studio units, and the one- and two-bedroom cottages feature designer furniture, queen size beds, air conditioning, tile floors, fans, fully equipped kitchen with refrigerator, two-burner cook top stove, microwave, toaster, coffee maker, purified drinking water system, private covered porch, tele/computer hook-up, cable TV, ironing board, hairdryer, queen-size beds, and pull-out couches in all one- and two-bedroom cottages.

Rates start at $143 per night, depending upon the season, for an ocean-side studio and rise to $506 per night for a two-bedroom, ocean-side cottage. PO Box 29137, George Town, Exumas; 888-396-0606, 242-336-2787, fax 242-336-2770, info@PalmBayBeachClub.com, www.palmbaybeachclub.com.

Two Turtles Inn, on Main Street in George Town, 242-336-

2545, www.exumabahamas.com/twoturtles.html. The inn, right in the center of town, features 14 comfortable guest rooms, three with kitchen units; all are air-conditioned. There's also a patio bar shaded by palm trees, and a restaurant where you can sample a variety of Bahamian dishes. The hotel staff will arrange diving, bonefishing, and deep-sea fishing excursions. Bicycles, jeeps and mopeds are available for rent on the premises. The rates start at $88 per night, per person; EP only.

Three Sisters, Queen's Highway, Mt. Thompson, 242-358-4040 is right on the ocean. It has 12 air-conditioned rooms and three luxury villas complete with kitchenettes. All rooms have television sets. The dining room offers fresh seafood dinners and a spectacular view of the ocean. The staff can arrange fishing, sailing and diving excursions, and you can go snorkeling among the Three Sisters – three large rocks in the ocean – right off the hotel beach. Rates are around $100 per night; EP only.

Regatta Point, Kid Cove, George Town, 800-688-0309, 242-336-2206, www.regattapointbahamas.com. Regatta Point is surrounded on all sides by water. A vacation here is like staying on a private island, but still you're only a few minute's walk from George Town. Each guest apartment is fully equipped with a kitchen, and you'll have use of a skiff that can be tied up at your own private dock. Rates start at $115; EP only.

Club Peace and Plenty, Harbourfront, George Town, 800-525-2210, www.peaceandplenty.com. The Club has 35 deluxe, air-conditioned rooms, all with tiled floors and private balconies. The restaurant offers fine dining in a candle-lit atmosphere, and a menu featuring both American and traditional Bahamian dishes. There's free ferry service out to the Club's own Stocking Island Beach Club for snorkeling. Windsurfers and Sunfish sailboats are available too. Rates at the Peace and Plenty start at $120 per night; an MAP plan is available for $32 extra.

Peace and Plenty Beach Inn, Harbourfront, George Town, 242-336-2551, www.peaceandplenty.com. The Beach Inn has 16 deluxe rooms, all with air-conditioning, TVs, refrigerators, and private balconies. The restaurant offers a choice of international or traditional Bahamian cuisine. Tropical drinks from the bar are served around the freshwater swimming pool and on the fishing dock. World-class bonefishing is available. Rates start at $130;

MAP is $32 extra.

Staniel Cay Yacht Club, Staniel Cay, 242-355-2024, www.stanielcay.com. The Yacht Club is in the heart of the island and caters mainly to private pilots, sailors, and vacationers looking for a little peace and quiet. The waters off Staniel Cay provide excellent scuba diving, and the Yacht Club staff will fill your tanks and provide rental scuba gear. The bonefishing is excellent, too. Rates run $195 per night, which includes FAP.

THE Other out Islands

Beyond the more well-known Out Islands of the Bahamas, there are many more that are not-so-well-known, just as beautiful, just as inviting, and just as welcoming. They are a little more difficult to get to, but that only makes them more of an adventure. You can spend hours on truly deserted beaches, walk for miles and never see another soul, fish, dive and snorkel to your heart's content. Package vacations to these islands, with the exception of Long Island and San Salvador, are not available. So you'll need to find a creative travel agent.

With the exception of American Airlines, no major US airline makes scheduled stops at these islands. You can fly into Long Island, usually via Miami, on American, and into the Berry Islands, Long Island, and Cat Island on Island Express out of Fort Lauderdale. But to get to the others you'll need to fly into Nassau via scheduled air, and then onward by Bahamasair, Gulfstream Air or one of the several local air charters.

Another option, one that's worth considering if you have lots of time to spare, is the mail boat. These boats make scheduled runs from Nassau to all of the Out Islands and, for a fee, they'll take you along. If you're truly the adventuresome type, this is the way to go. These little ships, often crowded and noisy, ply the waters between the islands mostly at night and will provide you with an experience you'll remember the rest of your life.

Mail boats leave Nassau, from the docks at the Paradise Island Bridge, for Andros, the Abacos, Eleuthera, the Exumas, Long Island, Cat Island, the Acklins, San Salvador, the Inaguas and others every other week.

The Acklins & Crooked Island

For a remote and tranquil vacation, you might choose a secluded getaway on the Acklins or Crooked Island. Located almost as far south as you can go in the Out Islands, south of the Tropic of Cancer, beyond Long Island and the Exumas, these islands are accessible only by private boat or regularly scheduled flights on Bahamasair.

Here you'll discover sun swept shores, scenic coves and hidden bays. On **Crooked Island** there are caves, miles of creeks, tidal flats populated by record tarpon and bonefish. Days on these islands are spent swimming, snorkeling, fishing, visiting tiny churches and historic buildings while you stroll the streets of quaint little towns and villages, such as Snug Corner, Lovely Bay, Delectable Bay Spring Point, Pompey Bay and, on Cat Island, Pittstown Point, Colonel Hill, Landrail Point and Albert Town. In the evening, you'll wander deserted beaches, and enjoy a cool tropical drink as you watch the sun go down in a blaze of glory.

History

The history of these islands lies hidden in the mists of time; what's known for sure is that **English** loyalists from Virginia, fleeing the aftermath of the American Revolution, arrived here at the end of the 18th century, bringing with them hundreds of slaves. Soon, more than 40 plantations had been established, but they were short-lived. By 1825, most of them were in ruins, the result of one crop failure after another.

Columbus Was Here

Today, the islands are a quiet little backwater, visited by few, but loved by all that do set foot ashore. Separated from Crooked Island by the Crooked Island Passage, an important shipping route during the early days when sailing ships used it en route to and from the New World, the Acklins are at the center of the "Columbus-landed-here-first" controversy. These islands entered the debate when *National Geographic* ran an article in 1986, pinpointing Crooked Island as the place where the explorer first set foot in the Bahamas; and the debate will, no doubt, continue.

Crooked Island is the hub of activities, such as they are. The island's capital is **Colonel Hill**, a colorful settlement of gaily painted buildings where everyone has a friendly word, and time goes by very slowly. No one's in a hurry here and that, after all, is the essence of a great getaway.

Getting There

By Air

From the US, take a regularly scheduled flight into Nassau with a connection to either Colonel Hill or Spring Point. **Bahamasair** flights (800-222-4262) leave Nassau on Tuesdays and Saturdays at 8:45 am, arriving at 10. Round-trip airfare from Nassau is $168.

By Mail Boat

Lady Matilda leaves Nassau's Potter's Cay Dock weekly for the Acklins, Crooked Island and Mayaguana. The schedule varies according to need and the season. Call the dock master at 242-393-1064. Sailing time is 15 hours or more, and the voyage is usually overnight. The fares are $65, $70 and $70 respectively.

By Private Boat

There are no marina facilities on Crooked Island or in the Acklins. There are, of course, lots of places where you can drop anchor for the night and pick up supplies – groceries and the like.

J Once you're on the ground and have cleared the small airport building, call your hotel for a ride – 344-2507 – or grab one of the few **cabs** that may or may not be waiting outside. If you're arriving by mail boat, the tele may be the only option.

Sightseeing

Bird Rock Lighthouse

If you're a lighthouse enthusiast, you should visit this one. Located on the Crooked Island Passage, it dominates a lonely land- and seascape where the only inhabitants are the gulls and ospreys that squawk and squabble among the rocks where they build their nests.

The rocky landscape and white lighthouse make this a must for photographers.

Crooked Island Caves

Most of the Out Islands are riddled with caves, and Crooked Island is no different. Many of the caves here are larger than those on other islands: narrow, underground passageways that suddenly open upon vast chambers where shafts of light filter in through holes in the roof. And then there are the bats – harmless enough, but scary even so.

It's best to explore the caves with a Bahamian guide. Pittstown Point Landing staff will be pleased to arrange this for you. 242-344-2507.

French Wells

This is one for the environmentalist adventurer. Here, close to the mangroves, is one of the few places in the Bahamas you can watch flamingos in the wild. It is very quiet here. You can almost feel the stillness. The waters are crystal clear – and the fish are fearless. Sit long enough, and you're almost sure to see barracuda, rays and even sharks. Again, the staff at Pittstown Point Landing can arrange a visit.

Marine Farm

Once a British fort built to guard the Crooked Island Passage against marauding Spanish ships and pirates, Marine Farm has long since been abandoned and is now little more than rocks, ruins and rusted cannons. Still, if you have the time, it's well worth a visit to experience a little local history.

Dining

$ In Pittstown, **Ozzie's**, at Pittstown Point Landing, is the place to go. Open from 7 am until 11 pm, they serve three complete meals. Fresh seafood is offered daily, along with a variety of Bahamian dishes. You can even get a picnic basket for a day's outing. 242-344-2507.

Accommodations

Pittstown Point. Just 16 miles from Colonel Hill airport on

Crooked Island, this is the premier hotel on the two islands. The hotel has its own airstrip, and the management can arrange for you to be flown in direct from Nassau or Florida. It's an old-world type of establishment where the atmosphere is easy-going and quite colonial. The rooms, while a little austere, are comfortable, with nice bathrooms and two double beds. This is a friendly place where you'll soon get to know every member of the staff, as well as the other guests. Speaking of the staff, everyone pitches in: cooks double as waiters, bar tenders double as guides, or might even take you bonefishing. Dress is casual, and rates are reasonable, starting around $100 per night. 800-752-2322 or 242-344-2507, www.pittstownpointlandings.com. EP, MAP and FAP available.

The Berry Islands

Less than 35 miles to the north of Nassau, close to the fishing grounds on the eastern edge of the Great Bahama Bank, these little-known islands have long been a favorite stop for divers, anglers and yachtsmen. There's not much to them; just 12 square miles of land scattered across a dozen, or so, small cays, most of them privately owned. Small and isolated as the archipelago is, there's plenty for the outdoor enthusiast to see and do. Tiny communities with colorful names – Cockroach Cay, Goat Cay, Hog Cay, Devil's Cay – conjure images of James Bond. Divers can explore the coral reefs off **Mamma Rhoda Rock** and unidentified sunken ships.

Anglers know the Berrys are renowned for championship sport fishing and that they can hunt the "big one" on the Banks, or just off-shore in the deep blue waters to the east. Naturalists can walk the deserted beaches, ply the waters between the islands in a rented boat and perhaps visit the private bird sanctuary on **Bond's Cay**. These islands are perfect for yachtsmen; they lend themselves beautifully to inter-island day-sailing.

The largest of the Berry Islands is **Great Harbour Cay**, where most of the islands' 500 residents live on a narrow strip of land some 10 miles long by only 1½ miles wide.

Chub Cay is the southernmost island in the Berry group. It's a resort island, home to Chub Cay Club, with a 76-slip marina and almost all the modern conveniences you'd expect at a resort in Nassau.

Getting There

The Berrys are perhaps the most difficult islands to reach. Your options are limited to charter air, the mail boat and private boat.

By Air

Only private charters serve the Berry Islands. These can be arranged in Nassau or Florida: 800-688-4752 for information.

From Fort Lauderdale, **Island Express** operates direct flights into Great Harbour Cay. Cost is $200 round-trip. 954-359-0380 or fax 954-760-9157.

By Mail Boat

Champion II provides service between the Berry Islands and Nassau. The cost of the trip is $30. 800-688-4752 for information.

By Private Boat

Veteran sailors and yachtsmen will be very familiar with the **Great Harbour Cay Yacht Club and Marina**, a full-service marina with extensive facilities. These include 85 slips, repair facilities, fuel service, Laundromat, showers, shops, and a restaurant. The draft at high water is 10 feet; eight feet at low water. The maximum depth is 15 feet. The marina can accommodate boats up to 150 feet long and 70 feet wide. The 30-foot-high bank provides excellent storm protection. You can call for information at 800-343-7256, fax at 242-367-8115, or call on VHF channel 68.

> You may or may not find a **taxi** at the airport. If not, you'll find local numbers posted. Or you can call your hotel and request a ride.

On The Water

Boat Rentals

Great Harbour Yacht Club & Marina rents small boats and sailboats at rates from $40 per day. 242-367-8838 or 800-

343-7256.

Diving & Snorkeling

While there are a number of excellent diving and snorkeling sites in the Berry Islands, there are no dive operators. You take it as you find it. The barrier reefs are spectacular and unspoiled, ideal for scuba diving: visibility averages over 100 feet. And there are great underwater photo opportunities. Snorkeling is good almost everywhere, but especially so in the shallows off **Chub Cay**.

Dining:

$ Backside Lounge & Disco, Great Harbour Drive, Bullock's Harbour. Open Thursday through Friday, this is a great place for cocktails, dancing and relaxing.

$ The Beach Club. Overlooking the ocean on Great Harbour Drive, Bullock's Harbour, this restaurant is open daily from 7 am until 6 pm for breakfast and lunch.

$ The Tamboo Dinner Club. Located at the Great Harbour Cay Yacht Club, Tamboo is open Wednesday and Saturday for dinner.

$ The Wharf Restaurant and Bar at the Great Harbour Marina is open for breakfast and dinner daily, except Tuesday. It serves local dishes and seafood.

$ White Water Bar & Restaurant. Situated on the causeway into Bullock's Harbour, White Water is open daily for lunch and dinner. Great Bahamian food.

Accommodations

Chub Cay Club Resort & Marina. Located on the southernmost island in the Berry group, the resort features beachfront rooms, yacht club rooms, and two- and three-bedroom villas. Amenities include tennis courts, two swimming pools – one for members and one for guests – and two beaches. There's also a full-service dive shop where you can take scuba lessons or guided day-trips to the reefs or wrecks. Guest rooms are comfortable, and most have coffee makers and satellite television. There's a non-member's bar and a fine dining room that serves three meals every day. The fare includes such local delights as peas and rice, grouper and lobster, and not-so-local dishes such as lamb chops and steaks. At night you can while away the hours in the bar, playing pool or dominoes, or dancing. Rates start at $120 per night. EP only. 800-662-8555 or 242-325-1490, www.chubcay.com.

Great Harbour Marina. Expensive, but well worth it, the accommodations here on Great Harbour Cay border on the luxurious. It offers waterfront townhouses at the marina and beachfront villas on the eastern shore. All are comfortable, with air-conditioning, ceiling fans and fully equipped kitchens. Marina units all have private docks, and daily maid service is provided for all units. Facilities include three restaurants, as many bars, and a couple of small inns. Bicycles and motor scooters are available for rent; diving and snorkeling excursions can be arranged; small boats are also available for rent, as well as larger powerboats and sailboats. There's even a nine-hole golf course. Rates start at $120 per night. EP only. 800-343-7256 or 242-367-8005.

Cat Island

Named for a British sea captain, Cat Island is one of the most beautiful in the Bahamas: 50 square miles of tranquility, rolling hills and lush green forests. It's a peaceful retreat of great natural beauty, with a way of life that's quiet and relaxed.

You can enjoy endless miles of wind-blown beaches, explore the **Arawak Indian Caves** near Port Howe, and follow the stations of the cross to the island's highest point, the peak of **Mount Alverina** at 206 feet. At the top is **The Hermitage**, a miniature abbey built by Father Jerome Hawes, by hand, during the early part of the 20th century.

During the 17th century, the island was known as San Salvador, the same name as that of the tiny island just to the southeast where, so the story goes, Columbus first landed in 1492.

Cat Island is not on any list of tourist destinations. It's a distant stop on sailing routes southeast beyond Nassau and Eleuthera. Time goes by slowly; electricity and running water are luxuries. The island's residents make their living farming or fishing, and visitors spend their days quietly: swimming, hiking, visiting the ruins of Colonial plantations, or simply contemplating the great natural beauty of the island.

Getting There

By Air

Scheduled service by **Bahamasair** (800-222-4262) from Nassau to Arthur's Town. The fare is $120 round-trip. **Cat Island Air**, 242-377-3318, also flies. Charter service is available to New Bight from Fort Lauderdale, and is provided by **Island Express**, 954-359-0380; **Air Sunshine**, 800-327-8900; **Bel Air Transport**, 954-524-9814. Average charter cost per person is $200.

A 4,600-foot airstrip is within 300 feet of the Hawk's Nest Resort and Marina. Transport to and from the strip can be arranged by calling 357-7257.

Complimentary transportation to and from the airport is

provided by all of the major hotels on the island. Some require advance notice, so it's best to call ahead. **Cabs** *are also available at the airport, and at the dock to meet the mail boats; they will make the run between any and all of the hotels. They are also on call for sightseeing excursions.*

By Mail Boat

Cat Island is well served by Nassau's mail boat system. You can leave Potter's Cay dock either on Tuesday or Wednesday, and return either on Friday the same week, or on Monday the week following.

The ***North Cat Island Special***, leaves each Wednesday at 1 pm for Cat Island (North and South), Arthur's Town, Bennen's Harbour, Bluff, and Bight, and returns on Friday. Sailing time is 14 hours. The fare is $48.

Sea Hauler leaves each Tuesday at 3 pm for Cat Island (South), Smith's Bay, Bight, Old Bight, and returns on Monday. Sailing time is 12 hours. The fare is $48.

By Private Boat

You can arrive in your own boat and stay at **Hawk's Nest Resort and Marina** (see below).

Sightseeing

The Hermitage

Near New Bight, the Hermitage is set atop Mount Alvernia. Mount is, perhaps, a bit of stretch but, at an elevation of 206 feet, it does represent the highest point on the island. The Hermitage is a tiny abbey complete with round tower and cloister, all built of gray native stone by the hand of its founder, Father Jerome Hawes. The little abbey commands an outstanding view of the island, New Bight, and Fernandez Bay away to the north. The seascape as seen from the abbey is spectacular. The pale green shallows glow and sparkle in the sunlight, and the sandy shore is bright white.

From New Bight, take the dirt road, up the rise, through the old stone arch and on along the footpath up the hill. It's a strenuous hike of about 20 minutes, but well worth the effort for the gorgeous views.

The Deveaux Plantation

The Deveaux Plantation, in Port Howe, was once the scene of splendor and luxury. Today, it lies in ruins. This was the home of Colonel Andrew Deveaux, who settled with his family and slaves on Cat Island in the 18th century. It's worth seeing to experience the local history and the spectacular setting.

On The Water

Boat Rentals

Fernandez Bay Village offers guided boat rentals with captain only. Rates are approximately $450 for a half-day and $675 for a full day. 800-940-1905, 242-342-3043, www.fernandezbayvillage.com.

Greenwood Beach Resort. Charters only, from $250 per day for 16-foot reef fishing boats. 242-342-3053.

Diving & Snorkeling

There are two full-service dive centers on the island. Both

offer excursions to the reef, one has night dives and wall diving, and both have equipment rental.

Cat Island Dive Centre

At the Hotel Greenwood Inn. Facilities include equipment rental, PADI instruction, and local ocean dives. Tele/fax 242-342-3053.

Hawk's Nest Dive Centre

This facility is at the Hawk's Nest Resort. It is a full-service outfit offering equipment rental, instruction, day and night dive excursions and reef and wall diving. Rates are $45 for a one-tank dive. Snorkel equipment can be rented for $10 per day. 242-357-7257.

Best Snorkeling Sites

Both the Fernandez Bay Village and the Greenwood Beach Resort participate in the Jean Michel Cousteau "Snorkeling Adventures" program. The best sites are as follows:

Bains Town

An area of the reef with large quantities of sea fans, elk- and staghorns, and brain corals.

Dry Head

A large area of coral reef that includes sea fans, brain and lettuce coral formations, along with schools of grunts and yellow-tails.

Greenwood Beach

Adjacent to the resort, this is another section of the reef where you can explore a variety of coral formations.

Guana Keys

The Keys are a chain of reefs, close to a small island you can use for a base, where the water is unusually clear, and fairly shallow to the point where it approaches the drop-off. The marine life here is prolific.

Hazel's Hideaway

An area with lots of soft corals and multitudes of reef fish.

Lump of Limestone

Just a few minutes swim from the beach, this limestone formation is home to a number of large, friendly groupers.

Naked Point

An underwater cave and the home of a variety of marine life, including stone crabs. Lots of fun and an unusual snorkeling experience.

Shipwreck

An old wreck, half-in and half-out of the water. It's an unusual snorkel with lots of marine life, including lobsters, crabs and a variety of multi-colored reef fish.

Dining

$$ The Bridge Inn's restaurant is open for breakfast, lunch and dinner. The dining room is clean and attractive and there's a rustic bar where you can enjoy an evening cocktail. The menu is extensive, offering a variety of fresh seafood – steamed grouper, conch, lobster, crab – with garden-fresh vegetables, and peas and rice. 242-342-3013.

$$$ Fernandez Bay Village's restaurant is open daily for breakfast, lunch and dinner. The menu features Bahamian and international dishes served on the beach terrace. Appetizers and cocktails are available in the evenings before dinner from 7 pm. A reservation is required for dinner. 242-342-3043.

$$$ The Greenwood Beach Resort's oceanfront restaurant offers outdoor and indoor dining with a menu that features Bahamian and European cuisine along with extensive buffet dinners. 242-342-3053.

Accommodations

The Bridge Inn. Located in The Bight, this is a small, comfortable hotel hideaway. The rooms are spacious. Some have air-conditioning. The food is good, and free round-trip transportation from New Bight airport is provided. Rates start at $140 per night for a room without air-conditioning, and $190 for one with air-conditioning. To get there, you simply fly into New Bight. The hotel will take care of the rest. For reservations and information, 800-688-4752 or 242-342-3013; fax 242-342-3041; www.catislandbridgeinn.com.

The Greenwood Beach Resort & Dive Center. This 20-room resort in Port Howe is situated on an eight-mile stretch of pink sand beach. It's an ideal spot for diving and snorkeling – the coral heads are just off-shore from the hotel. All rooms have private baths, king-size beds, and patios. There's a large oceanfront restaurant serving Bahamian and international dishes, and there are beachfront gazebos where you can relax in the shade and enjoy a quiet afternoon with a good book. The full-service, on-site dive shop on the property can arrange trips for wall and reef diving. Fly into New Bight airport and call the hotel for transportation. Rates are reasonable, starting at $69 off-season; $79 during the peak winter months. 877-228-7475, 242-342-3053, www.GreenwoodBeachResort.com.

Hawk's Nest Resort & Marina. This resort has its own airstrip which, along with its marina and on-site dive shop, makes it one of the most accessible resorts on Cat Island. Accommodations are limited to just 10 rooms. The rooms are, however, comfortably appointed and, unlike those at most hotels on the island, are air-conditioned. Most rooms have king-size beds. Those that don't have two queen-size beds. Refrigerators are available on request, but there are no TVs in the rooms; satellite TV is available in the lounge. There's a broad sandy beach, just right for relaxing, swimming and shelling, fishing and bird-watching. Bikes and mopeds are available on-site. To get there, fly into Hawk's Nest via charter or private plane, or take Bahamasair into Arthur's Town Airport and call the hotel to make arrangements for transport to the hotel. The rates are on the expensive side, starting at $177 per night. 800-688-4752 or 242-342-7050, www.hawks-nest.com.

Fernandez Bay Village is a rather remote and rustic resort of nine villas situated on one of the finest stretches of private beach on the island. This small family-run resort specializes in, as they say, "the kind of hospitality you expect when visiting good friends." They do a little better than that, however. The rooms, though rustic, border on the luxurious. The floors are laid with terra-cotta tiles, the walls are made from fieldstone, and the furniture is dark, heavy and opulent. All rooms are cooled by overhead fans, and most have an outdoor garden bath as well as one indoors. All sorts of water-sports are available: sailing, water-skiing, snorkeling and fishing. Complimentary bikes are available, too. The food is outstanding, especially the homemade bread, and you can dine outside under the stars. Rates start at $255. 800-940-1095 or 242-342-3043; fax 242-342-3051, e-mail catisland@fernandezbayvillage.com.

The Inaguas

The most southerly and most remote of the Out Islands, the Inaguas, with fewer than 1,200 inhabitants living on **Great Inagua**, are also the most sparsely populated. Almost all of the locals work for the Morton Salt Company. Very few tourists make it this far out. Those that do are in for a rare experience. The third largest of the islands, this is the Bahamas' answer to the Galapagos Islands. Here is a land where wildlife still reigns over most of the rocky shorelines and uninhabited **Little Inagua** just to the north. This not the place for the casual vacationer in search of lazy days in the sunshine, nightlife and full-service hotels. If you're an outdoor adventurer, however, this is the place for you. You can walk for miles along the deserted, rocky coast (sandy beaches are few and far between) and spend long days bird-watching, fishing or bicycling. It's not the easiest place to reach, either. You'll need the services of a creative travel agent.

Getting There

You've a couple of options, neither of them very convenient.

By Air

Bahamasair, 800-222-4262, operates two flights weekly from Nassau during the winter months – Wednesday and Saturday – and three during the summer – Monday, Wednesday and Saturday. The airfare is $180 round-trip. **Cat Island Air**, 242-377-3318, charges $160 round-trip from Nassau.

By Mail Boat

The *Abilin* calls once every two weeks. The sailing time is a whopping 17 hours, but it's a nice ride, most of it overnight. The fair is $70 one-way. 242-393-1064 for schedules and information.

Taxis meets most incoming scheduled aircraft, and you can call the hotel of your choice to arrange a ride.

Sightseeing

Inagua National Park

Covering more than 280 square miles, this is a vast park

incorporating inland waters, rocky shoreline, saltwater flats, and large areas of shrub land and jungle. It's here you'll find Inagua's famous **flamingos**: huge flocks of bright pink, long-legged birds that rise and fly, almost as one, from their nesting grounds around **Lake Windsor**. Although the drive from Matthew Town to the National Park campground is only about 20 miles, it takes an hour.

The best time to visit is from early March through the middle of June. This is when the birds are nesting, and you'll be able to get up-close for bird-watching and photography.

Aside from the colonies of flamingos, more than 200 species of birds make their homes in the park. Lake Windsor itself is an unusual sight: the waters are pale pink, due to the salt content. Here and there, wild donkeys can be seen in the distance, but never up close.

Henri Christophe's Treasure

The donkeys were, according to legend, brought to the Inaguas by Henri Cristophe in the early 1800s. Cristophe was a Haitian revolutionary, and something of a rogue. Apparently, his revolution was initially successful, and he had himself crowned king. Then, perhaps as an afterthought, he loaded the Haiti's treasures, mostly gold, on pack animals – donkeys – and headed for the docks. Once there, he loaded everything onto boats, the donkeys included, and sailed away with his loot, finally landing somewhere in the Inaguas. But the story doesn't end there. Cristophe's vast cache of loot lies buried in a cave somewhere on one of the islands, and it's still there, waiting for some lucky adventurer to find it; you, perhaps.

If you want to rough it a little, camp out in one of the park's two rustic cabins. The accommodations are basic, to say the least, but bedding is provided, and there are a couple of fresh-water showers that make life in the outback tolerable. You will need to provide your own food, which you can cook in the park at a specially designated area.

Morton Bahamas Salt Company

Vast mountains of snow-white sodium chloride mark the

boundaries of this, the mainstay of Inagua's economy. Beyond the salt lie hundreds of acres of what appear to be ice-bound lakes, something of an enigma in this land where the temperature rarely drops below 70°. But the pink-tinged surface is in fact a thin crust of brine that sparkles and shines in the sunlight, more so at the lakeshore where the crystals build like the edges of some giant pie crust. The salt produced here is sold around the world to highway departments, fisheries, chemical plants, and the like. If you'd like to visit the plant, take Gregory Street and go north of Matthew Town. But make arrangements beforehand. Call the Bahamas Ministry of Tourism in Nassau for information: 242-322-7501, fax 242-328-0945.

Matthew Town Lighthouse

Located just beyond the Matthew Town limits, this picturesque lighthouse was erected in 1870 to light the way for ships using the Windward Passage between Inagua and the larger island to the south, Hispaniola, where Haiti and the Dominican Republic are located. It's a lonely spot, fit only for bird-watching, but there's something indefinable about lighthouses that draws people to them. This one is no exception. The climb to the top is a long one and, perhaps, not really worth the effort. The view is of a lonely, rocky shoreline with only Matthew Town to break the monotony of the flat, almost featureless, land- and seascape. Interesting, though, is the machinery that drives the light, and its great Fresnel lens.

On The Water

The Inaguas are not on the list of top dive spots in the Bahamas. Far from it. There is little information available as to dive sites on and around the islands. The waters are crystal clear, but the rocky shoreline is less than inviting.

Dining

$ Tops. This small bar and restaurant on Astwood Street in Matthew Town, is open for lunch and dinner. It's the most popular eatery on the island. The food is traditional Bahamian fare with island vegetables, peas and rice, fried plantain, chicken and fresh seafood – conch, lobster, grouper, etc. The atmosphere is definitely "island home." The tables are set family style, and everyone is friendly and pleased to meet you.

$$ The Main House. This is the hotel restaurant. Off Gregory Street in Matthew Town, it serves three meals a day. The dining room is small and bright, the tables are dressed with linen cloths, and the food is typically Bahamian. 242-339-1267.

$ The Cozy Corner serves good, wholesome Bahamian cuisine in a neat little restaurant. The menu includes seafood, plantain and curry.

Accommodations

Great Inagua is better provided with accommodations than you might expect. There are three small hotels/guest houses on the island, all of them fairly inexpensive.

The Main House. This pleasant inn is owned by the Morton Bahama Salt Company. It's a homely place with five air-conditioned rooms, two with private baths, the rest sharing a couple of well-kept modern bathrooms. There's a nice, bright dining room, a comfortable sitting room with satellite TV, a balcony with a view, and a lounge where guests can gather and relax over a drink before dinner. The rate is $50 per night. 242-339-1267.

Ford's Inn. This small two-story inn is run by an ex-Detroit policeman and his good lady. Originally from Inagua, Leon Ford spent some 20 years in the Motor City before returning to his homeland. This is one of the best places to stay in the islands. The two-story, block-built inn boasts five brightly decorated rooms. They share modern bathrooms and a comfortable sitting room with satellite TV and a spacious balcony. The only meal they offer is breakfast, but it's served in an atmosphere that rivals the traditional bed & breakfast inns of Europe. The inn is closed March through July. The rate is $50 per night. 242-339-1277.

Long Island

Long Island is, well, long. How long is debatable; nobody seems to know, exactly. Some references say it's 60 miles long; others say 70 miles; still others say it's 100 miles long. But if you get hold of a good map, you'll see by the scale that it is a little more than 60 miles from one end to the other, and not more than a mile wide; in places, no more than a half-mile wide. It is, however, one of the most scenic of the Out Islands, with starkly contrasting coastlines east and west. On the Atlantic side the coast is a lonely, rocky stretch more reminiscent of New England than the Bahamas. On the Caribbean side, long stretches of sugar-white beach stretch for miles in either direction. They are mostly deserted and rank among the best beaches in the world. Best of all, the beach at **Cape Santa Maria** is truly a paradise, a four-mile crescent of pristine white powder that almost encircles a magnificent stretch of turquoise water, and the chances are you'll have it all to yourself. It must be seen to be believed.

The terrain inland is hilly and, here and there, jagged cliffs of coral drop steeply to meet the surging ocean. This is the garden island of the Bahamas. Fertile fields produce a variety of vegetables and local fruits. Beyond the fields, among the hills, the island is riddled with limestone caves and blue holes.

Christopher Columbus made Long Island his third stop on passing through the Bahamas in August, 1492. His journals describe the rocky cliffs, isolated beaches and the scent of the flowers, "delicious and sweet." He called the island Fernandina in honor of King Ferdinand of Spain.

This is a must for divers and snorkelers, not to mention those that simply like to spend long lazy days on the beach. There are some 30 sunken shipwrecks within easy distance of the **Stella Maris Resort Club**, the local gathering place for those to whom all-things-wet are important. And, as you might imagine, the sea is the source of wonderful culinary delights, presented as only the Bahamians can.

History

During the centuries that followed **Columbus**, Long Island was virtually forgotten, visited only by pirates and freebooters.

But the American Revolution changed all that. The years following 1776 saw large numbers of **English loyalists** leaving Virginia and the colonies for new homes all over the Caribbean, and especially the Bahamas.

The Adderleys

The Adderlys fled the American Revolution and settled on Long Island, bringing with them large numbers of slaves. They established a cotton plantation and, for a while at least, prospered. So the story is told, old man Adderley discovered his son was in love with one of his slaves. It's difficult to imagine why the old man was so shocked by his discovery. Liaisons between slaves and their masters were an accepted fact in those days, so one has to wonder exactly what it was that drove the senior Adderley to take his own life. But the event apparently had little effect on his son for the relationship between the two lovers continued. Today, their descendants are still a major part of the population of Long Island. And the ruins of the once-proud Adderley mansion are all that's left of the family's glory days of the early 1800s.

Getting There

Getting to Long Island is quite easy but, once again, you will need to enlist the services of a creative travel agent. The main port of entry is **Stella Maris** at the northern end of the island.

By Air

Long Island is served from Fort Lauderdale, Miami and Nassau. You'll need to take a scheduled flight to one of those cities, and then make the local connection. Round-trip airfare from Nassau on **Bahamasair** is $128, and $170 from Miami; flights are scheduled daily. 800-222-4262.

American Eagle also operates scheduled flights from Miami into Stella Maris. Rates are comparable to Bahamasair. 800-433-7300.

Island Express serves Long Island out of Fort Lauderdale. Rates are approximately $200 round-trip. 954-359-0380.

By Mail Boat

The ***Sherice M*** leaves Potter's Cay Dock in Nassau on Mondays at 5 pm for North Long Island – Salt Pond, Deadman's Cay, and Seymour's – and returns the following Thursday. Sailing time is 15 hours, overnight, and the one-way fare is $45.

The ***Abilin*** sails from Nassau for Clarence Town on Tuesday at noon and returns the following Saturday. Sailing time is 17 hours and the one-way fare is $65.

See *Mail Boat Schedules*, page 335, for more information.

Vacation Packages

Important Note: All of the packages listed below were active and correctly priced at the time they were researched. You should be aware, however, that all are subject to change without notice. Please check with the provider at the Phone numbers listed for up-to-date packages, rates, and information.

American Airlines FlyAAway Vacations can fit you up with a vacation package for two nights or longer, and from almost any major US and Canadian gateway city. Rates, depending on the city of departure, start at $594 per person, and include an ocean-view room at the Stella Maris Resort Club, round-trip airfare from Miami, and round-trip airport/hotel transfers on Long island.

For more information, call American Eagle, 800-433-7300, and ask for American FlyAAway Vacations. Visit their website at www.aavacations.com.

>The resorts all offer transportation at no charge from and to the airport; just call ahead to make arrangements. Failing that, taxies do meet the mail boats and all incoming scheduled flights from Nassau and the mainland.

Sightseeing

The Adderley Plantation

Little is left of this once-stately mansion. The roof-less shells of three buildings, a tall stone chimney, remnants of old stone walls, and large blocks of hand-cut stone scattered here and there belie the opulence of what once was a prosperous and bustling plantation. Even so, it's not difficult to let the imagination wander and conjure images from the past as you wander among the old buildings with their decaying cedar frames and the vegetation, growing wild, threatening to overwhelm what little is left. North of the old house, just a short walk through the undergrowth, is the slave burial ground. You can still see the mounds, though they have all but been reclaimed through neglect and erosion.

Columbus Point

To the north of Stella Maris, near the bridge to Newton's Cay, is a narrow dirt road that leads to Columbus Point. It's an enjoyable walk. It was at the Point that, according to legend, Columbus first set foot on the island in October, 1492. On top of the cliff, with a spectacular view of the ocean, a plaque commemorates the landing.

Conception Island

Northeast of Stella Maris, off the tip of the island, lies tiny Conception Island. It's protected by the Bahamas National Trust as a wildlife sanctuary and is home to many species of wild birds and the endangered green turtle. The island can be reached only by boat, and the surrounding waters offer great diving. Check with the dive center at the Stella Maris Resort Club.

Deadman's Cay Caves

Like to go caving? This is the place for you. Deadman's Cay is close to the center of the island, south of Stella Maris. To get there, rent a car at the Stella Maris Resort Club. Two caves are worthy of note. The first is the Deadman's Cay complex of caves itself. This is an extensive system that's never fully been explored. The other is **Dunmore's Cave**. Used extensively by Arawak Indians in prehistoric times, it later became a refuge and hideaway for pirates. Legend has it that they used to store loot here taken from ships at sea.

Churches

There are several churches on Long Island; all are unique. Three, however, are of special interest. In **Clarence Town**, Father Jerome Hawes, the Catholic missionary who built the Hermitage on Cat Island, was also responsible for two of the town churches, one Anglican, the other Catholic. Both show his inimitable style. If you have the time they are well worth a quick look. The Spanish Church in **The Bight**, once part of an early Spanish settlement, is the oldest Spanish Church in the Bahamas.

On The Water

Diving & Snorkeling

Locals will tell you that the diving at Long Island is some of the best in the Bahamas. From reef to wreck diving, and shark to wall diving, the island has it all. If you like to stay top-side or in the shallows, the snorkeling opportunities, too, are good. The shallow waters of the reefs on both sides of the island abound with wildlife. Coral formations differ from the Atlantic side, where the waters are more aggressive, to the Caribbean side, where life beneath the ocean is much quieter. The Cousteau Program is available at the Stella Maris Diving dive shop, 800-426-0466 or 242-338-2053, along with an assortment of dive options.

Best Dive Sites

Grouper Valley

The best time to visit the Valley is in November, when the groupers school in vast numbers. This is a rare opportunity to observe one of nature's wonders. The groupers congregate in vast numbers and seem to hang in the watery sky like an invasion fleet from another world.

Grouper Village

Here in the Village, you'll find six or seven tame groupers that will greet you like old friends. True, they're after a hand-out, but it's fun just the same. Be sure to take along some food for them.

Also in the Village, you may be lucky enough to see Brutus, a huge jewfish that weighs in at more than 350 pounds.

Shark Reef

Shark Reef is one place where you can get up-close with a shark. The reef is a 30-minute boat ride from the Stella Maris Resort Club. The dive masters at the shop will be pleased to arrange a visit.

Ship's Graveyard, Cape Santa Maria

The remains of many a ship lie beneath the waters off Cape Santa Maria. The best site is the wreck of the ***MV Comerback***. The ship was sunk in the summer of 1986 to provide a safe and interesting dive for guests of the Stella Maris Resort Club. The 103-foot British freighter lies upright and intact at a depth of 100 feet; the deck is at 65 feet. The hatches, portholes and doors have all been removed to provide safe and easy access to the ship's interior. Visibility, even at maximum depth, is prime; and currents are minimal. There's even a 1975 Ford van in one of the holds. All this makes it an ideal site for the novice diver – under supervision, of course – and for underwater photography.

H.M.S. Southampton

This wreck has only tentatively been identified as the *Southampton*, an English 32-gun frigate under the command of Sir James Yeo that foundered on the reef in November, 1812. All the evidence indicates that the wreck dates from around that time, but a definitive identification has not been made. The wreck lies scattered over a wide area, with only her boilers, engine, propeller shaft, four anchors, three propellers and a pile of rusty anchor chain showing. She offers some rare photographic opportunities.

> To visit the Southampton, you need to make arrangements with Stella Maris Diving, 800-426-0466 or 242-338-2053.

Conception Island Wall

This is a dive for veterans. Not far from the beach, the reef drops away from a depth of about 40 feet into the ocean darkness. If wall diving is for you, this is as good a place as any, and better than some, so the experts say.

Southampton Reef

This is a grand stretch of reef. From shallow waters less than 10 feet deep, descending gently to more than 90 feet at its edge, the reef is a veritable garden of elk and staghorn coral, brain coral and seafans, populated by colorful reef fish.

Rum Cay Wall

Yet another amazing drop-off where the crystal-clear waters

at the reef's edge, at a depth of 40 feet, accentuate the feeling of extreme depth as they plunge downward.

Best Snorkeling Sites

Snorkeling can be done just about any place you can walk into the water, from the beaches at Cape Santa Maria, along the western shore, almost as far south as you can go. Some of the best spots, however, are as follows:

Columbus Harbour

This is where Christopher Columbus first landed on Long Island.

Poseiden Point

The Point is one of the few places in the Bahamas where you can see big tarpon.

Coral Gardens

A reef site with valleys, caves, corals and turtles.

Eagle Ray Reef

A reef where you swim among an amazing variety of coral formations and make friends with a giant grouper.

Flamingo Tongue Reef

This site is home to thousands of colorful reef fish, anemones, crabs and even a large green moray eel.

Rainbow Reef

This reef is famous for its sponges and coral formations.

Rock Pools

A collection of tidal pools where you can observe smaller fish and crabs that inhabit the shallows of the reef.

Watermelon Beach

An easy site just right for the novice snorkeler.

Dive Shop

The single dive shop on the island is at the **Stella Maris Resort Club**. The operator offers full- and half-day scuba diving excursions and participates in the Jean Michel Cousteau snorkeling program. The cost for a basic four-day excursion with up to three dives included, depending on how many people are participating, starts at $75 per person. If you add a specialty dive, such as a shark dive or wall dive, the extra cost is $20 per dive, per person. The cost for a basic half-day dive excursion also depends on the number of people participating; rates vary and are available on request. Snorkeling excursions start at $35 per person and that includes the use of mask, snorkel and fins. 800-426-0466 or 242-338-2052, fax 954-359-8238, www.stellamaris.resort.com.

Sport Fishing

Long Island is the angler's ultimate destination. The bonefishing here is as good as it gets. Great schools of the silver fish flit this way and that over the flats where the water rarely is deeper than a couple of feet. You can spend hours casting into the schools and, when you hook one of the little demons, you're in for the fight of your life.

Rarely does the bonefish weigh in at more than 10 or 12 pounds but, pound-for-pound, it's the strongest fighter in the ocean.

A seven-hour reef fishing excursion will put you right on the spot where the best sport bottom fish are found. From the boat, you'll see all that's happening in the water. You can expect to catch barracuda, grouper, yellowtail snapper, horseye jacks, amberjack, king mackerel and tuna.

For the deep-sea angler, charters are available at the Cape Santa Maria Beach Resort, the Stella Maris Resort Club, and the Stella Maris Marina. You can take a seven-hour excursion out into deep waters where the "big ones" lurk: trophy-sized white and blue marlin, kingfish, shark, tuna, grouper, dorado and sailfish.

Boat Rentals

Cape Santa Maria Beach Resort. Guided rentals only, from $250 for seven hours. 242-338-5273, www.capesantamaria.com.

Stella Maris Resort Club. Charter boats with guide only, starting at $200 per day. 800-426-0466, www.stellamarisresort.com.

Dining

$$$ Cape Santa Maria. This restaurant is part of the resort complex and features a full-service bar where you can enjoy a cocktail before dinner. Open for breakfast, lunch and dinner daily, it's best to make a reservation, especially in the high season. The menu includes continental, American and local dishes, as well as a wide range of fresh seafood dishes such as lobster, grouper and conch. A fine selection of imported wines is also available. 242-338-5273.

$$ Conchy's. Located in the Stella Maris shopping district, Conchy's is open for lunch and dinner and offers a choice of indoor or patio dining. The menu is mostly Bahamian and the food is good. Reservations for dinner are preferred. VHF channel 16 only.

$$ Salty's is in the Stella Maris Marina main building. If you're an angler, the staff will be happy to prepare and serve your catch. The menu includes Bahamian and American dishes, and the restaurant is open for breakfast, lunch and dinner weekdays only. Reservations are required for dinner. VHF channel 16 only.

$$ Stella Maris Resort Club Dining Room and Garden serves lots of fresh seafood. American, Bahamian and European dishes are offered for dinner, along with full breakfasts and lunches. Specialties include patio cookouts, moonlight dinner cruises, a cave party, and the weekly Bahamian night. You must make a reservation for dinner. 242-338-2051.

$$ The Tennis Club. Set on the hillside in Stella Maris, the Club is open only for dinner. The menu is European, and you have a choice of indoor or outdoor dining; both options offer spectacular ocean views. 242-336-2106.

Accommodations

Cape Santa Maria Beach Resort. This resort has a fabulous, crescent-shaped stretch of beach. The resort itself is small and exclusive. Accommodations consist of one- and two-bedroom beachfront cottages. Each is air-conditioned and tastefully decorated, with cool marble floors and comfortable furniture. There are no teles, radios or televisions in the rooms; the emphasis is on uncomplicated luxury and stress-free living. Amenities for guests include use of a small catamaran, Sunfish, sailboards, snorkeling gear, and bicycles. Rates start at $235 per night in the off-season, and go up from there. 800-663-7090, fax 242-338-6013, www.capesantamaria.com, e-mail obmg@pinc.com.

Stella Maris Resort Club. Set in the middle of a garden estate, just a few steps from the beach, this resort has a lot to offer. The full-service dive shop is the only one on the island, and you can go wreck diving at more than 30 locations. For the angler, there's deep-sea, bone, and reef fishing. The club even has its own guest air service. Accommodations range from one-bedroom apartments to two- and four-bedroom villas and bungalows, all with ocean views, refrigerators and ceiling fans; every room is air-conditioned. Rates start at $148 for a single room ($175 for a double) in the off-season (May through August) and go up from there. American Airlines Vacations arranges all sorts of air-inclusive packages with the resort. 800-426-0466, fax 242-338-2051, www.stellamarisresort.com, e-mail smrc@stellamarisresort.com.

San Salvador

Northeast of Long Island, on the outer reaches of the Great Bahama Bank, lie two small islands, San Salvador and Rum Cay. They are just a couple of dots on the map. Fewer than 600 people live on San Salvador, and even fewer on Rum Cay. San Salvador is six miles wide and 12 miles long. It's a strange place where there's almost as much water inland as there is *terra firma* – brackish lakes joined one to the other by narrow, man-made waterways.

The island's one and only sizable community is **Cockburn Town** (pronounced "Coburn"). Named for Sir Francis Cockburn, Royal Governor of the Bahamas from 1837 until 1844, it's the capital of San Salvador and Rum Cay, its smaller, sister island just to the west.

History

They say it was here, in 1492, that Christopher Columbus first set foot ashore in the New World. Did he? There's a certain amount of evidence to support the theory, but some at National Geographic might beg to differ. Their choice is an island 65 miles farther south, Samana Cay.

At the time when Columbus made his historic landing, many of the islands, San Salvador included, were inhabited by **Lucayan Indians**. The explorers, and those that followed, quickly enslaved the Indians, shipped them out, and worked them to death. As an added bonus, they introduced the luckless Lucayans to a whole range of new diseases against which they had no defense. And so, by the mid-1500s, the Lucayans had been exterminated.

Today, once a year, on the weekend closest to October 12, visitors converge on the island for the **Columbus Day** celebrations. There's always plenty to eat, dancing in the streets, and lots of fun in the sun. If you can make it, this is a good time to visit.

John Watling

An extraordinarily bloodthirsty, but pious, English pirate, John Watling made San Salvador his base of operations during the latter part of the 17th century. In fact, for many years, San Salvador was known as Watling's Island. It was renamed only in 1926, thanks mainly to the efforts of Father Chrysostome Schreiner, a Catholic missionary who lived here until his death in 1928. The impressive ruins of Watling's Castle, at Southwest Point, are all that remain of what is reputed to be the pirate's home. Archaeologists, however, say the ruins are not that old, dating only from the early 19th century. Stories of buried treasure on the island abound, as they do throughout the Out Islands. As to John Watling, he came to sticky end, like most of his contemporaries – at the end of a rope.

Getting There

By Air

Island Express, 954-359-0380, offers service from Fort Lauderdale and **Bahamasair**, 800-222-4262, provides scheduled air service daily between Nassau and Cockburn Town – the round-trip fare is $12. **Riding Rock Inn** operates a charter air service from Fort Lauderdale on Saturdays only. Flights depart from Fort Lauderdale at 10 am and leave the island at 12:30 pm. Round-trip fare, $289. 800-272-1492.

By Mail Boat

Your other option is to take the mail boat. The ***Lady Frances*** leaves Potter's Cay Dock in Nassau weekly, on Tuesday, at 6 pm and makes the 12-hour trip overnight. She returns on Friday, which means you could pre-book two nights' accommodations at the Riding Rock Inn, spend a couple of days enjoying the sights and sounds of the island, then return to Nassau and finish your vacation. The fare is $80 round-trip. Call the dock master at 242-393-1064.

By Private Boat

Riding Rock Inn & Marina, 800-359-8254, near Cockburn Town, is the main port of entry and maintains seven slips with a maximum depth of 12 feet; there are no width restrictions. There's also 415 feet of docking wall where visiting boats can stock up on fuel, water, ice and off-site groceries. Sailors have access to the Inn's restaurant, showers, accommodations and laundry. The VHF frequency is 16.

Package Vacations

Only two operators offer vacation packages on San Salvador: one is Club Med (800-258-2633, www.clubmed.com), the other is locally operated by the Riding Rock Inn (800-272-1492, www.ridingrock.
com). A good travel agent should also be able to put something together for you.

*If you arrive on a Club Med or Riding Rock Inn package, someone will meet, greet and transfer you to the resort. If you arrive by scheduled air or private charter from Nassau or the mainland, you'll need a **taxi**. These are usually available at the airport. Most drivers depend heavily upon arriving and departing flights for a major portion of their income. The same goes if you arrive by mail boat. If drivers are not ready and waiting, they're only a call away; ask at the harbour master's office. If all else fails, call your resort and they'll arrange transport for you; Riding Rock Inn is quite close to the airport, so you should experience no difficulties.*

Sightseeing

Small and isolated as it is, there's plenty to see and do on San Salvador. While many of the sites are within easy walking distance of both Club Med and Riding Rock Inn, you'll need a car to see all of the island. Your hotel staff will be pleased to arrange one for you. An even better option would be to rent a bike or moped for a couple of days, then head in one direction one day, the other the next day. Make arrangements with your hotel to supply picnic lunches; there are plenty of places along the way to stop and enjoy them. Also, be sure to take along plenty to drink and something to snack on.

The main road around the island is the Queen's Highway – 35 miles of white road. Although the word "highway" is sometimes a bit of a stretch, it is well-maintained and provides a fairly smooth ride. Side roads branching off the highway are neither marked nor always easy to negotiate, especially on a bike or moped. Sometimes they lead to a deserted sandy beach where you can enjoy a swim, snorkel or picnic. Sometimes it's a rocky escarpment with a seascape, ideal for bird watching and nature photography. Often, it's an inland lake, quiet and mysterious, surrounded by palms and seagrass. Sometimes they just end.

On a small island such as this, it's difficult to imagine getting lost. But, with none of the roads marked, not even the highway, you can become disoriented. After a while, all roads seem to lead northward. If you do get lost, ask a local for help.

Cockburn Town

Although it's the capital of San Salvador, Cockburn Town (pronounced "Coburn") is one of the smallest communities in the Out Islands, and definitely old-world Bahamian. Two miles south of Riding Rock Inn and 2½ miles south of Club Med, it's little more than a collection of clapboard and cinder block houses. Most of the sights are on or close to Fifth Avenue, just across the street from the dock. It's here you'll land if you decide to visit the island via mail boat. Aside from the **Public Library**, which stands on the corner of Fifth Avenue and Queen's Highway, there's a pub, the **Ocean View Club**, where you can drop in for a cold beer, even breakfast or lunch. The **San Salvador Gift Shop** is the place to stock up on film, candy, local crafts, books and all sorts of other odds and ends, including newspapers (sometimes a day old). The **Hanover Square Club** is a bar run by Marcus Jones, a friendly and well-traveled host. His wife, Faith, runs the **Three Ships Restaurant** just across the street. The food is good, reasonably priced, and decidedly Bahamian. In fact, Faith is a talented cook: her cracked conch, peas and rice, and fried grouper have made her something of a celebrity among the island-hopping, sailing fraternity. If you want to eat dinner, you'll need to make a reservation; she only cooks to order. 331-2787.

There are a couple of churches in Cockburn Town, both of which are worth a visit: **St. Augustine's Anglican Church** and the **Holy Savior Catholic Church**, famous for its image of Christopher Columbus above its entrance. The **San Salvador Museum**, next door to Holy Savior, once was the island jail. Today, it houses a collection of artifacts that interpret the history of San Salvador from pre-historic through Colonial times to the present day. If you want to visit, call in advance. 331-2676.

Sandy Point

Sandy Point is at the extreme southern end of the island, about six miles south of Cockburn Town, eight miles from Riding Rock Inn, and 8½ miles from Club Med. Here you'll find Watling's Castle, Lookout Tower, and Dripping Rock Cave.

Take the Queen's Highway south from Cockburn Town and go six miles to Mile Marker 9. This will put you very close to Watling's Castle.

Watling's Castle

There's little left of the one-time thriving plantation that bears the name of one the most bloodthirsty buccaneers in the history of piracy. Watling, for whom the island was once named, is said to have lived here during the 17th century. It's doubtful, however, that any of the structures now in ruins were there during his tenancy. They date from the early 19th century and were probably built by Loyalist refugees fleeing the aftermath of the American Revolutionary War.

Wrecking

Aside from his terrorist activities on the high seas, Watling engaged in another nefarious activity: wrecking. He and his men would lure passing ships onto the rocks by flashing lights, board the doomed vessels, slaughter the survivors and then pick the wreck clean. Not a nice character.

Today, nothing is left that can be attributed to Watling. The plantation, however, thrived well into the 20th century. In the early days it was worked by slaves. The remains of the slave quarters can still be seen in the undergrowth that is slowly reclaiming the land upon which they stood.

Lookout Tower

Also once a part of the Watling's Castle Estate, the old tower is now reached via the road to the west of the estate. It was used to watch for ships bringing supplies from Nassau. One can't help but wonder, though, if this might have been the spot from which Watling conducted his wrecking enterprise.

Dripping Rock Cave

At Sandy Point itself, Dripping Rock is a limestone cavern surrounded by fruit trees. There's a fresh-water well inside the cave, and a secluded beach just to the north. It's an ideal spot for snorkeling or a romantic picnic.

Graham's Harbour

On October 12 each year, Graham's Harbour plays host to the **Discovery Day** celebrations. Everyone gets together for a grand time: boat races, dancing, kite flying and picnicking.

The huge natural harbor located on the northernmost tip of the island is said to have inspired Columbus to comment that it was big enough to take "all the ships in Christendom."

There's a nice beach; the waters are calm most of the time, making it the ideal spot for an afternoon picnic.

Father Schreiner's Grave

From Graham's Harbour, take the rocky path to Father Schreiner's Grave. This was the man who was responsible for changing the island's name from Watling's Island to San Salvador. He is also responsible for the image of Columbus on Holy Savior Catholic Church in Cockburn Town. Father Schreiner died in the church in 1928. Of special interest is the circular stone block next to the grave; it's thought to have been either a slave whipping post or an auction block.

North Victoria Hill

North Victoria Hill is a small community on the coast a couple of miles north of the Riding Rock Inn and Bonefish Bay. Its main claim to fame is that it's the home of Ruth Durlacher Wolper, widow of movie producer David Wolper. Her beachfront estate is where you'll find the New World Museum.

New World Museum

This relatively small museum houses the Wolpers' private collection of New World relics that help to interpret the history of the islands and their Spanish occupation, including pre-

Columbian and Native American artifacts, and pieces of Spanish origin that date to the late 15th century. The museum is within walking distance of Club Med and the Riding Rock Inn. It's open during daylight hours every day and is free. The walk and the museum, along with a visit to the beach, make a very pleasant afternoon.

The Columbus Monuments

There are several permanent monuments that commemorate Columbus' first landings in 1492. He is said to have come ashore at all four. Whether or not he did so is debatable. Today, the monuments present a unique opportunity for exploration. It's doubtful that you could visit them all in a single day, but a couple of afternoons should see the job through. The first and best known is the much-photographed **white cross** that stands on the beach near Mile Marker 6 on the Queen's Highway south of Cockburn Town.

A **second monument**, erected in 1951 by the Tappan gas company, is near Mile Marker 5. The **third monument** lies close by somewhere on the ocean floor; you'll need your snorkeling gear to find it. The **fourth monument** was erected on the eastern shore of the island, close to Mile Marker 25, by the *Chicago Herald* in 1891. The Chicago monument is not easy to find. If you like to explore, however, the search can be quite entertaining. Take along your swimming and snorkeling gear, lots to drink, sunblock, and allow a full afternoon for the excursion. Go to Mile Marker 24 on the Queen's Highway. From there take the side road to **East Beach**, a great snorkeling spot. When you reach the beach, park your vehicle and walk two miles south along the beach and be on the lookout for a path leading off the beach to the right. From there it's a short walk along the path through lush green vegetation to the old limestone monument. This trip also presents a good opportunity to visit the Dixon Hill Lighthouse.

Dixon Hill Lighthouse

Built in 1856, Dixon Hill is a traditional lighthouse in every sense of the word. Its light, more than 160 feet above sea level, is the highest point on the island. The snow-white tower stands on a limestone plateau, and the view from the top is spectacular. Far into the distance, the sea, land and lake are laid out in sharp relief. The sea to the east stretches endlessly, starting as the palest green in-shore and changing to the deepest indigo of the ocean out beyond the reef to the horizon. The light itself is one of only a few kerosene-fueled, hand-operated lamps left in the world. To make the climb to the top you'll need to be in good shape. Once there you can view the lamp itself. You'll be amazed how small it is. Small or not, it does the job. Twice a minute it sends out a 400,000 candle-power beam of light that can be seen more than 19 miles at sea.

Going on Foot

Walking & Hiking

San Salvador is a great place for hikers. From Cockburn Town, Club Med or Riding Rock Inn, set off in any direction. Take your time and explore the sights and beaches along the way. Once you've seen the local area, rent a car or moped and head to the extreme ends of the island. Park your vehicle, and set out again on foot.

> Be sure to take along plenty to drink. There's little available on the outer reaches of the island.

Even with such a tiny population, San Salvador's roads are not quite as deserted as you might imagine. You can go long periods without seeing a soul, but you can also count on a friendly face to appear just when you need it most. The gently rolling terrain, dusty roads and narrow trails lined with a profusion of local flora, and the little, colorful communities, all make for a delightful walking adventure.

On The Water

Diving & Snorkeling

San Salvador is one of the most exciting diving locations in the Bahamas. It's doubtful that there's a comparable diversity of locations anywhere other than the Cayman Islands or Bonaire. Visibility is from 100 to 200 feet, currents are minimal and, whether you're an experienced diver or just learning, there something here for you. For experienced divers, the reef wall, on the leeward side, starts at a depth of less than 40 feet and runs more than 12 miles from one end of the island to the other.

The Riding Rock Inn participates in Jean Michel Cousteau's "Snorkeling Adventures" program, which includes 10 sites, one of them a shipwreck.

Best Dive Sites

Most of the sites involve the reef that runs the entire length of the leeward side of the island. Veteran divers will tell you, it's a rare day that the reef doesn't yield some new and rare experience. Some of the best-known sites are listed below.

Devil's Claw

This site includes three large craters, side by side, that start at a depth of 45 feet, then descend fairly slowly to 80 feet, before dropping off into the darkness. Lots of small marine life inhabit the crevices in the crater walls, while larger fish such as groupers, barracudas and sharks can be seen lurking in the deeper waters.

Frascate

The *Frascate* was a German-built English freighter that ran aground in 1902 while steaming south from New York to Jamaica. Built in 1886, she measured some 260 feet by 35 feet. Her bones lie in shallow waters off Riding Rock Point, and are a favorite spot for beginning divers, and snorkelers too. She lies scattered across a wide area in 15 to 20 feet of water. The ocean floor is sandy and the visibility is usually 100 to 150 feet. The wreck is home to all sorts of marine life, including a large green moray eel that lives in her boiler. The boiler and stern section are excellent for underwater photography.

The Hump

This is a fun dive suitable for both beginner and veteran divers. It's a shallow reef dive with the coral heads starting less than 15 feet from the surface to a maximum depth of 40 feet. The hump itself is an underwater hillock some 80 feet long, 40 feet wide, and 20 feet high, covered in coral of various types. It's a microcosm of the greater reef itself. There are angels, clowns, sergeant majors, crabs, lobsters, morays, snappers, groupers, parrotfish, anemones, octopus, and shrimp; even the odd barracuda has been known to drop by.

Vicky's Reef

This is really a wall dive. From 40 feet at the edge of the reef, the wall drops away. This is not a dive for the fainthearted. At 60 feet the reef is undercut. Here, the coral heads are at their best. It's also home to moray eels, yellow stingrays, grouper and snappers. If you are not subject to vertigo (the drop-off is alarming!), this is a fabulous site.

Best Snorkeling Sites

East Beach

From Crab Cay almost to Graham's Harbour, there's a deserted, six-mile stretch of beach that reminds one of the Outer Banks off North Carolina. With waving seagrass, soft white sand and sea the color of Colombian emeralds, it's an ideal snorkeling site. Visibility stretches well beyond 150 feet, and the coral formations teem with wildlife. Take along something to shield you from the sun; there's no shade along the entire length of the beach.

Elkhorn Gardens

A reef site where the main feature is the extensive growths of elk and staghorn coral, along with several acres of turtle grass. Lots of marine life.

The Flower Gardens

An area of the reef with large coral heads, caves, and ledges. You can snorkel down among the heads and get up close with the reef creatures.

The Movie Caves

This nice snorkeling site is close to where Columbus is thought to have first set foot ashore in 1492.

Natural Bridges

This is a fun site, with lots of natural bridge formations to explore and swim through.

The Rookery

A great site for shellfish, especially conch.

Snapshot Reef

This is one of the most popular snorkeling sites on San Salvador. Here you can enjoy the best of life on the reef. The site is home to millions of sea creatures, most too small to see. The reef fish are friendly, and will take time out from their daily chores to meet and greet.

Staghorn Reef

Very similar to Snapshot Reef. Life on the reef is full of fun and danger, for the local inhabitants, of course.

Also, see **The Hump** and **Frascate** above under *Best Dive Sites*.

Dive Operators

Guanahani Divers Ltd. are based at the Riding Rock Inn and Marina. They operate three dive boats, each with a capacity for six divers. Certified instruction, equipment rental, underwater camera rental and instruction, and one-day film processing are all available. You can also take a course in underwater photography and videography. They offer three boat dives daily, and a night dive once a week. Dive packages are available through the Inn. Rates are $50 for a one-tank dive. The beginner's one-day certification course is $150 and full PADI certification is $450. For more dive information, and for dive-inclusive vacation packages, 800-272-1492 or 242-331-2631.

Dining

$$ The Riding Rock Inn's oceanfront restaurant in Cockburn Town is open daily for breakfast from 7:30 am until 9:30 am, for lunch from 12:30 pm until 2:30 pm, and for dinner from 6:30 pm until 9:30. The menu includes American, European and Bahamian cuisine. The specialty of the house – conch chowder and bread – is served daily for lunch. In the evening, you can enjoy a cocktail before dinner out on the oceanfront terrace of the inn's **Driftwood Bar**. Reservations are required. 242-331-2631.

Also in Cockburn Town, you can eat breakfast and lunch at the **$ Ocean View Club**, or you can eat breakfast lunch or dinner at the **$ Three Ships**. The Three Ships is owned by Faith Jones, a lady with the magic touch where cooking is concerned. She cooks only to order, so you'll need to make a reservation, but her cracked conch, fried grouper, and peas and rice are to die for. 242-331-2787.

Accommodations

As previously mentioned, accommodations on San Salvador are quite limited. Club Med is, of course, the best resort on the island. Then there's a small inn/hotel comprising three cottages and little else. Finally, there's the Riding Rock Inn, a moderately priced, comfortable inn in Cockburn Town.

Riding Rock Inn Resort & Marina. This small resort is dedicated to divers and diving. There is a full-service dive shop on the premises and guided dives, instruction, and equipment rental are all offered.

Guest rooms – 30 oceanfront rooms and 12 standard rooms – are located along the shore. All are air-conditioned, with cable television, teles, ceiling fans, patio or balcony, chaises and refrigerators. The furnishing are rather plain, but functional. Unfortunately, time and tides take their toll on most small island hotels and motels, and this one is no exception. Although maintenance work on the buildings and rooms is ongoing, there's always that little something that can give cause for complaint. On the whole, this resort offers real value for money, but make allowances for its remote location and exposure to the elements. There are tennis courts and a pool, with plenty of room and furniture for lounging. Rental bikes, mopeds and cars are available on-site. The beach is a 50-yard walk from the hotel.

The dining room is clean, the service prompt and friendly. The menu features all of the popular Bahamian dishes – conch, fresh fish, lobster, peas and rice, even turtle – along with American and European cuisine. The home-baked bread alone is worth the trip. The **Driftwood Bar** is the watering hole on the island. Its oceanfront deck is a great place to enjoy a beer or tropical drink after a long day out on the water. The atmosphere is lively and friendly and the locals will make you welcome. Wednesday night is live music night; Friday night is when most of the locals drop in to round off the week.

Rates start at $141 per night for a deluxe oceanfront room, and $114 per night for a standard poolside room; both are based on double occupancy.

The hotel runs its own charter air service from Fort Lauderdale on Saturdays. Better yet, they also offer **packages**: some specifically for divers, some for those who just want a vacation far away from the hustle and bustle of life in the city. An all-inclusive dive package – with round-trip air fare from Fort Lauderdale, three dives per day for six days, round-trip airport/hotel transfers, seven nights' accommodations, all meals and gratuities (alcoholic beverages are not included) – costs $1,750 with a deluxe oceanfront room, or $1,500 with a standard poolside room.

For non-divers the package includes all the above except the dives. The seven-night all-inclusive package with a deluxe oceanfront room costs $1,300, and the same package with a standard poolside room costs $930. 800-272-1492, www.ridingrock.com.

Club Med Columbus Isle. Club Med has a reputation for service and quality and their Columbus Isle resort more than lives up to it. Billed as one of their "finest" and most exotic locations, it certainly has a lot to offer. Situated right on one of the best stretches of beach, it's a tropical village of gaily painted Bahamian cottages built very much with the local ecology in mind. Narrow footpaths lead to all corners of the resort to ensure walkers don't disturb or damage the rolling dunes and vegetation. The public access rooms house a wonderful collection of art and artifacts brought in from around the world: Asia, the islands of the Pacific, South America, Turkey, Thailand, India and Africa.

Although this particular location is not one of Club Med's designated family villages, kids of all ages are welcome, and there is plenty for them to do.

The guest rooms are tastefully and comfortably furnished and decorated with international handicrafts. All are air-conditioned, have televisions, teles, safes, refrigerators and hair dryers. Each has its own private balcony or patio, private bathroom, and shower with desalinated water. Some offer spectacular views of the ocean, others look out over the gardens; each has a character all its own.

Because the cottages are situated along the beach, some are quite a long walk from the public rooms, dining rooms and facilities.

The resort boasts three restaurants and a spa where you can have a wonderful full-body overhaul. There are tennis courts, three of which are lighted, and a fitness center.

As at all Club Med resorts, the emphasis here is on organized activities. If you want to get involved, and the powers that be will do their best to make sure you do, there's aerobics, bocce ball, deep-sea fishing, horseback riding, sea kayaking, ping pong, sailing, scuba diving, snorkeling, softball, soccer, swimming, tennis, volleyball, basketball, water exercises, water-skiing and windsurfing – more to do than you could possibly manage in a single week. And, as if all that's not enough, you can take a day excursion to Nassau for shopping, a snorkeling day-trip that includes a beach picnic lunch and a speedboat ride, or a sunset cruise.

The resort also features one of Club Med's exclusive **Dedicated Dive Centers**. All this really means is that it's a full-service dive center where everything is available, from guided dives to rental equipment. The Club Med Dive Center offers up to six days of diving per package, up to two boat dives per day, up to three dives per day, one night dive per week, snacks on board the boat and, if required, the supervision of a Club Med guide. Diving does carry an extra charge over and above the regular package charge, in this case $160 per person per week, and that includes two dives daily and one night dive.

Club Med packages usually start and end on Saturdays. Rates begin at $1,499 in the off-season (August 29 through December 12), $1,699 in the high season. The rate includes airfare from Boston, Los Angeles, New York, San Francisco and Washington, DC. You can fly out of other major cities, but air add-ons will raise the base rate accordingly. If you've not been to a Club Med resort before, you will be required to pay a one-time $50-per-person initiation fee, and an annual membership fee of $30 per family. You can have your travel agent make arrangements for you – probably the most painless way to do it – or you can book the trip yourself: 800-CLUBMED, www.clubmed.com.

Rum Cay

This tiny island to the west of San Salvador has a population of less than 150. It's a pleasant, though remote, spot on the map, accessible only by private boat and mail boat. Unless you're a sailor with a boat of your own upon which you can live while you're there, Rum Cay is not the place for an extended vacation. You could visit by mail boat, but that would mean a stay on the island of slightly more than two days, and the only hotel was, at the time of writing, closed indefinitely.

Ecologists will find Rum Cay to be something special. Completely unspoiled, and just as it must have been when Christopher Columbus first set foot on San Salvador, it's a microcosm of the islands: gently rolling hills, deserted beaches, limestone caves, deserted farms, salt ponds, and seas where the visibility underwater approaches 200 feet.

If you do decide to come here, be sure to visit **Port Nelson**. It's a friendly little place where you're sure of a warm welcome, and the opportunity to stock up on supplies. The town is reminiscent of those featured in movies of a type that were made only in the late 1940s and early 1950s; *Donovan's Reef*, starring John Wayne, and *The Coral Reef*, starring Gilbert Roland, are two that come to mind. There are a couple of places to eat where you can sample good food made only as the locals can.

There are no s on the island – islanders communicate by VHF. If you've been at sea for a while, you'll probably want to hike. You can leave your boat at anchor, take to the road, and walk to the far side of the island, where you will find a beautiful beach. You can do the whole island in a single day. Bikes and cars are available for rent in Port Nelson.

Mayaguana island

Finally, we come to the one island in the Bahamas that I love best of all, Mayaguana. I was lucky enough not long ago to spend ten days on Mayaguana. Paradise Lost, could almost be a better name for it. No more than a tiny spot on the map of the western Atlantic, it is one of our planet's last undiscovered gems. Mayaguana is a sun-drenched tropical island surrounded by jewel-hued waters and swaths of sugar-white beaches. It beckons irresistibly to those who are looking for something a little out of the ordinary, whether that be the back-to-nature, exploratory vacation of a lifetime, or something a little more permanent.

The island is the outdoor adventurer's dream: scuba diving, snorkeling, bonefishing, deep-sea fishing, bird watching, sailing, hiking – it has all this and more, and is totally unspoiled. The colors of the reef are more vibrant and the reef-life is fearless. The fish are bigger, they bite harder and faster, and they fight like the devil. If you like to bonefish, don't miss a fishing experience on Mayaguana. Looking for solitude? You can wander endless miles of deserted beaches in a place so peaceful you might think it is your own private retreat.

If you've spent a lifetime looking for the perfect place to get away from it all, and a new place to get into, you have found it in Mayaguana; I promise.

Mayaguana is an island of quiet mystery and tranquility; a land bypassed by time and tide; a beautiful uncharted island of The Bahamas, a secret waiting to be discovered. It boasts a warm, year-round climate with mostly sunny days, cooling trade winds, more than 50 miles of unspoiled beaches, and stunning scenery.

One of the largest of the Out Islands, Mayaguana is almost 27 miles long and some six miles at its widest point. It sits 52 miles northwest of Providenciales (Provo) in the Turks and Caicos Islands, and is the most easterly of the Bahamian Island chain.

Like many other remote, virtually uninhabited Out Islands, Mayaguana is a mostly forested strip of low-lying land ideally suited for fishing and minimal agriculture. Its eastern end is an unspoiled wilderness where vast tracts of lignum vitae (the official tree of The Bahamas), low-growing hardwood forests of casuarina, mahogany, black mangrove flats and seagrape blanket the landscape. There are no roads here, just a few barely discernable tracks through the dense undergrowth that have all but given themselves back to nature. The greater portion of the island is accessible only by boat.

Eastern Mayaguana is ringed on three sides by a magnificent coral reef whose shallow, emerald Atlantic waters are home to a dazzling and vibrant undersea world of tropical fish, giant lobsters, conch, barracuda, sea turtles, bone fish and more. The shoreline is one long, powder-white sandbar after another: untouched, unspoiled. All of this makes the eastern side of the island attractive to hikers that enjoy the challenge of exploring without developed trails.

The western half of the island is inhabited by a laid-back population of about 300, more than half of whom are schoolchildren. The islanders are happy people who make an effort to attend the three-times-weekly visits by Bahamas Air.

Hours before each flight is due – whether they are flying or not, meeting travelers or not – island residents gather in force at the terminal to sit, chat, discuss island affairs, play dominoes and enjoy a plate of home-made macaroni and cheese.

Mayaguanians live a seemingly idyllic, but very quiet life, in three quaint settlements that are unquestionably old-world Bahamian, in appearance and in spirit. Abraham's Bay sits on the edge of a shallow water flat on the south coast. Betsy's Bay is a tiny settlement on the west coast. Pirate's Well is a vibrant little community on the western side of the north coast.

Farming is an important occupation on the island. Farming produce is not grown for revenue but primarily for eating and bartering with other islanders.

While the island has long been a favorite stopover for yachting enthusiasts, tourists have still to discover this tiny paradise. Located far from the beaten path, guidebooks mention it only in passing, usually saying little of its wonders.

Tourist Information

There is no tourism representation on Mayaguana. You'll

need to deal directly with The Bahamas Ministry of Tourism, PO Box N-3701, Market Plaza, Bay Street, Nassau, Bahamas, 242-322-7501; fax 242-328-0945.

Communications

The islanders have cell Phone service via Bahamas Telecom. Those with international roaming chips work best. If your flight to Mayaguana involves a stopover in Nassau, consider obtaining a prepaid Bahamas Telecom cell Phone . This will certainly provide you with service all over the western portion of Mayaguana, and limited service if you're heading east. **Wireless Internet is available only in the Baycaner's lobby and bar.**

Accommodations

There are four places to stay on Mayaguana, including The Baycaner Beach Resort in Pirate's Well and Reggie's Guest House, Paradise Village and Mayaguana Inn in Abraham's

Bay. The Baycaner Beach Resort, a comfortable guest house with 16 rooms, is owned by Earnell Brown, called Shorty, all the locals.

Baycaner Beach Resort, Pirate's Well

It's wonderful to find a reasonable place to stay this far off the beaten path in The Bahamas. There is a restaurant and a bar, but other amenities are minimal.

Guestrooms have a bed or two, a night stand, a TV and a small air-conditioner that does a great job of keeping the rooms cool. You can relax totally, as there are no telephone s in the rooms and Internet access is available only in the main lobby and bar. The TV is controlled from the bar, so whatever is being watched in the bar is what's available in your room – but why would you be watching TV on beautiful Mayaguana?

The bathrooms are functional, clean and well maintained. Towels and small bars of soap are supplied – you'll need to take all other toiletries with you.

The lobby adjoins the dining room and bar, which is popular with locals. There's rarely a bartender on duty, so the honor system applies. Simply help yourself, note what you've taken, then settle up at the end of your stay.

The dining room is spacious, clean and cool, and you might

find that you have it all to yourself. Breakfast, which is ordered the night before, usually consists of eggs, bacon and French toast. Dinner is also served on a casual, as-needed/as-ordered basis and always includes the Bahamian staple of peas 'n' rice. Most evening meals feature conch – perhaps in a chowder or freshly made salad – and grouper, the most popular fish caught off island. The hotel cook makes delicious fresh bread daily and will happily turn your catch into a delicious dinner. The Baycaner's beach is truly private. You can lay out and enjoy the sun, sand and sea, and a good book with never a thought of being disturbed.

Rates for a double at the Baycaner are $106 September-April; $88 May-August, including taxes. Breakfast, lunch, and dinner can be included for an extra $80 per person, and it's well worthwhile, because there's really nowhere else offering a meal every day. MasterCard and Visa only are accepted. The Baycaner Beach Resort, Pirate's Well, Mayaguana, Bahamas, 242-339-3726, www.baycanerbeach.com. Alternately, you can stay at one of the island's tiny Bahamian homes, where the people are friendly and ever-willing to please, but facilities are minimal. Those who have stayed at guest houses often return. Try Captain Brown, 242-339-3116.

Dress

To overdress on Mayaguana is to wear shorts and a shirt with long sleeves. Bring lightweight shirts and shorts and at least a couple of bathing suits. If you burn easily, cover up. A good pair of walking shoes is a must, and a strong pair of water shoes is also recommended – if not water shoes, then a strong pair of sandals, not flip-flops.

Medical

The majority of Bahamian islands are blessed with an excellent health service. Hospital facilities – both public and private – are available in Nassau and Freeport, and most of the larger Out Islands are served by health centers, clinics and general practitioner doctors. On Mayaguana, the clinic in Abraham's Bay is staffed by three nurses capable of performing most minor medical procedures. They are on call 24 hours a day. Additionally, a doctor from Inaugua flies in three days each month. Serious injuries involve an emergency flight to either

Nassau's Princess Margaret Hospital, or to Provo only 52 miles away. Medical attention is expensive, so check your insurance coverage first.

Money Matters

Legal tender is the Bahamian dollar, which is always equivalent in value to the US dollar. Both US and Bahamian dollars are accepted interchangeably, and visitors are likely to receive change in mixed American and Bahamian paper and coins.

On Mayaguana, credit cards are accepted only at the Baycaner Beach Resort. And while traveler's checks are accepted throughout The Bahamas and may be cashed at banks and hotels, Mayaguana has no banks, meaning cash is king.

There are no ATMs on Mayaguana, so be sure to carry enough cash to get you through your stay. If you are traveling through Nassau and need a bank, their hours are 9:30 a.m. until 3:00 p.m., Monday through Thursday, and 9:30 a.m. until 5:00 p.m. on Friday. ATMs are located at strategic spots in the town, including the casinos.

Photography

There's no place quite as photogenic as Mayaguana. The ocean changes color from emerald green to sapphire blue, the sand from pristine white to the most delicate shades of pink. Add the amazing Technicolor decor of the typically Bahamian buildings – from delicate pastels to riotous shades of red, yellow, green and blue – the eclectic mix of ramshackle architecture, the flora and fauna, the magnificent sunsets.

As the digital age advances from one stage to the next, photography is easier than ever. If you own a digital camera, simply put the machine on auto, and then point and shoot. You'll get some great images. Remember that the best light for photography is in the early morning and late afternoon, when the colors are warmer. If you're using film, make sure you pack a supply as you may not find any on Mayaguana.

Things You Need to Know

DISABLED TRAVELERS: As of this writing there are no provisions for disabled travelers to Mayaguana. Bahamas Air flights are, of course, equipped to carry disabled passengers, but once on the island nothing is available.

ELECTRICAL: All U.S. and Canadian appliances can be used without adapters. Visitors from the United Kingdom will need adapters to 120 volts.

TIME: Time on Mayaguana... stands still (joking). Time on Mayaguana is the same as the rest of The Bahamas: the same as the Eastern United States. If it's noon in New York City, it's noon here.

How to Get There:

All roads to Mayaguana lead through Nassau. Bahamas Air flies into Mayaguana, and out again, on Mondays, Wednesdays and Fridays each week. Your travel agent can connect the dots for you. If, however, you feel like planning and booking the vacation yourself, you can do it easily enough. Me? I booked my own trip: one night in Nassau, 9 nights on Mayaguana, and one more night in Nassau.

Mail Boat Schedules

Mail boats leave Potter's Cay, Paradise Island bridge, in Nassau, weekly heading to Mayaguana. You can find out when and for which destinations by calling the Dockmaster's office in Nassau, under the Paradise Island Bridge on Potter's Cay, 242-393-1064.

At a Glance

This section serves all the Islands of the Bahamas, including New Providence and Nassau. It's included because much of the information is helpful to visitors with plans to visit places other than Nassau.

Airlines Serving the Islands

Airline Telephone Numbers

Air Canada:...................................888-247-2262, www.aircanada.com

Air Sunshine: ....800-327-8900, fax 954-359-8211, www.airsunshine.com

American Airlines: 800-433-7300

American Eagle: ....800-433-7300, www.aa.com

Bahamasair: ....800-222-4262, fax 305-593-6246, www.bahamasair.com

Bel Air Transport: ....954-524-9814, fax 954-524-0115

Chalk's Ocean Airways: ....800-424-2857, www.chalksoceanairways.com

Delta:...800-359-7664, www.delta.com

Gulfstream (Continental): .... 800-525-0280, www.continental.com

Island Air Charters: ....800-444-9904, fax 954-760-9157

Island Express:............................954-359-0380, fax 954-359-7944

Jet Blue Airways:.........................800-538-2583, www.jetblue.com

Lynx Air: ....954-491-7576, fax 954-491-8361

Major Air: ....242-352-5778, fax 242-352-5788

Pan Am Air Bridge:.....................800-424-2557, fax 305-371-

3259

Sandpiper Air: ....242-328-7591, fax 242-328-5069

Southern Air: ....242-323-6833, 242-300-0155 (toll-free)

Spirit Airlines: 242-377-6150

Twin Air: ....954-359-8266, fax 954-359-8271

USAirways Express: ....800-622-1015, www.usairways.com

Virgin Atlantic: 800-744-7477

Package Operators

American Airlines Vacations: 800-321-2121, www.aavacations.com.

Air Jamaica Vacations: 800-523-5585, www.airjamaicavacations.com.

Apple Vacations: www.applevacations.com.

British Airways Vacations: 800-AIRWAYS, www.britishairways.com.

Classic Custom Vacations: sold only through travel agents, but you can visit their website at www.classicvacations.com.

Continental Airlines Vacations: 800-301-3800, www.covacations.com.

Delta Vacations: 800-221-6666, www.deltavacations.com.

Liberty Travel: 888-271-1584, www.libertytravel.com.

Tour Scan, Inc: 800-962-2080, www.tourscan.com.

Travel Impressions: www.travelimpressions.com (book through travel agents only).

USAir Vacations: 800-455-0123, www.usairvacations.com.

Vacation Express: 800-309-4717, www.vacationexpress.com.

Charter Airlines - Florida

Dolphin Atlantic Airlines: 800-353-8010, fax 954-359-8009

Trans-Caribbean Air: 888-239-2929, fax 954-434-2171

Resort Charter Airlines

Deep Water Cay Club: 954-359-0488, fax 954-359-9488

Fernandez Bay Village, Cat Island: 800-9490-1905fax 954-474-4864
Great Harbour Cay, Berry Islands: 800-343-7256
Greenwood Beach Resort, Cat Island: 242-342-3053
Hawk's Nest Club, Cat Island: 242-357-7257
Riding Rock Inn, San Salvador: 800-272-1492
Small Hope Bay Lodge, Andros: 800-223-6961
Stella Maris Resort, Long Island: 800-426-0466

Getting There
Nassau/New Providence
Many direct flights are available, as follows: **Air Jamaica** flies from Newark and Philadelphia; **American Eagle**, from Fort Lauderdale, Miami, Orlando and Tampa; **Bahamasair**, from Fort Lauderdale, Miami and Orlando; **British Airways**, from London; **Comair**, from Cincinnati; **Continental**, from Fort Lauderdale, Miami and West Palm Beach; **Delta**, from NY/Laguardia, Boston and Atlanta; **US Airways**, from Philadelphia, NY/Laguardia and Cleveland.

Freeport/Grand Bahama
Direct flights include: **AirTran**, from Atlanta; **American Eagle**, from Miami and Fort Lauderdale; **Bahamasair**, from Miami; **Continental**, from Miami, Fort Lauderdale and West Palm Beach; **TWA**, from NY/JFK.

Getting to Abaco		
Airport	From	Airline
Marsh Harbour	Ft. Lauderdale	Island Express, Gulfstream, Air Sunshine, Bel Air Transport
	Miami	American Eagle, Gulfstream
	Orlando	USAirways Express

	Freeport	Major Air
	Nassau	Bahamasair
Treasure Cay	Ft. Lauderdale	Island Express, Air Sunshine, Twin Air, Gulfstream
	Miami	Gulfstream
	Orlando	USAirways Express
	West Palm Beach	USAirways Express
	Freeport	Major Air
	Nassau	Bahamasair

Getting to Andros		
Airport	From	Airline
Andros Town	Ft. Lauderdale	Island Express
	Freeport	Major Air
	Nassau	Bahamasair
Congo Town	Ft. Lauderdale	Island Express, Lynx Air
	Freeport	Freeport
	Nassau	Bahamasair
Mangrove Cay	Ft. Lauderdale	Island Express
	Freeport	Major Air
	Nassau	Bahamasair
San Andros	Ft. Lauderdale	Island Express
	Freeport	Major Air
	Nassau	Bahamasair

Getting to the Berry Islands

Airport	From	Airline
Great Harbour Cay	Ft. Lauderdale	Island Express

Getting to Bimini

Airport	From	Airline
North Bimini	Ft. Lauderdale	Pan Am Air Bridge, Chalk's Ocean Airways
	Watson Island, Miami	Pan Am Air Bridge
	Paradise Island	Pan Am Air Bridge
South Bimini	Ft. Lauderdale	Island Air Charters

Getting to Cat Island

Airport	From	Airline
Arthur's Town	Nassau	Bahamasair
New Bight	Ft. Lauderdale	Island Express
	Nassau	Bahamasair

Getting to Crooked Island

Airport	From	Airline
Crooked Island	Nassau	Bahamasair

Getting to Eleuthera

Airport	From	Airline
Governor's Harbour	Ft. Lauderdale	USAirways Express, Air Sunshine, Bel Air Transport
	Miami	American Eagle
	Freeport	Major Air
	Nassau	Bahamasair
North Eleuthera	Ft. Lauderdale	Gulfstream, USAirways Express
	Freeport	Major Air
	Nassau	Bahamasair, Sandpiper Air
Rock Sound	Ft. Lauderdale	Island Express
	Freeport	Major Air
	Nassau	Bahamasair

Getting to Exuma

Airport	From	Airline
George Town	Ft. Lauderdale	Island Express, Air Sunshine, Lynx Air
	Miami	American Eagle, Bahamasair

	Freeport	Major Air
	Nassau	Bahamasair
Staniel Cay	Ft. Lauderdale	Island Express

Getting to Long Island		
Airport	From	Airline
Stella Maris	Ft. Lauderdale	Island Express, Bel Air Transport
	Miami	American Eagle
	Nassau	Bahamasair

Getting to San Salvador		
Airport	From	Airline
San Salvador	Ft. Lauderdale	Air Sunshine
	Miami	Bahamasair
	Nassau	Bahamasair

Getting to the Turks & Caicos		
Airport	From	Airline
Provo	Miami	American Airlines
	Atlanta	Delta
	Toronto	Air Canada
	Nassau	Bahamasair

Mail Boat Schedules

The following schedules and one-way fares were current at the time of writing but are subject to change without notice. Mail boats leave Potter's Cay, Paradise Island bridge, in Nassau, weekly.

To	Route	Times & Fares

Abaco	Marsh Harbour, Treasure Cay, Green Turtle Cay, Hope Town	*Miz Desa* leaves Tuesday at 5 pm and returns on Thursday at 7 pm. Sailing time is 12 hours. The fare is $45.
	Sandy Point, Moore's Island, Bullock Harbour	*Champion II* leaves Tuesday at 8 pm and returns on Thursday at 10 am. Sailing time is 11 hours. The fare is $30.
Acklins, Crooked Island & Mayaguana		*Lady Matilda*, schedule varies, 242-393-1064. Sailing time is upwards of 15 hours. The fare is $65, $70 and $70 respectively.
Central Andros	Fresh Creek, Stafford Creek, Blanket Sound, Staniard Creek, Behring Point	*Lady D.* leaves Tuesday at 12 noon and returns on Sunday. Sailing time is five hours. The fare is $30.

North Andros	Nicholl's Town, Majestic Point, Morgan's Bluff	*Lisa J. II* leaves Wednesday at 3:30 pm and returns on Tuesday at 12 noon. Sailing time is five hours. The fare is $30. *Lady Margo*, leaves Wednesday at 2 am and returns on Sunday at 5 pm. Sailing time is five hours. The fare is $30. *Challenger*. 242-393-1064 for schedule. Sailing time is five hours. The fare is $30.
South Andros	Kemp's Bay, Bluff, Long Bay Cay, Driggs Hill, Congo Town	*Captain Moxey* leaves Monday at 11 pm and returns on Wednesday at 11 pm. Sailing time is 3½ hours. The fare is $30. *Delmar L.* leaves Thursday at 10 pm and returns on Monday at 5 am. Sailing time is seven hours. The fare is $30.
Bimini & Cat Cay		*Bimini Mack*. Schedule varies. 242-393-1064. Sailing time is 12 hours. The fare is $45.
Berry Islands		*Mangrove Cay Express* leaves Nassau Thursday at 10 pm. Return arrives 7-9 am on Sundays. Fare is $30.
Cat Island, North & South	Arthur's Town, Bennen's Harbour, Bluff, Bight	*North Cat Island Special* leaves Wednesday at 1 pm and returns on Friday. Sailing time is 14 hours. The fare is $40.
Cat Island, South	Smith's Bay, Bight, Old Bight	*Sea Hauler* leaves Tuesday at 3 pm and returns on Monday. Sailing time is 12 hours. The fare is $40.

Eleuthera	Rock Sound, Davis Harbour, South Eleuthera	*Bahamas Daybreak III* leaves Monday at 5 pm and returns on Tuesday at 10 pm. Sailing time is five hours. The fare is $20.
	Governor's Harbour & Spanish Wells	*Eleuthera Express* leaves Monday at 7 pm and returns on Tuesday at 8 pm. She also leaves on Thursday at 7 am and returns on Sunday. Sailing time is five hours. The fare is $20.
The Exumas	Ragged Island, Exuma Cays, Barraterre, Staniel Point, Black Point, Farmer's Cay	*Ettienne & Cephas* leaves Tuesday at 2 pm. 242-393-1064 for return. Sailing time is 21 hours. The fare is $50.
	George Town	*Grand Master* leaves Tuesday at 2 pm and returns on Friday at 7 am. Sailing time is 12 hours. The fare is $40.
Grand Bahama	Freeport	*Marcella III* leaves Wednesday at 4 pm and returns on Saturday at 7 pm. Sailing time is 12 hours. The fare is $45.
Inagua		*Abilin* leaves Tuesday at 12 noon and returns on Saturday (time varies). Sailing time is 17 hours. The fare is $70.
Long Island	Clarence Town	*Abilin* leaves Tuesday at 12 noon and returns on Saturday (time

		varies). Sailing time is 17 hours. The fare is $65.
North Long Island	Salt Pond, Deadman's Cay, Seymours	*Sherice M* leaves Monday at 5 pm and returns on Thursday (time varies). Sailing time is 15 hours. The fare is $45.
Mangrove Cay	Cargill Creek, Bowen Sound	*Lady Gloria* leaves Tuesday at 8 pm and returns on Thursday at 10 am. Sailing time is five hours. The fare is $30.
	Hatchet Bay	*Captain Fox* leaves Friday at 12 noon and returns on Wednesday at 4 pm. Sailing time is six hours. The fare is $25.
San Salvador	United Estates, Rum Cay, Cockburn Town	*Lady Francis* leaves Tuesday at 6 pm and returns on Friday. Sailing time is 12 hours. The fare is $40.

Other Sailings

Mail boats also leave Nassau at unscheduled times. You can find out when and for which destinations by calling the Dockmaster's office in Nassau, under the Paradise Island Bridge on Potter's Cay, Phone 242-393-1064.

Fishing Guides on all the Islands

Abaco

Will Key, Marsh Harbour, 242-266-0059.

Robert Lowe, Hope Town, 242-366-0266.

Maitland Lowe, Hope Town, 242-366-0004.

Truman Major, Hope Town, 242-366-0101.

Creswell Archer, Marsh Harbour, 242-367-4000.

Orthnell Russell, Treasure Cay. 242-367-2570 or 242-365-0125.

The King Fish II, Treasure Cay, 242-367-2570.

Lincoln Jones, Green Turtle Cay, 242-365-4223.

Joe Sawyer, Green Turtle Cay, 242-365-4173.
Trevor Sawyer, Cherokee, 242-366-2065.
Andros
Cargill Creek Lodge, Cargill Creek, 242-368-5129.
Andros Island Bone Fishing Club, Cargill Creek, 242-368-5167.
Nottages Cottages, Behring Point, 242-368-4293.
Bimini
The Bimini Big Game Fishing Club, Alice Town, 242-347-2391.
The Bimini Blue Water Resort & Marina, Alice Town, 242-347-3166.
The Bimini Reef Club & Marina, South Bimini, ☐05-359-9449.
The Sea Crest Hotel & Marina, Alice Town, 242-347-3071.
Weech's Dock, Alice Town, 242-347-2028.
Eleuthera
Coral Sands Hotel, Harbour Island, 800-333-2368.
Valentines Inn & Yacht Club, Harbour Island, 242-333-2080.
Spanish Wells Yacht Haven, Spanish Wells, 242-333-4255.
Spanish Wells Marina, Spanish Wells, 242-333-4122.
Hatchet Bay Marina, Hatchet Bay, 242-332-0186.
Harbour Island Club & Marina, Harbour Island, 242-333-2427.
Exuma
Club Peace and Plenty, George Town, 242-345-5555.
Grand Bahama
Captain Ted Been, Freeport, 242-352-2797.
Captain Tony Cooper, Freeport, 242-352-6782.
Captain Steve Hollingsworth, Freeport, 242-352-2050.
Captain Elon "Sonny" Martin, Freeport, 242-352-6835.
Captain John Roberts, Freeport, 242-352-7915.
Captain Doug Silvera, Port Lucaya, 242-373-8446.
New Providence

Brown's Charters, Nassau, 242-324-1215.
Captain Arthur Moxey, Nassau, 242-361-3527.
Captain Mike Russell, Nassau, 242-322-8148.
Born Free Charter Service, Nassau, 242-363-2003.

Dive Operators
Abaco
Brendal's Dive Shop International, Green Turtle Cay, 242-365-4411, www.brendal.com.
Dive Abaco, Marsh Harbour, 800-247-5338, fax 242-367-4779, www.diveabaco.com.
Dive Odyssea, Great Abaco Beach Resort, Marsh Harbour, 242-367-3774.
The Hope Town Dive Shop, Hope Town, 242-366-0029.
Walker's Cay Undersea Adventures, PO Box 21766, Ft. Lauderdale, FL 33335, 800-327-8150, www.nealwatson.com/Walkers/WalkersTransportation.html.
Andros
Small Hope Bay Lodge, PO Box 21667, Ft. Lauderdale, FL 33335, 800-223-6961, 242-368-2014, www.smallhope.com.
Bimini
Bimini Big Game Fishing Club, Alice Town, North Bimini, 242-347-3391.
Bill and Nowdla Keefe's Bimini Undersea Adventures, PO Box 21766, Ft. Lauderdale, FL 33335, 800-348-4644, www.biminiundersea.com.
Bimini Undersea, 242-347-3089.
Cat Island
Cat Island Dive Center, 242-342-3053.
Greenwood Beach Resort & Dive Center, 242-342-3053.
Eleuthera
The Ocean Fox Dive Shop, Harbour Island, 242-333-2323.
Valentine's Dive Center, Harbour Island, 800-383-6480, 242-333-2080, www.valentinesdive.com.
Exuma
The Club Peace and Plenty, George Town, 242-345-5555,

www.peaceandplenty.com.

Exuma Fantasea, George Town, 800-760-0700.

Staniel Cay Yacht Club, Staniel Cay, 242-355-2011, www.stanielcay.com.

Grand Bahama

Under Water Explorers Society (UNEXSO), PO Box 22878, Ft. Lauderdale, FL 33335, 800-992-DIVE, 242-373-1244, www.underwater-explorers-society.visit-the-bahamas.com.

Xanadu Undersea Adventures, PO Box 21766, Ft. Lauderdale, FL 33335, 800-327-8150, 242-352-3811, www.xanadudive.com.

Deep Water Cay Club, Grand Bahama, 242-359-4831, www.deepwatercay.com.

Sunn Odyssey Divers, Freeport, 242-373-4014, www.sunnodysseydivers.com.

New Providence

Bahama Divers, Box 21584, Ft. Lauderdale, FL 33335 800-398-DIVE, www.bahamadivers.com.

Custom Aquatics, Box CB-12730, Nassau, 242-362-1492, www.divecustomaquatics.com.

Dive Dive Dive, 1323 SE 17th St., Ft. Lauderdale, FL 33316, 800-368-3483, www.divedivedive.com.

Diver's Haven, PO Box N1658, Nassau, 242-393-0869, www.divershaven.com.

The Nassau Scuba Centre, Box 21766, Ft. Lauderdale, FL 33335, 800-327-8150, www.nassau-scuba-centre.com.

Stuart Cove's Dive South Ocean, PO Box CB-11697, Nassau, 800-879-9832, 242-362-4171, www.stuartcove.com.

Sun Divers, PO Box N-10728, Nassau, 242-325-8927.

Sunskiff Divers, PO Box N-142, Nassau, 800-331-5884.

Turks & Caicos Islands

Accommodations

Many of these hotels have websites as well. To find them quickly, go to the search engine, www.google.com, and type in the hotel name. If it has a website, the address will come up.

The Abacos

The Abaco Inn, Elbow Cay, 800-468-8799, $120, MAP $33 extra.

The Bluff House Club & Marina, Green Turtle Cay, 242-365-4247, $90, MAP is $34 extra.

The Club Soleil, Hope Town Marina, 242-366-0003, $115, MAP $32 extra.

The Conch Inn, Marsh Harbour, 242-367-4000, $85 EP only.

The Great Abaco Beach Hotel, Marsh Harbour, 800-468-4799, $165 EP only.

The Green Turtle Club, Green Turtle Cay, 242-365-4271, $165, MAP $36 extra.

The Guana Beach Resort, Great Guana Cay, 242-367-3590, $140, MAP $35 extra.

Hope Town Harbour Lodge, Elbow Cay, 800-316-7844, $100, MAP is $33 extra.

Hope Town Hideaways, Elbow Cay, 242-366-0224, $140 EP only.

The Inn at Spanish Cay, Spanish Cay, 800-688-4725, $180 EP only.

Island Breezes Motel, Marsh Harbour, 242-367-3776, $75 EP only.

The New Plymouth Inn, Green Turtle Cay, 242-365-4161, $120, includes MAP.

Pelican Beach Villas, Marsh Harbour Marina, 800-642-7268, $145 EP only.

Schooner's Landing, Man-O-War Cay, 242-365-6072, $150 EP only.

The Sea Spray Resort & Villas, Elbow Cay, 242-366-0065, $150 EP only.

The Tangelo Hotel, in Wood Cay, 242-359-6536, $66 EP.

Walker's Cay Hotel & Marina, Walker's Cay, 800-432-2092, $125, MAP $32-50 extra.

Andros

Andros Island Bone Fishing Club, Cargill Creek, 242-329-

5167, call for rates, EP only.

Cargill Creek Lodge, Cargill Creek, 800-533-4353, $275, includes all meals and unlimited fishing.

Emerald Palms by the Sea, Driggs Hill, 800-688-4752, $90, MAP $40 extra.

Green Willows Inn, Nicholl's Town, 242-329-2515, $65, EP only, includes taxes.

Mangrove Cay Cottages, Mangrove Cay, 242-3680, $88 MAP and EP.

Moxey's Guest House, Mangrove Cay, 242-329-4159, $60 EP, FAP.

Small Hope Bay Lodge, Fresh Creek, 800-223-6961, $150 per person per night, meals and activities included.

Bimini

Bimini Big Game Fishing Club, Alice Town, 800-327-4149, $150 EP.

Bimini Blue Water Resort, Alice Town, 242-347-2166, $100 EP.

The Compleat Angler Hotel, Alice Town, 242-347-3122, $85 EP.

Sea Crest Hotel, Alice Town, 242-347-2071, $90 EP.

Eleuthera

Cambridge Villas, Gregory Town, 242-335-5080, $55, MAP $25 extra.

Coral Sands Hotel, Romora Bay on Harbour Island, 800-333-2368, $160 MAP and EP available.

The Cove-Eleuthera, Gregory Town, 800-552-5960, $110, MAP $38 extra.

Palm Tree Villas, Governor's Harbour, 242-332-2002, $105 EP only.

Palmetto Shores Villas, South Palmetto Point, 242-332-1305, $100 EP only.

Pink Sands, Harbour Island, 800-OUTPOST, $300, MAP $55 extra.

The Romora Bay Club, Harbour Island, 800-327-8286, $160, MAP $38 extra.

The Runaway Hill Club, Harbour Island, 800-728-9803, $125, MAP $40 extra.

Unique Village, North Palmetto Point, 242-332-1830, $90, MAP $35 extra.

Valentines Inn & Yacht Club, Harbour Island, 242-333-2080, $125, MAP and EP available.

The Exumas

Club Peace and Plenty, George Town, 800-525-2210, $120, MAP $32 extra.

Coconut Grove Hotel, George Town, 242-336-2659, $128, MAP $38 extra.

Latitude Exuma Resort, 877-398-6222, George Town, Exuma, from $190.

Palms at Three Sisters, Mt. Thompson, 242-358-4040, $100 EP only.

Peace and Plenty Beach Inn, George Town, 242-336-2551, $130, MAP $32 extra.

Regatta Point, George Town, 800-327-0787, $115 EP only.

Staniel Cay Yacht Club, Staniel Cay, 242-355-2024, $195, includes FAP.

Two Turtles Inn, George Town, 242-336-2545, $88 EP only.

Grand Bahama

Castaways Resort, Box 2629, Freeport, 242-352-6682, $75 EP.

Coral Beach Hotel, Box F-2468, Freeport, 242-373-2468, $75 EP.

Club Fortuna Beach Resort, Freeport, 800-847-4502, $240 EP.

Deep Water Cay Club, Box 40039, Freeport, 242-353-3073, $350 per night for a minimum of three nights.

The Oasis, The Mall at Sunrise Highway, Freeport, Bahamas. 800-545-1300. Rates from $118 through $350.

Our Lucaya, PO Box F-42500, Royal Palm Way, Lucaya, Grand Bahamas. 800-LUCAYAN. Rates from $155 through $490.

Port Lucaya Resort & Yacht Club, Box F-2452, Freeport, 800-LUCAYA-1, $95 EP.

Running Mon Marina & Resort, Box F-2663, Freeport, 242-352-6834, $90 EP.

Nassau-New Providence

The Atlantis on Paradise Island, Paradise Island, 800-321-3000, www.atlantis.com, $325 EP.

Breezes, Cable Beach, 242-327-8231, $200 all-inclusive.

British Colonial Hilton, 1 Bay Street, Nassau, 800-445-8667, www.hilton.com, $200 EP.

The Buena Vista Hotel, Delancy Street, Nassau, 242-322-2811, www.buenavista-restaurant.com/hotel.htm, $95 EP.

Casuarina's of Cable Beach, Box N-4016, 800-325-2525, $105 EP.

The Comfort Suites, Box SS-6202, Nassau, 800-228-5150, $150 EP.

Club Land'Or, Box SS-6429, Nassau, 800-363-2400, $230 EP.

The El Greco Hotel, W. Bay & Augusta Streets, Nassau, 242-325-1121, $100 EP.

The Graycliff Hotel, Box N-10246, 242-322-2796, Nassau, $170 EP.

Holiday Inn Junkanoo Beach Hotel, Box N-236, Nassau, Phone800-465-4329, $70 to $100.

Nassau Beach Hotel, Cable Beach, 800-627-7282, $125 EP.

Nassau Marriott Resort & Crystal Palace Casino, Cable Beach, 800-222-7466, $225 EP.

The Nassau Harbour Club Hotel & Marina, Box SS-5755, Nassau, 242-393-0771, $90 EP.

Ocean Club Golf & Tennis Resort, Box N-4777, Nassau, 800-321-3000, $280 EP.

The Radisson Cable Beach Casino & Golf Resort, 800-333-3333, www.radisson.com, $180 EP.

Sandals Royal Bahamian, Cable Beach, 888-SANDALS, www.sandals.com, $200 all-inclusive, adults only.

The South Ocean Golf & Beach Resort, 808 Adelaide Drive, 800-228-9898, $140 EP.

I sincerely hope you enjoyed this book. Thank you so much for purchasing it.

If you have comments of questions, you can contact me by email at blair@blairehoward.com. I will reply to all emails. And you can also visit my website www.blairhoward.com to view my blog, and for a complete list of my books.

If you enjoyed the book, I would really appreciate it if you could take a few moments and share your thoughts by posting a review on Amazon. Here's the link to post your review: *http://amzn.to/YD4YmW*

Other Books by this Author:

The Visitor's Guide to Florida – A complete Guide to the Sunshine State

The Visitor's Guide to Bermuda – A Complete Guide to the Islands

The Visitor's Guide to the Bahamas – Grand Bahama Island and Freeport

The Visitor's Guide to the Bahamas - Nassau

The Visitor's Guide to the Bahamas – The Out Islands: The Abacos, The Exumas, Eleuthera, The Acklins and More

Photography Books:

How to Take Better Photographs: Quick and Simple Tips for Improving Your Photographs

Stock Photography: How to take Great Photographs and Sell them Online to Stock Photo Agencies

The Photo Feature: How to Make Money with your Camera… and MS Word:

Civil War Books

Great Battles of the American Civil War - Chickamauga

Touring Southern Civil War Battlefields: From Vicksburg to Savannah

The Visitor's Guide to the Bahamas – Grand Bahama Island and Freeport

Photography Books:

How to Take Better Photographs: Quick and Simple Tips for Improving Your Photographs

Stock Photography: How to take Great Photographs and Sell them Online to Stock Photo Agencies

The Photo Feature: How to Make Money with your Camera... and MS Word:

Civil War Books

Great Battles of the American Civil War - Chickamauga

Touring Southern Civil War Battlefields: From Vicksburg to Savannah